THE BUTLER DID IT

Paul Pender is a Scots-born writer who now lives and works in Hollywood. He wrote and co-produced the movie *Evelyn* starring Pierce Brosnan and is currently head of television at Infinity Media, the company that produced the Oscar-winning film *Capote*.

The Butler Did It

My True and Terrifying Encounters
with a Serial Killer

PAUL PENDER

MAINSTREAM
PUBLISHING

EDINBURGH AND LONDON

First published in Great Britain in 2012 by
MAINSTREAM PUBLISHING COMPANY
(EDINBURGH) LTD
7 Albany Street
Edinburgh EH1 3UG

ISBN 9781780575612

A catalogue record for this book is available
from the British Library

Printed in Great Britain by
CPI Group (UK) Ltd, Croydon, CR0 4YY

1 3 5 7 9 10 8 6 4 2

CONTENTS

Preface
2B or not 2B

> You can always rely on a murderer for a fancy prose style.
>
> Vladimir Nabokov, *Lolita*

THIS BOOK IS IN one sense the record of a friendship, if friendship can be held to include death threats. To this day I cannot sharpen a pencil – and as a writer I sharpen a lot of pencils – without experiencing a frisson of fear. Roy is once again thrusting the pencil's needle-sharp point towards my retina, threatening to ram it through my eye and into my brain, as he helpfully informs me *'This'll kill you outright, you cunt!'*

Medical experts I have subsequently consulted tell me he was right: that is indeed a very effective way of killing someone. One of the many strange things about Roy is that though he may have been a pathological liar, in his own peculiar fashion he was a stickler for the truth.

Despite the fact that a sharp object through my eye would have been a very literary way to go (oh so Christopher Marlowe), I realised even then that the finality of the act would greatly outweigh any posthumous glamour.

That was to be the first of many threats Roy would make, either in person or through surrogates. Other threats were less anatomically precise but no less frightening. Once, late at night, I saw that the light on my home phone's answering machine was blinking. I had a message. I pressed the play button, only to hear *'Pender, I'll have your balls for garters!'* delivered in a rasping, guttural and strangely other-worldly voice, reminiscent of the Devil in *The Exorcist*. Fear mingled with admiration as I marvelled that Beelzebub had somehow managed to adapt his cloven hoof to the delicate art of dialling.

I do not wish to tax your patience, dear reader, by speculating on the feasibility of converting balls into garters. Fortunately, at the time of writing my testicles are mercifully intact. Suffice it to say that such threats take on extra credibility when they are made by a man who, with no sign of remorse, has killed and killed again.

Why was it, then, that ten years later, safely ensconced in California, at the other end of an ocean and a decade, I felt genuinely saddened when I read of Roy's death? I had expected to feel only relief, yet I remembered him with something like affection.

I realised that I missed our conversations, which were quite unlike those I have had with anyone else, before or since. California was in the midst of a heatwave, and as I looked out on the parched landscape, Roy's death made me reflect that in our society of spin, doublespeak and political correctness, an authentic conversation between two people is as rare and as welcome as desert rain.

I left my office and walked along Santa Monica beach, where I picked up a large flat stone, thinking fondly of our discussions about skimming the stones we called 'skiters' in Rothesay Bay on Scotland's Isle of Bute, the lost paradise of Roy's childhood and of mine. The fun we'd had, generations apart, the simple joy of making those stones dance defiantly across the waves.

'This is for you, Roy,' I thought, as I threw the stone with all my might. It skimmed the surface of the Pacific, hopping and skipping several times before it sank.

'You danced across the waves, Roy!' I said to myself with a smile. 'Just like you said you would.'

I turned back to my office and went to my writing desk.

I had a promise to keep.

I braced myself and sharpened a pencil.

1

The Bogie Man

Polonius: What do you read, my lord?
Hamlet: Words, words, words.
                    Shakespeare, *Hamlet*, Act 2, Scene 2

A S THE TAXI MEANDERED through a leafy English lane in the sleepy cathedral town of York, I felt my pulse racing. Soon I would be face to face with him. I was excited and a little nervous. I'd never met a murderer before.

I hope you found those opening sentences arresting, dear reader. Arrests and sentences feature largely in the narrative that follows. But I jump ahead of myself. I hate to drag that sweet English rose Julie Andrews into this tale of death, deceit and debauchery, but as she so memorably trilled, 'Let's start at the very beginning, a very good place to start.'

As in all good books, in the beginning was the Word.

When this adventure began, words were my bread and butter. I was gainfully employed as a television script editor in the drama department of BBC Scotland, where my job was to work with writers, unknown and established, in an effort to get their scripts into shape for broadcast as TV drama. Having written some plays myself, I was to an extent a poacher turned gamekeeper: the job enabled me to revive my own dormant career as a writer.

I had spent the low dishonest decade of the 1980s in a squalid London bedsit trying to write the Great Novel. It was to be about the rise of Hitler, and humanity's apparent inability to resist the glamour of evil. When I'd spent longer researching the book than Hitler took to lose the war, I began to suspect that, like him, I was fighting a losing battle. But I persevered, trying to convince myself, like the little moustachioed man in the bunker, that tomorrow belonged to me. I would be the great writer or bust.

For the bulk of the decade, I was on the verge of going bust. When I ran out of money for the electricity meter (a regular occurrence), I would sit freezing in the dark, pondering the unsolved mystery of why my bedsit smelled of cat's piss and gas leak, even though the room was all-electric and I didn't have a cat.

The nadir came when I found myself taking mouldy bread out of my rubbish bin, scraping off the mould and toasting it to make it more palatable. My early love affair with London had rapidly turned sour. The metropolis had become the City of Dreadful Night.

So it was with joy, pride and a reborn sense of purpose that I finally swallowed my artistic pride, got real, applied for the script editor's post at BBC Scotland and, to most people's amazement, landed the job.

I was lucky. Bill Bryden, who ran the drama department, was brave enough to take a risk on me. I vowed I would finish off the Hitler book later. After years spent in the Teutonic twilight, it was time for me to climb out of the bunker.

It was early in January of 1993 when the call came that changed everything. Scotland was recovering from its collective New Year's hangover and I had settled into my BBC job in Glasgow. Convinced I was striking a blow for the Romantic tradition, I dedicated myself to what I called 'shaving the day'.

I defined my working day as beginning at ten. I would work till twelve-thirty, then have lunch with a writer at the Trattoria Trevi, the delightful restaurant around the corner from my office. Fine Italian wines often contributed to the creative flow of ideas. When I got back, I would ensconce myself in my swivel chair, prop a script up on my desk and instruct my secretary that I was only to be interrupted if the call were urgent. This was euphemistically known as my 'afternoon read'.

I would swivel so that my back was to the door. By placing the wastepaper bin at a strategic angle, anyone entering would clatter it. This was usually enough to arouse me from the sleepy penumbra into which I would inevitably have drifted as a result of my long lunch. Startled into consciousness, I would immediately resume my pose as a dedicated reader of scripts.

On particularly cold days, such as that icy January afternoon, I would wallow in a compensatory fantasy which involved me, an unspecified Mediterranean island, and Maria, the island's most sensuous woman, a sultry golden-brown Latin beauty.

In the comfort of my warm room, I would daydream that I had morphed into a hugely successful writer, a kind of heterosexual Somerset Maugham, now living abroad for tax purposes. Maria, who combined the literary sensibility of F.R. Leavis with the body of a *Playboy* centrefold, would mop my creatively fevered brow as she gently critiqued my day's literary output.

I would show my gratitude by rubbing copious amounts of sun lotion onto her voluptuous breasts, accompanied only by the chirruping of the cicadas in the Mediterranean haze.

But on that fateful morning the cicadas were chirruping longer and more loudly than usual – so much so that they pulled me out of my dream state – and I realised that it was not the cicadas that were chirruping but my office telephone.

I lunged towards the offending implement, cleared my throat and tried to sound businesslike. The voice at the other end of the line had a clipped cut-glass accent: 'Hello, may I speak to Paul Pender?'

'Oh no,' I thought. 'It's the Director General of the BBC, about to reprimand me over his memo on the great shit/shite debate.'

A few weeks earlier I had received a memo from BBC headquarters in London, from the office of the Director General himself. Such memos were met with a degree of enthusiasm hitherto matched only by those receiving the black spot in *Treasure Island*. They always began with the dread phrase 'In the opinion of London'.

Whenever BBC Scotland employees received an 'In the opinion of London' memo, we felt as we were meant to feel – like humble functionaries in a distant outpost of Empire, receiving a command from Caesar to be obeyed on pain of death. The subtext was 'Listen, Jocks. We know you enjoy your delusions of independence, but never forget we are your Lords and Masters. Yes, wear tartan skirts. Paint your faces blue if you like. But never forget who's running the show! Tug your forelock and do as we say, or the crucifix awaits.'

The memo concerned a script I was editing – a working-class TV drama very much in the then fashionable tradition sometimes described as 'prolier than thou'. You know the kind of thing. Every Scotsman is hard, angry, drunk, drugged and violent, given to slashing men with razors and pummelling women with his fists. The anti-heroes of these dramas spent their lives shooting up, throwing up or beating up. Such dramas gave our effete lords and masters in London a frisson of danger, the literary equivalent of a bit of rough. The lives of Glaswegian hard men seemed to offer an authenticity their own safe, soft little buttoned-down lives lacked.

My memo from London read as follows:

> In the opinion of London, the language used in the drama in question may be deemed offensive by the majority of the viewing public. Although we appreciate that the language must reflect the harsh life of the characters, it is the opinion of London that 1 'shite' is as offensive as 2 'shits'. Using a points system on that basis (1 point for a shit, 2 points for a shite) the script must contain no more than 10 points' worth of the offensive material.

My job was to communicate this profound insight to the writer whilst maintaining credibility, not to mention a straight face.

I had found this memo so entertaining that in a well-oiled moment of festive exuberance I had passed a copy round at the Christmas party. I now assumed some quisling had leaked it and I was about to be fired.

When I said 'This is Paul Pender speaking', in what I hoped was an educated Scots accent, to my amazement the voice on the other line instantly became working class and guttural. It was as if Begbie from *Trainspotting* had just headbutted the Director General and grabbed the phone from his hand. I was, to say the least, confused.

'Ah knew ye must be a Glesga Boy!' the voice on the other end raved. The words poured out in a torrent. 'Ah loved yir film *The Bogie Man*. That Robbie Coltrane's some actor, so he is! Funny as fuck! You're the boy to write my story! None of thae English wankers can get it right! I'll tell you all about all my fantastic scams, my stings, my cons. *The Sting* was a great film, but none of their scams were as good as mine. I pulled off one of them a week. My name's Roy, by the way. Roy Fontaine.' After a short pause, he obligingly spelt it for me.

'Oh, hello, Roy,' I said, nonplussed. This was to be the beginning of a very peculiar friendship.

The Bogie Man was a TV film that I had adapted from the graphic novel of the same name. Remember when we use to call graphic novels 'comics', before we started pretending they're literature?

The film, which had been broadcast over the Christmas season on BBC2, brought together in comedic form the themes of criminality and madness, and featured a flamboyant, charismatic character who was convinced of his own genius.

Its hero, Clunie, played by Robbie Coltrane, escapes from a Glasgow lunatic asylum in the belief that he is Humphrey Bogart. He thinks that everything that happens to him is part of a Bogart movie. Hence the title 'The Bogie Man'.

I wrote lines like, 'Clunie had a troubled childhood. His father was a heather beater. Unfortunately, Heather was his mother.' That line was delivered by Craig Ferguson, who went on to become famous in the USA as a late-night TV chat-show host.

OK, I never said it was *Citizen Kane*, did I? It was never intended to be anything more than a bauble on the BBC's Christmas tree, a little festive present to the nation.

Clunie the Looney was a madman with a swaggering style, a mastery of accents and an unshakeable belief in his own destiny. I didn't know it at the time, but that was the story of Roy's life.

'You've probably heard of me,' he said, as if the name Roy Fontaine were famous.

'I'm sorry, I haven't, Roy,' I replied.

After a brief pause to massage his bruised ego, he continued.

'I was Britain's top jewel thief and confidence trickster,' he said proudly, 'until I was detained permanently at Her Majesty's pleasure. Looking at Her Majesty's sour old face, I'd say she needs as much pleasure as she can get: it's obvious Prince Philip isn't giving her any!'

I smiled at the thought. Whoever this Roy might be, he was already entertaining me.

'My story's funny,' he added. 'Funny as fuck. I just need somebody to write it. Somebody who gets the humour. I'm convinced you're the man for the job. Come down and see me in the next couple of weeks.'

Telling him this was all a bit sudden, I said I'd do a little research and we'd speak again in a few days. After a brief pause (was there something he wasn't telling me?), he agreed. We set a time for him to call me back and bade each other a fond farewell.

I was intrigued. I wanted the Cole's Notes version of Roy's story to see if it was as promising as he'd claimed. I needed what Auden called 'A Shilling Life' to give me all the facts. I called down to the BBC library, one of the research wonders of the pre-digital world. This was 1993, remember, and though it now seems incredible, Google did not exist, 'You Tube!' was a term of abuse in Glasgow (politely translated it means 'You Idiot!'), and the information superhighway was still a dirt track. Fortunately, the BBC library was its very own Ministry of Information.

A couple of hours later, Moira the librarian called back, apologising for the delay. 'Sorry it took so long. He was filed under Archibald Hall. It took us a while to work out that Roy Fontaine and Archibald Hall are the same person.' That was my introduction to Planet Roy, where nothing is what it seems.

Moira delivered a buff-coloured folder bulging with press cuttings. I untied the red ribbon like an excited kid opening a Christmas present and saw a bunch of headlines screaming out at me: I had my shilling life all right, and some golden guineas to boot.

I stared at the photographs of the man to whom I had just been speaking. His forehead was high, suggesting intelligence, and he had the full, sensual lips of a libertine. He was handsome and looked self-confident, even arrogant, with a rakish grin and an undeniable charm. The headlines made it clear that everything he had told me was true.

Yes, he was a great confidence trickster. Yes, he brought panache, imagination and (I can't resist it) sparkle to the world of jewellery theft, pulling off several of the most inventive, ingenious and funny scams in the history of crime. He was, up to a certain point in his criminal career, a loveable rogue, a real-life Raffles.

Roy had, however, left out one tiny but significant detail.

He'd murdered five people.

2

Interview with the Vampire

All the world loves an outlaw. For some damn
reason we remember 'em.
        Jesse James in Bill Bryden's *The Long Riders*

THE HEADLINES SCREAMED OUT at me: 'Mass Murder Horror',
'Bones in the Glen' and, most intriguingly, 'Sex Secrets of
the Killer Butler', with the sub-heading 'Evil butler claims to
have had sex with 3 MPs'.

You didn't need to be a script editor to realise that this was a hell
of a story, with its very own murderous Mephistopheles. I spent a
few hours going through the cuttings, making notes and preparing
to pitch it to my boss Bill Bryden as a possible fast-track project.

Of course, from the point of the television company, the murders
made Roy more interesting, not less. I was already seeing this as a
potential vehicle for Robbie Coltrane – the charismatic Scots actor
who was the star of *The Bogie Man*. He would go on to achieve
national renown in the TV show *Cracker* and worldwide fame as
Hagrid in *Harry Potter*.

I went to Bill Bryden to tell him about our potentially exciting new
project. He loved Roy's theatricality, larger-than-life personality and
re-invention of himself. Bill said that if we agreed the story was worth
telling, I must write it not in the usual anodyne style of the true-crime
saga but with a verve and flamboyance worthy of its subject.

'Tell it with style, dear boy,' he said, every inch the literary gent.
'For after all,' he opined, 'as Henry James once said, "Style is what
a kiss lends to a dipstick."'

Dipstick? I believe the actual quote is 'Style is what a kiss lends to a greeting', but Bill, with his butterfly mind, had an endearing habit, when groping for a word, of substituting the word 'dipstick'. Surreal as this sounds, it became addictive. After a few months of exposure to it, I was 'dipsticking' all over the place myself.

Bill thought that Robbie Coltrane would make a great Roy Fontaine. Coltrane's star was in the ascendant, and we were keen to work with him again.

So the deal was done. I would visit Roy and dig as deep as I could. As deep as the policemen who dug the frozen hills around Perthshire looking for the remains of his victims. We would then decide if there was enough material for a one-off film or a multi-part series.

Roy called me back at the prearranged time and I told him that we were interested.

'Great!' he said. 'I'll make out a visitor's pass for you. I'll sit near a window, as far away from the screws as possible.' I asked him why that would be necessary, and he replied, 'Because I want you to slip me a packet of fags with a twenty-pound note in it. I have expenses to cover in here.'

He had another requirement: 'Bring me some cigars! Romeo and Juliets. They're Cuban, of course. My favourites. They were Churchill's favourites, too.' It was a command rather than a request.

I told him that I was sure the BBC expenses department could cover it. He laughed and said they were very expensive: 'You have to pay for quality, son. Never settle for second best. If you're writing my story, you have to understand that. I've never settled for second best in anything.'

'That's good to know, Roy,' I replied. 'I'll remember that. See you in two weeks!'

Next day, I went to the best tobacconist's shop I knew, near Glasgow's city centre.

The apparently prosaic act of going into a tobacconist's is for me a minefield of mixed emotions. From the age of five, I had grown up without my father, a courageous firefighter who had been awarded several medals for bravery. I remember him, cigarette in mouth, cursing the popularity of smoking and all the troubles it caused him in his job: the great majority of domestic fatalities were

The Butler Did It
The Butler Did It

the result of people falling asleep whilst smoking in bed.

Tobacconists' shops have therefore always held a great fascination for me, as well as a certain poignancy. It's only when I enter them, with their sweet-smelling aroma which I associate with manhood and their array of tiny tobacco-shredding knives, that I become acutely aware that I grew up without my father.

This is where I would have bought my dad cigarettes and fancy cigars for his birthday, and a pipe in his ripe old age. This is where he'd have bought a couple of cigars for my 21st, one for me and one for himself. This is where we'd have talked of his hopes for my future and my pride in his past.

It was impossible to enter such a shop without those tiny tobacco knives shredding my heart. Hence I choose not to visit them – the shops or the emotions – very often.

I consoled myself with the thought that it was better to have the memory of a brave father, whom I could mythologise, than the sad reality of a real one: those disappointing, defeated men who had married the unfortunate mothers of most of my friends.

So I didn't linger in the tobacconist's when I purchased Roy's smokes. I bought a box of Cuba's finest Romeo and Juliets and got out quicker than Fidel and Che on a guerrilla raid.

I cleared the cigars with the BBC's expenses department, who raised eyebrows at the cost. Strangely, they seemed convinced by the argument that the expense was justified since the cigars were for a serial killer. I would have had more difficulty persuading them if they had been for a mid-level TV star. Indeed, when an actor who played an unsavoury character named Dirty Den in the Corporation's most successful soap opera, *EastEnders*, was revealed as a killer in real life, he became a much bigger star overnight. Ah, the cult of celebrity!

◊

Two weeks after that initial phone conversation, I found myself on a train to Full Sutton prison, just outside York. I was armed with my cigars, neatly arrayed in their wooden box like bullets in an ammo belt. As the train neared its destination I saw an old-fashioned carved wooden signpost for 'Full Sutton'. I found myself wondering, 'Why *Full* Sutton? Is there an Empty Sutton? A Half-full Sutton? A Partial Sutton? An Incomplete Sutton?'

The place sounded like something out of an Ealing comedy, one of those great films Britain made when it still had a proper indigenous film industry. The nearest village of note, my guidebook told me, was Pocklington, which again sounded like the feeble creation of a screenwriter trying to invent a quaint-sounding English village.

From what I knew of it courtesy of the BBC library, Roy's career did have elements of an Ealing comedy, in the tradition of *Kind Hearts and Coronets*, where members of the ruling class are dispatched by a jealous social inferior. But real people died in Roy's story. Perhaps we would pioneer a whole new genre – the Ealing tragicomedy.

Full Sutton's quaint name was misleading. It might have been better described as Full Term, because for several of its inmates, Roy being the most senior, life meant life with no prospect of remission. I was wondering what it must feel like to know that you will never taste freedom again when the taxi from the train station pulled up in front of the prison gates.

From the outside it looked unremarkable. I had played football on the playing fields near London's Brixton prison, which looked dark and foreboding, like Glasgow's Barlinnie, which I'd passed many times as a schoolboy. I somehow assumed that a prison is meant to look gothic and menacing.

Instead, Full Sutton was a modern redbrick building that at first glance seemed more like a post-war technical college. Despite housing prisoners who had committed extremely violent crimes, including murder, its exterior suggested that it might be a fairly liberal, open prison, the kind of place that elicits angry letters to the Conservative press from retired colonels, claiming that too many prisons are like holiday camps.

Yet despite Full Sutton's comparatively benign exterior, I knew its denizens of darkness included not just Roy but other members of that select league of murderous supervillains whose horrific crimes haunt the dark, dank corners of the collective psyche. The roll call of inmates in its Hall of Shame included Dennis Nilsen,

19

who murdered and dismembered 15 men in his north London bedsit, putting various body parts in his fridge and under his floorboards. Nilsen said he felt lonely and 'needed the company'.

Life in a London bedsit got you like that. Nilsen's behaviour in response to his confinement in bedsitter land made me feel positively well balanced. The grossest thing I ever did with a knife, as previously noted, was to scrape the mould off some bread. Perhaps Nilsen felt that he needed a decomposing corpse or two under the floorboards to get rid of the smell of cat's piss and gas leak. Now why didn't I think of that?

Roy spent many long years claiming that the Establishment was victimising him for washing its dirty laundry in public. He was in correspondence with campaigning radical journalist Paul Foot regarding the perceived inhumanity of his incarceration. As the oldest of the whole-life tariff prisoners – those who are imprisoned for life with no prospect of release – he was the subject of heated public debates on the morality of his continued confinement. As you form your own opinion of Roy, dear reader, you can decide for yourself whether his punishment fitted his crimes.

I headed for the prison's reception area and joined a small group of visitors who were being searched by guards. In those innocent days before 9/11, being frisked by a complete stranger still felt shockingly intrusive.

A bleeper went off as my briefcase passed through the scanner. The guard opened it and removed a pencil sharpener from my shiny new pencil case. He tutted disapprovingly.

'No blades allowed! What were you thinking?'

'Sorry,' I replied, 'I didn't realise . . .'

He took out a packet of cigarettes and the large box of cigars, and his attitude immediately softened.

'For Roy, eh?'

'Yes, special request,' I said, forcing a smile.

He opened the cigarette packet and I thanked God that I hadn't as yet slipped any cash inside. He looked me up and down. I'd dressed in a suit for the occasion, trying to look as respectable as possible: the BBC's good and faithful servant.

'Are you his lawyer?' he asked.

'No,' I replied, 'I'm conducting an interview.'

'You're not allowed to record interviews. You'd need special permission from the Governor. Besides, Roy doesn't like being taped.'

I told him I only had a pencil and notebook, and that I planned to take notes. He nodded approvingly.

'Notes are fine,' he said, 'just as long as you don't try to slip him any of the cash variety.'

I smiled nervously, as if that were a ridiculous suggestion. My mouth was going dry. I could feel myself blush. I hoped he didn't notice.

He was too busy admiring the Cuban cigars. He opened the box, smiled and put them back in my case as he said, 'He loves his smokes, does our Roy.'

Our Roy? The affection was obvious. Roy's charm, evident to me over the phone, seemed to have worked its magic here too, even with those responsible for keeping him under lock and key.

The guard told me to follow him to a heavy metal door, which he unlocked. We walked down a long narrow corridor, our progress interrupted at regular intervals by more metal doors, all of which were painted a garish blue. They were as blue as the ocean, as blue as the sky: taunting reminders of the freedom the prisoners had lost.

The final door was opened using an electronic keypad. The guard punched in the code, and we entered the waiting area. Around 20 other visitors were already there, of whom the majority were women. I was taken by surprise by the sexiness of these women, who were visiting their savage sweethearts. I didn't know what to expect on my first visit to prison, but I certainly didn't expect sexual tension.

A dark-haired young woman in her mid-20s pouted provocatively whilst checking her lipstick in her vanity mirror. A sub-Marilyn blonde sat in the corner wearing a very short split microskirt of the type colloquially known as a 'fanny pelmet'. She kept crossing and uncrossing her legs à la Sharon Stone in *Basic Instinct*. As Full Sutton specialised in housing violent criminals, I concluded that this raging undercurrent of sex was testimony to the powerful aphrodisiac qualities of Grievous Bodily Harm.

I have always been baffled by women who write love letters to killers. Is it further evidence of the glamour of evil? I was now confronted with that uncomfortable truth.

The women were sexy rather than beautiful – there was a certain hardness about them – but they had dressed to excite their men, and, speaking as a man, they had succeeded.

Respectability had been left outside the prison gates. Inside was a different moral order, more primal than the one we'd left behind.

It occurred to me that a prison was a kind of pressure cooker protecting us from our darkest impulses, designed to keep a lid on the monsters from the id that threaten to erupt through the thin veneer of civilisation.

I wrote in my notebook: 'Prison: a lid for the id.' Some day, I thought, I might add a couple of words and publish that sentence as a haiku. Maybe it was a haiku already. I wrote myself another note: 'Check definition of a haiku.'

My fellow visitors and I stood at the last locked door before the visiting area, like a bunch of eager horses at the starting gate. I've always resented the casual yoking together of sex and violence, but as those provocative women panted in anticipation of their horny heart-throbs, the phrase kept resonating in my head: 'Sex and violence. Sex and violence.' I was about to meet a man who had a huge appetite for both.

Suddenly the door was opened from the inside by another guard, a female this time, who ushered all of us through. We found ourselves in a large room with about 30 tables and chairs arranged in tidy rows. I looked around, searching as agreed for the window that was 'as far away from the screws as possible'.

That's when I saw Roy in the flesh for the first time. I was already writing the screenplay in my head, thinking like a screenwriter, making camera notes for the director. I know directors hate to get notes from the writer, which is of course why I like to do it.

(Note to Director: cue swelling music, as when two lovers meet.)

Roy stood up, smiled and gave a little wave in my direction, looking astonishingly vital for a man approaching his 70th year. I had some caricatured notion about prisoners wearing special uniforms, but the truth was very different. Casual clothes were the order of the day.

Roy was wearing a tight-fitting red cashmere sweater designed to show off his powerful upper torso. He had the robust body shape of the elderly Picasso, with something of the same animal magnetism. His bearing immediately conveyed power and self-confidence. He exuded the charisma of evil, as if he knew he was Scotland's very own Hannibal Lecter.

I walked towards him. *(A slow tracking shot here please, herr director! I said slow, please, director! Oh well, you're the boss.)*

As I got closer, I noticed that the man whose life was about to become enmeshed with mine had the lifeless, predatory eyes of a shark. He smiled with all the sincerity of a politician or a TV game-show host.

It's only when you see a smile done badly that you realise the eyes are supposed to be involved as well as the mouth. Roy's mouth and eyes seemed to have undergone an acrimonious divorce and were now engaged in a bitter custody battle for his face.

He held out his hand and gave me a very firm handshake.

(CLOSE SHOT of his HANDSHAKE.

RAPID CUT to ROY'S HANDS strangling the life out of one of his VICTIMS.

RAPID CUT to ROY'S HANDS holding a pillow over the face of a 2nd VICTIM.

RAPID CUT to ROY'S HAND holding a chloroformed rag over the mouth of a 3rd VICTIM.

CUT BACK to Roy, his smile and his shark eyes.)

'Hello, my young friend. Pleasant trip?'

'Yes, thanks, Roy. York looks nice.'

'It's a beautiful city. So they tell me, anyway. Can't say I've seen that much of it,' he laughed. 'No a patch on Glesga, though, eh? Glasgow's the best city in the world. City of culture, eh? In my time it was a city of vultures.' He laughed at his own joke. I remembered to laugh too.

I opened my briefcase and handed him the box of cigars.

'Here, Roy – a wee present.'

With great delicacy, he took out a cigar and breathed its aroma deep into his lungs. He gave a satisfied sigh. Then he did something very peculiar. He ran his tongue suggestively along the length of the shaft, lightly licking it. He smacked his libertine lips in appreciation, like Hannibal Lecter anticipating a fine bottle of post-prandial Chianti.

'Thank you, young man. Very good.'

'The best,' I said.

I had unwittingly challenged his expertise. He instantly re-established dominance, like a gorilla flashing its backside at a younger male.

'No – not the best. Just very good. They were Churchill's favourites. In fact, it was Churchill's son-in-law who introduced me to them, just before I had sex with him.'

This remark stopped me in my tracks, as it was no doubt intended to do. I took the ambiguous 'him' with whom he'd had sex to refer to the son-in-law and not to the great man himself.

Flustered, I stammered, 'Oh, you had sex with Churchill's son-in-law, did you?'

'I did, yes. He was my first, actually. Penetratively speaking.'

Penetratively speaking? We'd obviously skipped the conversational formalities.

As usual when flummoxed, I took refuge in humour.

'I suppose having sex with Churchill's son-in-law was your finest hour, eh?'

'Hour? No, son, in those days I could stay up all night.'

There was a pause. Then he got the joke.

'Oh, I see, son! Churchill! Finest hour! That's funny. Quick too. That's why I told you to come and see me.'

Told me? I thought he'd asked me. But on Planet Roy, I would discover, only he had free will. The rest of us were merely his satellites.

'You brought the cigarette packet too?' he asked, winking.

This of course was code for the money-in-the-cigarette-packet. I nervously said that, yes, I had the cigarettes with me.

'Good,' he said. He politely ushered me to sit at the Formica table. 'Now we can begin.'

We sat down and I took out my notebook, trying to look as if I interviewed serial killers every day. He said he didn't mind if I took notes, but taping the interview was an absolute no-no. When I asked why, he replied, 'Plausible deniability, son. No man in his right mind would let himself be taped.'

My research had revealed that Roy was not in fact in his right mind, having been officially declared insane several times in his stellar career. For the time being, I let this pass and nodded sagely, like a TV interviewer hamming it up for the camera's cutaways.

As I did so, he asked if the BBC was seriously interested in his story.

'Absolutely,' I replied. 'We all think it's remarkable. But of course we only know the bare bones.'

I regretted the phrase as soon as it had left my lips.

He smiled grimly. The newspaper reports had gone into grisly detail about the bones of his victims being gnawed by wild animals.

(Note to director: cut to fox on Scottish hillside with knee-bone of ex-Government minister in its jaws.)

He waved at a guard, who came over on cue and handed him an ornate gold lighter. 'Thank you, John,' said Roy, smiling.

'I'll collect it at the end, Roy!' replied John, chummily. It was a strange ritual to behold, as if the normal hierarchical order had been turned on its head.

He explained that one of the perks of being the elder statesman of the prison was that the authorities would lend him his lighter for the duration of the visit and remove it at the end, since, as he jokingly put it, 'They trust me, but not enough to risk me arson about!'

'This lighter has been with me since I was 17 years old,' he said, lighting up his first cigar. 'We've been through heaven and hell together. So many memories . . .'

He caressed its elegant art deco shape as his eyes moistened. Were these crocodile tears, designed to signal to me that I was dealing with a sensitive man? I tried to move briskly on and begin the interview proper.

Roy loved to talk and proved to be a consummate storyteller. Words were the web with which he ensnared his hapless victims. He liked nothing more than spinning those gossamer strands that lured so many to a sticky end. He caressed words, made them sparkle, bent them to his will.

Diamonds and sex were the twin peaks of his heart's desire, and words formed the bridge between them. I came to realise that diamonds, sex and words constituted the holy trinity of his life.

Roy's facility with words and his ability to spin a good yarn bring us to the thorny question of the truth of this tale, so let me address it now, for the question of truth runs through our narrative like the trail of the worm through the apple's beautiful core.

3

True Crime and Other Fictions

All this happened, more or less.
        Kurt Vonnegut, *Slaughterhouse-Five*

I HOPE THIS BOOK IS difficult to categorise. I am suspicious of categories, the easy pigeonholing of the exotic. There's always the tendency to spray-paint the bird of paradise to make it look like a pigeon. We try to domesticate and make palatable that which is beyond our comprehension.

Roy was a rare bird of exotic plumage, albeit a bird of prey. He challenged my complacency and I hope he challenges yours, as only very good or very bad people are capable of doing.

Inevitably, I suppose, this book will find itself in the true crime section of the bookshop, a section I have to admit I rarely visit. Can this be true crime when it's based on the unreliable memoirs of a pathological liar and marinated in the creative juices of an author whose primary job is to invent stories?

Before I am 'Freyed' alive by Oprah, like the author of *A Million Little Pieces*, let me say this in my defence. This book is Roy's truth as filtered through the prism of my truth. It is not a prison diary. It's a prism diary.

Can we call it a work of faction and move on?

The writer is a kind of gardener, pruning the tricky thorns of reality so that we can appreciate the fragrant beauty of the rose beneath. Most stories we take as true have had a thorough going-over with the secateurs.

True crime, that subset of the true story, is a notion which belongs to the old Newtonian world where the author is a detached observer, objectively recording the facts. It is a truism of the New Journalism that the journalist is part of the story. We now live in the Einsteinian universe where the experimenter is part of the experiment, crucially affecting its outcome.

What follows, then, is primarily an account of the extraordinary life and times of one of Britain's most colourful and charismatic career criminals, but it would not be complete without a small yet significant aspect of the story being my own part in the matter.

Roy and I had many discussions about truth, so let him have the last word on the subject. When I asked him how much of the story he was about to tell me was true, he shrugged and quoted the Bible: 'What is truth, asked Pilate? And would not stay for an answer.'

He puffed on his cigar and added his own Biblical gloss: 'What did Pilate do? He washed his hands. See, son, Pontius Pilate was a busy man. He didn't have time to decide on all those big questions about truth and lies. Me, I've got all the time in the world. OK, Pontius Pilate was a cowardly bastard, I'll give you that. But I'll say this for him. He was clean. I respect a man who takes care of his personal hygiene.'

As he spoke, a whiff of his pungent aftershave wafted its way towards me as if to prove his point.

4

Roy the Boy

The child is father of the man.

William Wordsworth

'So, Roy,' I said crisply as I consulted my background notes, trying to be brisk and businesslike, 'you were born in Maclean Street in Glasgow. You were christened Archibald Thomson Hall, son of Archibald Hall senior and Marion Hall (née Thomson). You grew up in Govan on Glasgow's south side. Is that correct?'

He looked suddenly pained. Had I said something to upset him? He stared hard at me. A cold, impenetrable, implacable, murderous stare. When he spoke, it was in a threatening whisper.

This was my first exposure to scary Roy and to the look that I came to know as the Stare of Death. It was a stare capable of turning the blood to ice. The friendly face gave way to the furious face and suddenly it felt like the friendly face had been a mask all along.

He spoke coldly and deliberately, accentuating each syllable as if each word were a sentence. 'Don't. Call. Me. Archie! Don't. *Ever*. Call. Me. Archie! OK?'

'OK,' I said, not being one to disagree lightly with a murderer.

'My father was big Archie and I was wee Archie. "Wee Archie" – that's what they called me, "Wee Archie", or worse "Wee Erchie". Can you believe it?'

I could, but I tried to look like I couldn't.

'They would say, "Is Wee Erchie comin' out tae play? Wee Erchie – do ye want a game of fitba?" As if I could possibly be an Erchie!'

He winced at the memory.

OK, I told myself. I got the message. No more Archie or Erchie.

29

Roy it would be from here to eternity.

I decided to change the subject.

'So, Roy, you went to school in Jordanhill and Pollokshields. What are your memories of school?'

He puffed on his cigar, reflected for a moment and replied, 'I loved books and learning, but I wanted to be out having adventures in the real world where exciting things were happening. I found my classmates and lessons a bit boring. I suppose I was just too intelligent.'

He said that with no hint of irony. For him it was a given. And frankly I think he was right. All the evidence suggests that he *was* a very precocious child.

The man who was once that child now puffed on his cigar and said, 'I did learn one thing, though, that was to serve me well all my life.'

'What was that, Roy?'

'I learned about the sun and the wind. The teacher told us the Aesop fable about a man who was wearing a heavy coat, and the wind said to the sun, "I can make him take his coat off", and the sun replied, "No you can't, but I can."

'The wind blew and blew, but the man just pulled his coat tighter to his body. The wind got tired of blowing and gave up. Then it was the sun's turn. The sun gave a great big smile and the man felt warm and good and took his coat off right away.

'The teacher asked us what we thought the story meant. The class went silent. One boy put his hand up. Stupid little fucker, I think his name was Tommy, said, "It means you should never go out on a hot day with your coat on, Miss!"'

After a puff or two on his cigar, Roy continued, 'Well, that obviously went down like a cup of cold sick, so Miss Corrigan asked if anyone else had a better explanation of the story's meaning. For me, it was obvious. I put my hand up and said, "Miss, it means that if you want to obtain something, it's better to do so by smiling at people and being nice to them instead of shouting at them and being nasty. In other words, charm works better than force, Miss."'

Miss Corrigan beamed at the bright little boy and said, 'Exactly, Archie. Charm is the key to life. As I look around me I can see that it is in short supply in these parts. You, however, have it in abundance.

You could do very well here if you didn't keep disappearing.'

'Thank you, Miss,' he said, almost feeling guilty that he was already playing truant from school to expand his education in other areas. But he didn't have anything to worry about. He had Miss Corrigan wrapped around his little finger. Just by smiling like the sun.

I asked him if there was anything else of value he'd taken from school.

He said, 'Yes, there was a poem which foretold my life.'

Puffing on his cigar, he continued, 'It's spooky, but I often think you can foresee your whole life in something that you experience in childhood. The weird thing is that you know at the time it's something of enormous significance to you, even if you can't explain why. To other people it is of no particular importance.'

I asked him to elaborate.

'There was a poem in our reading book – "Lone Dog" by Irene Rutherford MacLeod. To the other kids it was just a daft wee poem, but I read it again and again, feeling it was some sort of omen predicting my future. How did I know that as a kid? I can't say. It's a mystery, but it's true. It was prophetic.'

He proceeded to recite the entire poem from memory. It's written from the point of view of a lone dog who hungers for adventure and loves to keep complacent souls awake at night by baying at the moon. It is perhaps significant that the dog describes himself as both bad and mad. Prophetic indeed.

'That's all I got from my education,' he added. 'A poem and a fable. But that's all I needed.'

I asked him if he had many childhood friends. 'No, I didn't,' he replied. 'My father said I was anti-social. He was always trying to get me to make friends by forcing me to go to the Boy Scouts, but I was too much of a loner. He made me go along a couple of times. The scoutmaster was the usual sweaty wee pervert in khaki shorts. In my book, all scoutmasters should be arrested on suspicion of being paedophiles. They're all guilty till proven innocent. Do you know what Baden-Powell, the founder of the Scouts, called his autobiography?'

'No,' I said.

'*Scouting for Boys*!'

He laughed uproariously, slapping his thigh in delight.

'If you ask me, every scoutmaster spends his life scouting for boys. Anyway, the wee wanker who ran our troop asked us to collect stuff from outside the scout hall that began with each letter of the word "Scout". I brought in some crabgrass, for the letter "c". He said, "That's no good, Hall, that's grass. There's no 'g' in scout."

'I said, "No, sir, it's *crab*grass." He laughed and said I was being ridiculous, and the other boys laughed too, the brown-nosing wee fuckers. That was my first experience of finding out that the proles don't like you to be clever. So fuck them, that's what I say. I had no interest in being a scout or a prole. After the crabgrass incident, I never went back. But I took their motto to heart: be prepared. Essential if you're contemplating a successful life in crime.'

I asked him if he got on well with his father, after whom he was named. I hesitated to use the offensive term 'Archie' again.

He took a puff on his cigar and said, 'My father was an upright, honest, God-fearing, hard-working man. In other words, a fucking loser! He was a devout member of the Scottish Presbyterian Church.'

Members of that church are worthy and righteous people, but they are rarely described as fun-loving. The doctrines of Calvin and Knox are not normally associated with the pursuit of carnal pleasure and sensual excess that were at the core of Roy's personal philosophy. Nor does his lifelong lust for sex, diamonds and the glittering prizes of the material world feature prominently in the Scottish Presbyterian book of prayer, which walks the primrose path of asceticism and self-negation.

Roy wanted to indulge his senses every bit as much as his Presbyterian father wanted to deny them. When he spoke of his dad, venom dripped from his lips like ash from the cigar that he was now smoking.

'My father worked at the post office in George Square, sorting the mail. He was a pious man. Fond of church-going and Bible-reading. He believed in the Good Shepherd and all that Christian shit.'

'I take it you don't believe in it then, Roy?'

'Don't make me laugh, son. There's no such thing as a *good* shepherd. What does a shepherd do? First he fleeces you, then he sends you to the fucking slaughterhouse. All that Good Shepherd shit was invented by the ruling class to keep the proles in their place. It's a slave mentality. Don't be a lamb, son. Be a lion!'

He warmed to his theme. 'All religions are there to keep you down, son. They all tell you to deny your senses. Fuck that! *Trust* your senses. Back in the '60s I picked up a badge from some hippy cunt's stall at a flea market in London. All it said was "Trust Lust". You could live by that motto. I *have* lived by it. Sight, sound, taste, smell, touch – the senses are all we've got. That's what I believe in, and that's what the Pope believes too. Every time he catches a cold he gets a team of the world's best doctors round him. He's in no fuckin' hurry to meet his Boss.'

Fascinating as his observations on Christianity were, I wanted to get back to the topic. I asked him to tell me more about his relationship with his father.

'He did his back in carrying mailbags. I'll tell you the difference between my father and me. He spent his life emptying his mail sack. I spent my life emptying my ball sac. When my mother wanted to annoy him, she would call him a second-class male.'

Roy smiled at the very mention of his mother. 'I get my wit from my mother,' he said with characteristic modesty.

'She was a wonderful woman. Different class. She worked as a waitress in the Malmaison restaurant at the Central Hotel. She was a whole lot better than the people she served. She was far too good for them!'

Roy spoke of his mother with a reverence he reserved for her alone. He became emotional as he remembered her. I came to realise she was the only person in his life whom he loved unconditionally. This filial devotion was surprising, even touching, in a man capable of murder, but as he spoke, something, or someone, was niggling away at the back of my mind: Roy's devotion to his mother reminded me of some other mummy's boy, someone who carried a photograph of his mother with him wherever he went. It took me a while to recall who that loving son was. Then I remembered. It was Adolf Hitler.

5

Oedipus Schmedipus

Oedipus schmedipus – what does it matter so
long as he loves his mother?
Joke about Jewish mother on being told her
son has an Oedipus complex.

MARION HALL WAS A tall, elegant woman who felt she was too good for her surroundings. This was one of the many characteristics she passed on to her son. She had what might be described as 'an artistic temperament'. She'd always wanted to be an artist of some sort, but motherhood intervened before she had time to find a satisfactory form of self-expression. She decided that her bright and charming little boy would be her greatest work of art: in him she would paint her masterpiece. She determined early on to imbue him with her own best qualities – an innate sense of style, a highly developed aesthetic sense, a love of literature and a passion for the good things in life. She believed that he would grow up to enjoy all of the above. And he did, though not necessarily in the way she had hoped.

She detested the guttural Glasgow accent and always spoke with a clarity of diction she had taught herself by imitating the cut-glass accents of announcers on BBC radio. Roy claimed that his mother imparted to him a lifelong respect for the BBC, which made him feel that I, as an employee of that organisation, was perfect for the role of his biographer. 'If my mother were alive today,' he said, 'she would be so proud to know that the BBC is interested in my story.'

(*The BBC wouldn't be so interested*, I found myself thinking, *if you hadn't topped five innocent people.* Naturally I deemed it safer to resist vocalising that uncharitable thought.)

Marion felt trapped and tormented by the confines of being a postman's wife living in the harsh environment of Govan, a working-class area of Glasgow whose principal claim to fame was ship-building. The landscape of Govan was striking, its tenements and terraced houses dwarfed by the shells of the luxury liners and huge ocean-going vessels being built in the adjacent shipyards.

Great names in shipbuilding such as Fairfield's and Harland and Wolff were based there, and were collectively known as 'The Pride of the Clyde'. The adjective 'Clydebuilt' was a guarantee of quality. Soon the citizens of Govan came to describe themselves as 'Clydebuilt', as a metaphor for strength, integrity and reliability.

When Marion married Archie Hall senior, she had mistaken his earnestness for ambition. She believed he would rise to a senior executive position in the post office and they would travel to exotic foreign lands. Instead, he spent his life sorting and delivering mail. When he got out of the office, his wife was embarrassed to see him staggering under a heavy sack. She felt she was carrying an even heavier load: the burden of unfulfilled dreams.

He was only allowed one two-week holiday per year – the Fair Fortnight as it was known – and the family went not to exotic foreign lands but down the River Clyde with the rest of the Glaswegian working class, to the Isle of Bute.

Marion dreamed of escape, and shared her dreams with her son in the hope that he might succeed where she had failed. Her dreams were bound up with the sea. She wanted to sail away, to a tropical island, to America, to freedom. To anywhere, as long as it was far away from Govan. She imbued her son with a lifelong love of poems about the sea, which he learned by heart. Sixty years later he could still recite them.

She had a fantasy of re-inventing herself as an actress on the Broadway stage, starring in one of her hero George Bernard Shaw's immortal plays with strong women characters like *Saint Joan* or *Major Barbara*. Once she'd found her freedom, Marion would rename herself Maisie and take the world by storm.

She thrilled little Archie with stories of exotic lands beyond the distant horizon. Her favourite book was *The Tales of the Arabian Nights*. It became his favourite too, with its magical tales of genies, thieves and sailors who had wonderful adventures.

As we sat in the harsh confines of that drab prison talking of his mother and their visits to the shipyards, the sea and its promise of freedom seemed very far away. But Roy brought them a little closer by suddenly reciting that perennial favourite 'Sea Fever' by John Masefield. The poem is a romantic daydream of ships, sky and the lonely sea.

His recital was strangely touching. Seeing that I was impressed, he quoted his favourite – 'Cargoes', by the same author, which plunged us into an exotic reverie of quinqeremes and Spanish galleons laden with precious cargoes of rare spices, diamonds and gold. He sighed. 'That poem conjured up a whole world of adventure and excitement for me. One I'll never get to experience now. Mother would recite it to me as we headed to one of the great launches that were a regular occurrence on the river.'

Roy's first glimpse of how the other half lives came when he watched the well-dressed local dignitaries applaud the smashing of an expensive champagne bottle against a ship's hull as it slipped into the river. He found the ceremony wasteful – that bottle of champagne must have cost a fortune – yet strangely alluring. When he grew up he wanted to be the kind of man who could smash a bottle of champagne without worrying about the expense.

Marion would also take young Archie to watch the great ships being built. He would see their giant hulls cradled in the yards, the worker ants busy beneath them in their drab work overalls. The welders wore goggles, and shot angry-looking flames from their blowtorches, which bounced off the steel and sent out dazzling, dangerous-looking shards of fire, reminding Roy of giant versions of the sparklers he would light on Guy Fawkes Night.

On such excursions, Marion would impress upon her young son that he must never end up working underneath the great liners like those common people in the welders' goggles. His destiny was to be *on* the great ships, not *under* them. It was a lesson he took to heart.

This desire to escape the shipyards was not unique to Roy: Govan produced a variety of sporting and showbiz celebrities. Sir

Alex Ferguson, the most successful of modern football managers, started as an electrician in the yards, and Billy Connolly, the greatest stand-up comedian of all time, once worked there as a welder. Connolly took to describing himself as 'the welder who got away'. Gus MacDonald, chief executive of Scottish Television before being elevated to the peerage in the Blair administration, also started out in the yards. Another one who got away.

Indeed, there was a time when it seemed that to succeed in Scottish cultural life a background of working in the yards was second only to being a convicted murderer. In the 1970s, Glasgow's tough Barlinnie Prison set up what it called the Special Unit, designed to rehabilitate hardened criminals, including murderers, through artistic pursuits such as writing, painting and sculpting. For years the Scottish press acclaimed the unit a great success. Ambitious to make my name in the Arts, I often wondered if it was too late for me to join a razor gang. There were practical issues involved, such as – would I have to trade in my battery-operated shaver for one of those old-fashioned open razors of the Sweeney Todd variety?

Roy, who would come to know Barlinnie very well, never needed the unit to make him feel special. His mother convinced him he was special at a very early age.

She was determined to show her son that even in what she regarded as the urban desert of Govan there were oases of beauty and artistic excellence. She tried to turn their trips to the shipyard into cultural events, delighting, for example, in taking her ten-year-old son to Fairfield's head office in the Govan Road. It was a surprisingly ornate building, and Marion had studied its history. She proceeded to educate him on its architecture: 'Archibald, we must appreciate beauty at all times. This building is beautiful. It was designed by the celebrated architect John Keppie, who was Scottish, but wisely he designed it in what is called the French Renaissance style. That is why it is so beautiful. The French love to make beautiful things.'

There were two sculptures that young Archie found intriguing, one on either side of the main doorway. Two men stood, holding strange objects that he did not recognise. He asked who they were and Marion told him they were a shipwright and an engineer. They were portrayed standing on the prows of ships holding the tools of their trade. There was a third sculpture, and this one fascinated young Archie most of all. It was a bearded face on the keystone over the door. 'Mummy, who is the beardy man?' he asked. Marion told him that the architect said the bearded man represented Neptune, the god of the sea, the spirit of the ocean. 'Doesn't that sound beautiful, son? The spirit of the ocean.'

'What's the ocean, Mummy?'

'Well, son, just think how big the River Clyde is. Even bigger than that is the Irish Sea that the great ships sail into. And beyond that there is something so big and so beautiful we can hardly comprehend it. The ocean. The ocean takes you all the way to America! You should go there when you grow up, son. I always wanted to go there, but I don't suppose I ever will, now. Would you like to go to America, son?'

'Is that where cowboys come from, Mummy?'

'It is.'

'Then I'd love to go, Mummy. I'll ask the beardy man to take me there.'

And he did. He passed the sculpture every day on his way to school and said a silent prayer to Neptune that some day the god of the sea would spirit him to America. Later he would tell me that in not reaching its fabled shore he had let his mother down. After some reflection he was to absolve himself and blame Neptune instead. The Roman god had proved just as disappointing as the Christian one. He concluded that all gods were a waste of time and never prayed for anything again.

In marked contrast to Marion, Archie senior, a firm believer in the dour Calvinist virtues of hard work and honest toil, took young Archie to visit a welder friend of his for a guided tour of Fairfield's shipyard. The idea was to convince his son of the dignity of labour, with a view to possible future employment in the yards. The visit had precisely the opposite effect. Young Archie was shocked to see shipyard workers emerging from under hulls and lining up at a long trough that dropped into the river. This trough was their toilet. Their bodily wastes, solid and liquid, slipped not so discreetly into the water. Young Archie was disgusted.

'It taught me a valuable lesson,' he said. 'When you're a prole, your life is not your own. Humiliation and shame are your daily diet.'

That might be fine for the meek of the earth, but his mother had installed in him a fierce pride, and he set his sights on higher things.

He told me, 'I decided that the dignity of labour was just another lie, like Gentle Jesus meek and mild, to keep the working classes in their place. It all seemed so obvious to me. I saw the lives those workers led and compared them to the lives of the leisured classes who'd smash bottles of champagne against the hulls of the ships that those workers had built with their sweat and their blood, but which the workers themselves would never get to enjoy. By the time I was 12, I said to myself, "To hell with the dignity of labour. I'm going to devote my life to the dignity of leisure!"'

And he did. He carried himself from the age of 12 like a gentleman of leisure waiting to come into his inheritance, in the hope and belief that it would be a self-fulfilling prophecy. If his inheritance didn't come along – well, he would just have to take it, even if that meant taking human life too.

6

The Perfect Gentleman

The Prince of Darkness is a gentleman.
Shakespeare, *King Lear*, Act 3, Scene 4

W HEN HE STARTED TALKING about his mother, Roy's words tumbled forth in a cascading torrent. He asked me how familiar I was with Glasgow's Central Hotel, where she worked for many years as a waitress. I told him I knew it well, as do most citizens of Glasgow. After refurbishment it has now been renamed the Grand Central Hotel, lest you be in any doubt that it's a swanky joint. It adjoins Glasgow's Central Railway Station and is noted for its Victorian grandeur. It had the added advantage, from Roy's point of view, of being ideally situated for a quick getaway.

He asked if I'd ever seen the view from its top floor. I had, when I attended several functions there as an undergraduate law student. After a Law Society event, I was in expansive mode (or drunk, as it's otherwise known) and was tipped off by one of the waiters that the view from the top floor was spectacular. He wisely cautioned me not to stand out on the fire escape in my inebriated state. I took his advice and was rewarded with a panoramic vista embracing the city and the River Clyde. It is a view that has inspired many ambitious young men and women, and Roy was no exception. He would frequently go there to experience godlike – or satanic – Master of the Universe moments.

'That's one of my favourite views in the world,' he said. 'When you stand there and see the twinkling lights of the city spread out underneath you, the tiny people milling around on the streets below, you feel that this is a world you were born to conquer. I remember my father reading me the story of Christ in the desert, looking down from the heights and being told that all this could be his. That's how I felt.'

Knowing Roy's antipathy to Christianity, it is unlikely he identified with Jesus. Though he discreetly neglected to mention Satan, it's a safe bet that he empathised more with the cloven-hoofed one. For him it was a case not so much of 'Get thee behind me, Satan' as 'Get out of my way, Jesus!'

The current hotel guide claims that 'behind its walls lie stories of ghosts and haunting, not to mention tales of humour and fame'. I hope this is one of the latter, despite the fact that the ghosts of Roy's victims haunt its pages.

Marion Hall continued her son's moral education by taking him to her workplace, the Central's Malmaison restaurant. In the early 1930s, the Malmaison was the very acme of fine dining in the west of Scotland, the exclusive province of the rich and powerful. Masters of industry, showbiz stars and even royalty dined in its art deco splendour. The roll call of such luminaries could fill a whole book. I will confine myself to mentioning only two – Elizabeth Windsor, Queen of England, and Roy Rogers, King of the Cowboys – both of whom will feature prominently in our (anti) hero's strange and wondrous tale.

Before she started work, Marion liked to take her boy to the restaurant's dining room, where she could demonstrate the skills she had acquired. 'Now, Archibald, watch how I place the soup spoon here, the fish knife here and the napkin there. Everything must be just so. The chef says we must be *très elegant. Très chic.*'

Young Archie looked puzzled. 'I don't understand, Mummy.'

'The chef's not Scottish like us, son. He speaks a different language. He's French.'

'Like the Fairfield's building?'

'Exactly. And the French are the most elegant people in the whole world.'

'What does elegant mean, Mummy?'

'It means stylish. Well mannered. That's why I've brought you up to have lovely manners.'

Her efforts were well rewarded. By the time he was ten years old, little Archie had exquisite manners. He could set a table fit for royalty and knew more about fine wines than any child had a right to know. He could also switch at will from the guttural Glasgow brogue he employed in daily life to an impeccable standard pronunciation, the result of his mother's relentless campaign to drum into him that he must not be the victim of what her hero George Bernard Shaw called the working classes being 'branded on the tongue'.

From a very early age, Roy had one accent for his school chums and another for his teachers. This was an occupational hazard of being a bright working-class Glaswegian schoolkid. My own pals at school used to claim that I spoke to my teachers in what they dismissively called 'your posh Shakespeare voice', while I spoke to my friends in the accent of the streets. I was not aware I was doing it. It was entirely subliminal.

I told Roy this, and he laughed. He had the same issues growing up in a tough neighbourhood. Our discussion on words and their social significance formed an early bond between us. We agreed that we spoke in a dual register not for any snobbish reason, nor for social advancement, but on aesthetic grounds. We both believed the English language was beautiful, England's greatest gift to the world.

As Roy grudgingly put it, 'Those Sassenach bastards had to get something right! Still, it doesn't justify them stealing our sheep and shagging our women. Or was it the other way round?'

The refined speech and delicacy of manners his mother taught him would prove invaluable in later life. As she ran her fingers affectionately through his hair, she liked to ask him, 'What did the nurse at school say when she checked your head for lice?'

'She said I was the perfect gentleman.'

'That's right, son, never lose your good manners. Don't grow up coarse like all those boys you play with. Promise me you'll always be the perfect gentleman.'

'I promise, Mummy. I'll always be the perfect gentleman.'

'That's my boy. *Mon parfait gentilhomme.*'

(FAST CUT to Victim's HEAD being SMASHED IN with POKER.)

◊

A voice said 'Five minutes, ladies and gentlemen.' Visiting time was about to end. The Formica table was now littered with polystyrene cups and chocolate biscuit wrappers. It was a long way from the formal beauty of the tables at the Malmaison.

Roy, perfect gentleman that he was, told me that, 'At night, after my father had droned on about the Bible, he would read me yet another sick story about God smiting his enemies. Was that supposed to impress me? It didn't. After all, it wasn't a very fair fight. And since God had created everything that walks and crawls upon the earth, surely it was His fault for creating those enemies in the first place! I put up with my father's Biblical ramblings so I could get to the fun part of the night.'

'What was that?' I asked.

'Mother would tuck me into bed and read me *The Arabian Nights*. I loved it. It was chock-a-block with tales of beauty and wonder. I wanted to be pals with Ali Baba.'

'And the 40 thieves, presumably?' I added, trying to find a link between his romantic past and his criminal present.

'I've met a lot more than 40 in my time, I can tell you,' he laughed, 'but they weren't a bit like Ali Baba's loveable rogues!'

Roy adored most of the characters in *The Arabian Nights*, but the one he was most fond of was Sinbad the Sailor.

Let me rephrase that. 'Fond' does not do justice to the depth of emotion Roy felt for Sinbad. 'Obsessed' comes much closer to the truth.

He leaned forward conspiratorially.

'I was an Arab in a previous life. A Potentate. A Sultan. My soul was born in Arabia. It was just my body that was born in Glasgow. Even as a kid I knew I wasn't wee Archie Hall from Govan. I wanted passion, beauty, adventure. I wanted to sail the Seven Seas! I wanted to be Sinbad.'

He paused for breath and took a meditative puff on his cigar.

'I thought about changing my name, but I realised that Sinbad Hall widnae have gone down too well in Govan.'

Trying to process this bizarre information, I found myself asking, 'Why Sinbad, specifically?'

He shrugged and looked at me as if the answer were obvious.

'Sin. Bad. Two of my favourite words.'

After a suitable pause for effect, he said, 'Fetch us a cup of tea before they close, son.'

He pointed towards the small tea bar at the other end of the room.

'You can put the cigarettes on the table when you get back,' he said. 'I'll slip the twenty-pound note out and that'll be that.'

My heart missed a beat. This was the moment of truth.

'Roy,' I said, my voice wavering, 'there's just one thing.'

He stared at me with a look that morphed in an instant from disbelief to contempt. His voice suddenly became cold and menacing.

'You haven't put the note inside the fag packet, have you? You have disobeyed me!'

'Roy, it's an offence to smuggle in money for prisoners. The guard at the door told me that. It would screw up this whole thing. They'd stop me visiting. I wouldn't be free to write your story.'

Roy's stare was unrelenting. It was the Stare of Death. It was, I imagined, the last thing his victims saw before he killed them.

'You've betrayed me!'

'I haven't, Roy. I never said I would do it. You agreed that we wouldn't be paying you.'

'I'm not asking to get paid for these interviews. But I have expenses.'

I didn't want to ask him what these 'expenses' might be. Condoms? Lubricant?

'I appreciate that, but you're supposed to earn money by doing tasks. If you *were* asking for payment, you know we wouldn't be doing these interviews at all. I personally wouldn't be happy with it, and the BBC wouldn't be happy either. It's illegal to profit from [I was a millimetre away from the 'M' word] . . . what you've done.'

His stare became even scarier. Again, he spoke slowly, each word a sentence in itself.

'I. Have. Expenses.'

'Roy, I'm not doing it. You can't corrupt everybody,' I said self-righteously.

He looked at me with a degree of mock innocence that was almost touching.

He thumped the table and rasped, 'Oh yes I fucking well can!'

I shot a nervous look towards the guard, who seemed unperturbed.

There was a deeply uncomfortable silence, which Roy broke, again speaking very deliberately to prevent any misunderstanding.

'Go up to buy me tea. Take out your fags. Smoke one. Take out some notes to pay for the tea and slip a twenty into the fag packet. Come back and put the packet on the table. I'll do the rest.'

There was another deadly silence as he stared unblinking at me. Now I knew what various witnesses meant about his scary hypnotic eyes – blazing, as one of them put it, with a demonic power.

I made my decision.

'Cup of tea then, Roy? No problem.'

I walked to the tea bar. It felt like the longest walk of my life. *(Ultra slo-mo here, director!)* I took the packet of cigarettes out of my pocket and put one between my lips.

I realised I didn't have a light. I asked the woman at the tea bar for one, along with two cups of tea. She lit the cigarette between my trembling lips. 'First time visiting, son?' she said. I nodded. 'Don't worry, you'll get used to it.'

I took out two notes, a fiver and a twenty, and paid for the coffee with the fiver.

With the twenty-pound note and two cups of tea in my hands and a cigarette between my lips, I turned and walked slowly back towards Roy, who was still staring at me with manic intensity.

If I slipped the twenty-pound note into the cigarette packet, I risked being apprehended by the guard and barred from all future visits. If I didn't, Roy might withdraw all cooperation and I'd have no story. What should I do? What would you have done?

It's easy to be righteous in the comfort of your armchair: much less so when you are confronted by the Stare of Death.

As I sat down at the table with my back to the guard, I slipped the twenty into the cigarette packet and handed it to Roy. I'm not proud to say it, but that's what I did. I believe most of you in my situation would have done the same.

Roy smiled – or rather he flashed his teeth in triumph, like a shark tasting blood.

As we drank our tea, the guard came over to us. I started

palpitating, believing he had seen me slip Roy the cash. I thought I was about to be arrested and charged with aiding and abetting a convicted murderer. Instead, he took Roy's lighter and with a smile informed us that our allotted time was at an end. I gasped with relief.

Roy shook my hand and said how much he had enjoyed himself. He looked forward to seeing me in a few weeks. I smiled and thanked him for his time, but I left feeling violated. I had the uncomfortable feeling that I was now his bitch.

On the train home, I was wrestling with mixed emotions: elation at the richness of the material and disappointment in myself for not having the courage to stick to my guns. I told myself that twenty pounds was a small price to pay for the marvels he had revealed, but I knew that wasn't the point. The point was that I had capitulated to his will. He had made me do something I swore I wouldn't do, just as he had, in the course of his career as a killer, turned petty criminals into murderous accomplices.

To console myself on the train, I read over my notes and consumed a few miniatures of Glenfiddich malt whisky.

As I look now at my notebook for that day, I see that under the title 'Masks', I have written:

> I am examining my own life through the prism of his. There are so many points of contact: the use of different voices, different accents, different registers depending on the audience. The sense of life as a performance.
>
> I don't know what my real voice is and neither does Roy. It depends on who we are talking to. Is identity itself a mask? W.B. Yeats wrote of the poet wearing a mask, but his definition was too narrow. Not only poets wear masks. We all do.

I looked at my bored-looking fellow commuters and felt I could brighten up their dull lives by recounting the adventure I had just had. I wanted to tell them, 'I've just spent an hour and a half with a murderer. How's your day been?' As I looked at their tired, defeated faces I wallowed in the outlaw dreams of a bourgeois boy – the rock and roll fantasy that bohemianism is the only authenticity.

I saw Roy and myself as two outlaws riding roughshod over reality, mocking the dull suburban lives of these good, solid, nine-to-five citizens who played by the rules. Roy and I knew that rules were there to be broken.

The train and the Scotch lulled me into rehearsing the elements of this project that appealed to me: the writer as vagabond, as outlaw, as one who lives on his wits and by his own rules, defying the conventional moral code which these sober citizens lived by.

'That's not something to brag about,' argued the responsible part of me. I defiantly sipped my whisky but experienced a pang of guilt as I began to suspect that I was being seduced by the glamour of evil.

Perhaps Roy saw my job as vindicating his crimes by sprinkling pseudo-intellectual magic dust over his murderous life. Was I like his aftershave, concealing the rancid smell of death? Was I baking a literary confection, lovingly putting the icing on his cake full of maggots? Was he using me as he had used everyone else in his life?

I took refuge in another Glenfiddich. The whisky soon kicked in, and I was lulled to sleep by the rhythmic rocking of the carriage.

I awoke as we approached Central Station. All that was left of my heroic outlaw fantasy was some drool dripping from the corner of my mouth and a ticket collector nudging me awake to punch my ticket.

I was no longer an outlaw. I was merely a servile employee of a giant corporation and I had chickened out of squaring up to a serial killer.

Roy had spent his life corrupting people. Now he was corrupting me.

7

A Review to Die For

Having the critics praise you is like having the
hangman say you've got a pretty neck.

Eli Wallach

I SPENT THE NEXT WEEK writing up my notes. Bill Bryden was delighted. He agreed that there was enough material to justify several more trips to Full Sutton. A few days after I came back, however, there was a sinister and disturbing new development.

Roy had somehow got hold of the worst review that *The Bogie Man* had received, which had appeared in one of Scotland's national Sunday newspapers. In keeping with our status as a self-loathing, thrawn (yes, we Scots have our very own word for 'twisted') wee nation, their television critic, Ms Becky Farr, decided to write a knocking piece badmouthing the film and the filmmakers.

Despite the fact that it was made on a minuscule budget, she compared it unfavourably to Hollywood epics and wondered why it couldn't measure up to their production values. Never intended as anything more than a festive decoration on the BBC's Christmas schedule, it achieved excellent viewing figures and won many rave reviews, yet she made the filmmakers feel like we'd just tried to inflict *Triumph of the Will* on an unsuspecting public. She had smilingly interviewed several of the principal players involved, including the star, the director and myself.

As a regular reader of her TV reviews, I admired her witty style of writing, which made the subsequent mean-spirited piece all the more disappointing.

In the interests of journalistic integrity (remember that quaint notion?) I should point out that Becky Farr is not her real name. I wish to spare her any post-traumatic stress she might experience were she to realise how close she was to suffering grievous bodily harm as a result of her hatchet job. Roy was about to make it clear that if he had anything to do with it, the hatchet would no longer be metaphorical.

On the Wednesday after I came back from Full Sutton, my phone rang. It was Roy, in Begbie mode. Dangerously angry Begbie mode. His tone of voice entirely lacked the charm of our previous telephone chats. There was no introduction. Formalities were dispensed with as he launched immediately onto the offensive.

'Did you read what that daft bitch wrote aboot you?' The caller had not announced his identity.

I thought it was Roy, but I had to make sure. 'Who am I speaking to?' I asked, like the good professional I was.

'Who the fuck do ye think it is? The Tooth Fairy? It's Roy, for fuck's sake!'

'Oh, hello, Roy,' I said, a little nonplussed. 'What can I do for you?'

'It's not what you can do for me. I'm goin' tae dae something for you, my friend. Did ye see the crap she wrote aboot *The Bogie Man*? How could she slag something so funny?

'That's what critics do, Roy,' I said, trying to sound unconcerned, even though a few weeks earlier when the review came out I had been seething. 'There are always one or two bad reviews. Most of the nationals gave us raves, so, to be honest, I'm not that bothered.'

'But *I* am bothered, son. If she kicks you, she's kicking me too, cos you're like family to me now. You're the son I never had.'

This struck me as a dubious honour. Whilst I was internally debating the merits and demerits of having a serial killer as a father, Roy delivered the knockout blow.

'Don't worry, son, she'll no be a critic for much longer. Mark my words. I've got associates on the outside who owe me favours.'

What was he saying? I felt the panic rising in my gorge. Was he threatening to *kill* the esteemed critic of Scotland's most prestigious Sunday newspaper? Or was he threatening to maim her in some way, as a warning? Kneecapping, perhaps? I tried to make myself feel better by telling myself that at least that if she were merely maimed it wouldn't necessarily interfere with her practising her nefarious profession. It might even enhance it, by forcing her to spend more time at home.

Deciding magnanimously that these thoughts were ignoble and that even a critic didn't deserve such a fate, I felt terror compress my chest like an anaconda. If Roy's 'associates' took action against her, would I be an accessory to the crime? Would I end up in the cell next to him?

'Roy, please, you don't have to do anything. I've had bad reviews before.'

'Aye, but she was really nasty. She got personal. She said you were wearing a big fucking watch! What's wrong with that? She said you were hoping for a Hollywood career! What's wrong with having ambition? She was slagging you for that? It's the kind of thing I've had to put up with all my life. These petty wee Scottish cunts are jealous of high achievers like you and me, son. In Scotland, as soon as you stick your head above the parapet, they try to shoot it off.'

In the current context, the image of a head being blown off was not one I wished to dwell on. Even though her vitriolic review had not endeared her to me, I took no pleasure from the thought of the brain matter of Scotland's wittiest critic being scraped off some dark alley.

'Please, Roy, don't do anything rash!' I beseeched him, in a voice that was on the verge of becoming a self-pitying whine.

'Don't worry, son,' he said, in what was meant to be a reassuring tone. 'I *never* do anything rash! Anyway, must go! Looking forward to seeing you next month!' he said brightly as he put the phone down, leaving me to wonder if I was on the verge of becoming an accessory to murder.

My vision swam and the room tottered as I asked myself what I should do. Contact the police? Call Becky Farr, the potential victim? Or would either course of action make me look paranoid, or worse, implicated? Nor did I want to risk getting Roy angry, since he might pull the plug on the whole project.

I decided to do what I normally do in moments of crisis. Nothing.

There was a fire bucket full of sand in the corridor outside my office. I resisted the urge to stick my head in it.

Over the next few days, my anxiety levels regarding the health and safety of Scotland's top TV critic went off the Richter scale. It was quite extraordinary that I was now feeling so protective of a woman who only a few weeks earlier had trashed my film.

On the Sunday following Roy's threats, I opened the review section of her paper. My heart froze. In the corner where her review normally appeared was a little black box, which bore an unfortunate resemblance to a coffin. Inside it, in funereal type, were the simple yet chilling words 'Miss Farr is indisposed'. All that was missing were instructions as to where to send the wreath. I had been reading her column for years, and this had never happened before. My breathing was becoming spasmodic. 'Miss Farr is indisposed.' Never have four short words struck such terror into the heart of a man.

I repeated it like a mantra, as if I might be vouchsafed a psychic vision of what had happened to her. The world of Glasgow literary types is small and largely confined to the city's West End, where both Ms Farr and myself lived. I knew from mutual acquaintances that she lived just a few streets away from me, and I often saw her walking along the leafy banks of the River Kelvin. I soon became convinced that she had been fatally assaulted there and dumped in the river by one of Roy's bloodthirsty little helpers.

I feared that poor Becky had been set upon as she walked along the riverbank, mentally polishing her next column, innocently sculpting an acidic bon mot with which to humiliate some other poor sucker whose only crime was to try to entertain the masses. Lost in her own thoughts, she probably didn't even see the glint of steel as the serrated edge of the knife penetrated her heart.

I had to find out the truth, if only to offer my condolences.

I called the newspaper and asked if they could tell me the exact nature of Ms Farr's indisposition. I was put through to someone on the features desk. I breathed a sigh of relief that it wasn't the crime desk. An anonymous male asked if I were a relative of hers. I immediately assumed the newspaper had been briefed by the police that only close relatives were to be informed of Ms Farr's untimely demise pending the announcement to the general public.

I told him that though I was not a relative, I was a 'colleague'. I had been interviewed by Miss Farr a few earlier weeks earlier in connection with a project of mine.

'What project? What's your name, sir?'

I realised that I had made a grave mistake. If I revealed my identity, they'd know that as the victim of her recent barbs I might bear a grudge. I would have a motive. Sweating, I put the phone down before I became the prime suspect.

On my way home, I took a detour to the street where she lived, or had lived, expecting her house to be cordoned off by yellow tape, with signs saying 'Crime Scene Investigation. No entry except for Forensics.'

But there was no sign of anything unusual. Just as I was about to turn back, I saw her door open. It was Becky Farr herself. Alive. And apparently fully mobile. She wasn't even limping.

I almost wept with relief. I hid in the shadows and let her pass on the other side of the street, following her at a discreet distance into a pharmacy around the corner. Now that I could see her in the full light, I quickly confirmed that she had no bandages, scars or missing body parts. I also noted that her nose was red and she sounded blocked up. She was buying flu medication.

She turned to leave. I tried to hide behind a revolving stand, feigning interest in a wide selection of reading glasses. Unfortunately, she spotted me. Obviously sitting square-eyed in the darkness for so much of her life had done nothing to weaken her eyesight.

'Hello,' she said smiling brightly, just as she had done when she was interviewing me for her hatchet piece. 'Did you enjoy my review?' she said, apparently oblivious to the fact that it was about as likeable as a piece of toxic waste.

'Enjoy it?' I thought to myself. I might have done if I were a raging sadomasochist. There are men who get off on hammering nails into their gonads, but I'm not one of them. When I was a kid, someone accidentally slammed a train door on my thumb. Her review was right up there with that in my league table of enjoyable experiences.

'To be honest, no, I didn't enjoy it,' I replied, annoyed at myself for sounding as if I were the one who should be apologising. 'It was well written, as ever, but no, I am afraid I found it a little . . . negative.'

'Really?' she said, sounding genuinely surprised, even hurt. 'I thought it was very positive.'

'Yes,' I thought, *'positive as in HIV positive.'*

'Oh well,' I said, 'we'll just have to agree to disagree, I suppose.'

'We should go out for a drink some time and talk about it,' she replied. I couldn't believe my ears. Was she now asking me out on a date, having created the lasting impression in Scotland that the film was a flop when the opposite was the case? My initial sense of the injustice of her piece welled up again.

'I've got a lot of work to catch up with, but I'll call you sometime,' I lied. I knew that going out for a drink was a dangerous suggestion. I might get hold of some hemlock.

Her insensitivity to the consequences of her words confirmed to me once and for all that critics live in a parallel universe divorced from normal human emotion. I was tempted to call Roy up and tell him I'd changed my mind. Instead, showing remarkable restraint, I held the door open for her and said, 'I hope you feel better soon.'

8

Arabian Nights

Sinbad picked up a bag, turned it over, and out came a shower of diamonds. His friends were dazzled. 'Diamonds! How beautiful!' his friends cried.

'The biggest diamonds I've ever seen!' said one friend. 'Where did you get them, Sinbad?'

Sinbad smiled. 'That's quite a story,' he said.

'The Tale of Sinbad the Sailor and the Valley of Diamonds' from *The Arabian Nights*

ON MY SECOND VISIT to Full Sutton, I felt more relaxed. I was enormously relieved that Roy had decided to heed my plea not to attack Ms Farr. In the visiting area I noticed how the prisoners' hair and fashion sense tended to be frozen at the time of their admission. Hence all the mullets and flared trousers. Roy was one of the few who seemed timeless, perhaps because he, as the oldest whole-life tariff prisoner, knew that he would die in prison. He had already made his accommodation with eternity.

Delighted that I wasn't occupying the cell beside him for colluding in the untimely demise of Ms Farr, I resumed where I had left off.

'So, Roy, why did *The Arabian Nights* mean more to you than the Bible?'

'Why wouldn't it? The Bible is a load of bloodthirsty nonsense. My father forced it down my throat like cough mixture, telling me it was good for me. Good for me? It made me want to throw up. The Old Testament is sadistic shit. Way too violent. As far as I'm concerned it's porn. Not good healthy porn that can give you a raging hard-on, but nasty evil porn that turns your stomach. Let's face it: the Old Testament is one long snuff movie.'

Intrigued by this killer's critique of violence, I asked him to elaborate.

'In the Old Testament, God is always angry, always killing somebody, always smiting them, and fathers are always sacrificing their sons. The God of the Old Testament is a fucking psycho! What's his problem? What kind of father lets his son be tortured and crucified? He should've been reported to child services. Classic case of child abuse if you ask me.'

I felt I had to intervene on behalf of Christians everywhere.

'But what about the New Testament, Roy? Doesn't it give us a moral code to live by? What about the Christ of forgiveness?'

'Well, he's a lot more appealing than the Old Testament God, I'll give you that. Younger and sexier. If he looked anything like Dali's Christ of St John of the Cross [a reference to the famous portrait of the Crucifixion which hangs in Glasgow's Kelvingrove Art Gallery] it's no wonder 12 fishermen followed him around, kissing the hem of his cloak. It wouldn't have been his cloak I'd have wanted to kiss, I'm telling you.'

He laughed lasciviously.

'So what's your problem with the New Testament, then?' I asked.

He puffed thoughtfully on his cigar.

'The problem is, son, that while the Old Testament is too violent, the new Testament is too meek and mealy-mouthed. All that Sermon on the Mount rubbish. It's a losers' creed. A creed for the sheeple. "The meek shall inherit the earth." Don't make me laugh. The only earth they'll ever inherit is six feet of it shovelled on top of them when they're finally planted. Our Lords and Masters encourage all that meekness cos it means we'll agree to be shafted till the day we die. When was the ruling class ever meek? When did they ever turn the other cheek? The only cheeks they turn are the cheeks of the arses they're trying to shag. They preach the Sermon on the Mount, but all they really believe in is mounting anyone and anything they can get their leg over – whether it be man, woman, or beast of the field. Believe me, I've studied them, lived with them, slept with them, sucked them and fucked them. I've served them and serviced them. I know what I'm talking about.'

When he put it like that, his argument did sound fairly persuasive.

I listened in fascination to this critique of Christianity from a man who had taken human life five times.

'Nietzsche was right: God is dead,' he added, 'but people still worship the corpse.'

I was intrigued by this reference to Friedrich Nietzsche, the German philosopher who proclaimed the passing of Christianity and the death of God. Roy said he'd discovered him via his mother's books on George Bernard Shaw. As he didn't have any of Nietzsche's books in his prison library, he said he'd love it if I could bring one or two. I told him I would.

I had read a great deal of Nietzsche's philosophy while researching my Hitler book, following the dance of ideas as it became the goosestep to global destruction. Nietzsche turned Wagner's world upside down, and Wagner provided Hitler with the Valkyrien soundtrack to genocide.

Sadly, it is difficult now not to convict Nietzsche as guilty by association, but one of the reasons for his continued appeal is that he ennobles loneliness, making you believe that you aren't just a sad and lonely bastard: you're a sad and lonely bastard for a noble reason, because you're a sensitive artist, a thinker, a misunderstood visionary. Hence his appeal to those of us who've been confined for years in a bedsit or a prison cell.

I asked Roy which of Nietzsche's books I should bring and ran a few possible titles past him. The ones he chose, inevitably, were *Beyond Good and Evil* and *Why I Am So Clever.*

Thus was born what we christened the Full Sutton Book Club. From now on, a part of our monthly discussion would be dedicated to the books and thinkers we admired. By the time we had reconvened, Roy-the-lifer came up with a suitable motto: 'Short sentences preferred'.

After our literary and philosophical digression, it was time for us booklovers to get back to what Roy regarded as the Not So Good Book.

'I left Bible-thumping to my father,' he said, 'but as a boy I had a deep religious sense.'

'Really?' I found this surprising in the light of what he'd just told me.

'Yes. I had my first mystical experience when I was eight years old. In the Argyle Arcade.'

The Arcade is an indoor shopping centre, a series of jewellers' shops located in a long winding corridor that joins two of Glasgow's main shopping arteries – Argyle Street and Buchanan Street. For the children of the dispossessed it is a glittering palace where you can marvel at the kind of sparkling gems hitherto only glimpsed adorning princesses in fairy tales.

Roy continued, 'To me, the Arcade was a winding serpent encrusted with precious jewels, like something out of *The Arabian Nights*. I was Aladdin and this was my cave. In later life, I often thought about robbing it, but that would have been like robbing a church.'

He saw his first jewellers' shop when he was eight years old. His mother took him on a shortcut through the arcade and he was transfixed. He stopped in his tracks and dragged her over to the shop window, where he stood in a wide-eyed state of ecstasy. Sixty years later, he still remembered the effect the experience had on him.

'Those diamonds were the most beautiful things I had ever seen. They took my breath away – the way they caught the light and transfigured it. I had to hold those diamonds in my hand, to possess them. I looked at them and saw another way to live.'

He continued to rhapsodise: 'I couldn't believe they used to be something as dirty and ordinary as coal.'

That transformational aspect, that alchemy, fascinated Roy, who spent his life trying to turn the dross of Archie Hall into the diamond of Roy Fontaine.

Young Archie pulled his mother into the shop and put on a diamond-encrusted watch under the wary eye of the shop assistant, who was not amused when the boy tried to leave the shop whilst still wearing it.

His mother dragged him back. The assistant took the watch off his wrist as the boy started bawling. An irate Marion dragged him out of the shop, cuffing his ear and telling him that stealing was bad. It was not a lesson he was to take to heart.

Roy was convinced he had met his destiny: 'I knew that some day I would hold such beauty in my hands. I only had to work out how. I kept dogging off school just to look at those sparkling gems. I even dreamed about them.'

'Really?' I asked.

'Yes. I had a recurring dream that I was dressed as Aladdin, in silken turban and robes, sitting cross-legged in the middle of the Arcade, as various shop assistants showered me with dazzling precious diamonds. Those dreams made me wake up with my first boyhood erections.'

Well, whatever turns you on, I suppose.

Diamonds were throughout his life a kind of aphrodisiac. We may ask ourselves why. Were they an emblem of eternal potency?

That's what Roy seemed to suggest when he told me: 'I love diamonds because they are so hard and so beautiful. Hard and beautiful as a proud cock.'

With the heightened linguistic sensitivity of the professional writer, I knew instinctively that the cock in question was not of the feathered variety.

9

By Any Other Name

What's in a name? That which we call a rose
by any other name would smell as sweet.
Shakespeare, *Romeo and Juliet*, Act 2, Scene 2

WHEN ROY WAS NOT being turned on by the sparkling gems in the arcade, he was gazing in rapture at glittering images on the silver screen. The cinema, like the Arcade, became a place of worship.

The 1930s saw him making regular pilgrimages to his local fleapit, where he would stare transfixed at the dramas unfolding in front of him, the light reflecting on his wide-eyed face.

'My life as Archie Hall was in black and white. I wanted it to be like the movies I loved – an epic in glorious living Technicolor.'

At the matinee one Saturday afternoon in 1938, as he ate his ice cream, he had a revelation that would change his life. He stopped in mid-lick as the soundtrack extolled the virtue of the charismatic cowboy riding across the screen. It was love at first sight.

'See Roy Rogers, King of the Cowboys, in *Under Western Skies*. He's a loner, an outsider. He lives by his wits. Thrill to his exploits. He's the smartest guy in the west.'

'That was it!' explained Roy. 'I'd wanted a new first name for ages. Anything was better than Archie. I'd run through the alternatives in my head. My original idea was to take something from *The Arabian Nights*. Sinbad, Aladdin, Ali Baba Hall were all possibilities. None of them was quite right for Govan. Now I had it! From that day on I knew I would be *Roy*. I too would live by my wits and have adventures every week.'

I couldn't believe my luck. Another brick was about to be cemented in the fortress of our bonding. I said proudly, 'I've actually met Roy Rogers!'

He seemed incredulous: 'You're kidding me!'

'No, really. A couple of years ago. On my first trip to the States.'

'How the hell did you manage that?'

'A friend of mine was making a TV documentary about him. I've got the photos.'

He seemed genuinely thrilled. 'That's amazing! You've got to bring them next time! Roy Rogers came to Glasgow, you know, in 1954. I missed him, cos I was pleasuring Her Majesty at the time. I was gutted. Have you seen the great photo of Roy riding Trigger up the steps of the Central Hotel?'

I hadn't, but I told him I would try to track it down.

'Make sure you bring the photos of you and Roy next time,' he said enthusiastically.

The only other person he knew who had met Roy Rogers was his mother, who had served the silver screen cowboy and his wife Dale Evans at the Malmaison.

'You met him, son, it's destiny! Destiny's telling me I was right to choose you!' My having met the cowboy had instantly elevated me into very select company. Now the Category A prisoner had his very own Category A visitor.

◊

Young Archie's controversial decision to call himself Roy originally met with strong opposition from his mother, though given her own tendency to think of herself as bohemian Maisie rather than respectable Marion, we can speculate that she secretly understood where he was coming from. Besides, she hated the name Archie too, reeking as it did of marital disappointment. She believed the name unworthy of the masterpiece she was creating in her beloved son. But for appearances' sake she had to show proper maternal concern.

'We can't call you Roy, son! Your daddy would be horrified. Your name's Archibald. You're not Roy Rogers, son, you're not from the

Wild West. You're Archibald Hall from Glasgow. I know Glasgow sometimes *feels* like the Wild West. They're both rough, violent places, but they're very different. At least the Wild West has a certain charm.'

Roy, as ever, was obstinate.

'But, Mum,' he said, 'Roy Rogers isn't the cowboy's real name either. I went to the library. It says in the film book that he's really called Leonard Slye.'

(In retrospect, Slye might have been the perfect name change for the master con man Roy was to become.)

Secretly pleased at her boy's diligent use of the local library's research facilities, Marion told him, 'Son, sometimes I think you're too smart for your own good!'

'If film stars can call themselves something else, why can't we? I want to be called Roy, Mum!'

'You're a determined wee soul, so you are! Sometimes you frighten me when you look at me with those big intense eyes of yours, do you know that? I suppose the name Roy might suit you. It's French for king, you know: *le Roi.*'

Roy greeted that information with joy.

'Is it? See, Mum? I told you it was perfect for me.'

She smiled and shook her head in resignation.

'I don't know where you get your confidence from, son. Certainly not from your father. Right then, we'll see if it'll stick.'

And stick it did. The only person who refused to call Archie by his new moniker was his father, Archie senior, who continued to call the boy Archie, which made life at home a little confusing.

◊

Now that we had bonded it would soon be time to tiptoe towards some sensitive issues – like the murders, for instance. For the time being, though, I decided to ask him something comparatively safe: 'Why have you chosen me, Roy? Why do you want me to tell your story?'

'Because you get me, son. You'll be able to do my story justice. What's the point of being a unique genius like me if no fucker can tell your story properly? You're the man to do it. Those English wankers just don't get my sense of humour. You can make my story funny as fuck! My life was a laugh, it was fun, it was exciting, it was a great adventure. I need somebody who can get that across. And that's you.'

After this touching vote of confidence, I felt empowered to take the plunge and raise the question of his brother and sister. This of course was delicate, since he detested one and adored the other. He took a deep meditative puff on his cigar and started telling me the tale of Violet and Donald. One he mollycoddled; the other he murdered.

10

The Devil's Disciple

Do what thou wilt shall be the whole of the
Law.

Aleister Crowley, *The Great Beast*

MR AND MRS HALL apparently could not conceive another child, so when Roy was 14 they adopted a pretty little girl. She was only six years old, and they named her Violet. She became the apple of her stepbrother's eye. He made dresses for her dolls, and she became his little doll, whom he dreamed of dressing up in all the jewellery he yearned to wear himself.

He reckoned that the kind of bejewelled flamboyance he had in mind would not be tolerated on the mean streets of Govan, where men were men and genders were as rigid as the girders with which the great ships were built. The kind of jewellery a Govan man would wear around the shipyards tended to be a Masonic ring, rather than, say, Roy's preferred tiara and pearls.

When he started to wax lyrical about little Violet, I decided to request a short break and have an early cup of tea.

I went up to the tea bar and returned with two teas and a couple of chocolate biscuits. I believed that Roy was now painting rather too rosy a picture of his childhood. I was, after all, a writer, and as someone once remarked, happiness writes white. I felt it was therefore time to edge towards the 'M' word. (M for Murder, for those of you who are a bit slow on the uptake.) As I unwrapped my chocolate biscuit, I took the first tentative step, summoning up the courage to ask him a blunt question: 'Roy, you seemed very happy at this time in your life. Where did it all go wrong? Where did you go off the rails?'

His affable features gave way to the menacing stare I had seen last time, when I had inadvertently called him Archie.

'Off the rails? I didn't go off the rails, son. I travelled first class.'

'What I meant, Roy, was why did you choose a life of crime?'

He sighed in exasperation. 'Let me set the record straight, son. I never *chose* a life of crime.'

I half expected him to come up with a trite 'crime chose me', but his explanation was more original.

'I chose a life of *leisure*, not a life of *crime*. Look around you, son. This is what a life of crime has brought me. Living in a tiny room. Occasionally seeing a little patch of sky. Never gazing on the sea. Sharing my life with a bunch of illiterate morons and degenerate perverts! Nobody in their right mind would *choose* a life like this!'

I dimly recalled that Roy's claim to being in his right mind was highly questionable, since he had been declared insane several times in his criminal career. I felt that to mention that now might seem churlish.

He continued: 'The good-for-nothing parasites who govern us are born into a life of leisure. Once you've seen how those leeches live, if you have any pride, any spirit, you'll want the same for yourself. But if you don't have property, investments or a trust fund, how else are you going to pay for your life of leisure except by making . . . some accommodation with criminality?'

I felt that to roll over and agree with this – though it would have been by far the easiest option – would have been dishonest of me. So I bit the bullet and said, 'But surely you could have got a job? A career? That's the usual method. You know – earning a living.'

'Don't give me that crap about a career!' he replied vehemently. 'My father had a "career" in the Post Office, and where did it get him? I'll tell ye, son. It got him a bad back and an electric clock. A clock that he put in pride of place on our mantelpiece. Can you believe it? That was his reward when he left the Post Office. A fucking silent electric clock. That's what all those years of devoted service got him, all those years of fighting his way through blizzards and rain with a heavy sack on his back, all those years of having the arse bored off him trying to read illiterate cunts' handwriting as he sat in a wee room sorting the mail. For all that torment what did he get? A clock! A clock that wasn't even honest enough to tick and remind him that time was slipping by and his life was ebbing away like sewage water down the drain! No, son, any time I was tempted to get a "proper" job or pursue a career I just had to think of my father and that fucking clock.'

I decided to backtrack.

'What I meant was that everything seemed to be going fine – till that bad business at the Army camp.'

'What bad business?' he asked, scowling.

My voice started to quiver as I said, 'You know, the pictures of Hitler and all that.' I knew I was in dangerous territory. The very mention of Hitler carries with it the stench of death and evil: two subjects in which Roy could have held a masterclass.

I had planned to introduce these topics later in our relationship. I hoped I hadn't blown it.

He stared at me with those dead eyes, which had a curiously paralysing effect, producing the kind of reaction a cat's stare has on a mouse.

'Who have you been talking to?' he said, with the rumbling restraint of a volcano waiting to erupt.

'Nobody. It's in my research notes. It's mentioned in several newspaper reports.'

There was a menacing Pinteresque pause, while he made up his mind on how to play this. He stared at me with a mixture of exasperation and contempt, and said, 'OK, let's get this straight. It was 1939. The world was at war. The Post Office decided that my father was so boring he'd make a wonderful telegraphist, whatever the fuck that was, so they sent him to the Army camp at Catterick, in the north of England. We all had to go with him. Mum, me and Violet. My mother wasn't too happy about going there. Until,' Roy said through gritted teeth, 'she met Major Morris.'

'Major Morris? Who was he?'

He took a long puff on his cigar and winced visibly. He was either experiencing cigar-induced heartburn or was recalling a painful memory. It soon became clear that it was the latter.

Whilst his father was busy learning the finer points of telegraphy and his mother was otherwise engaged, Roy would babysit little

Violet. One night, when his father came in exhausted, presumably from excessive telegraphing, Roy offered to go fetch his mum from the dance hall, where she had taken to spending a great deal of time allegedly with new women friends she'd made at Catterick.

The strains of Glenn Miller's 'In the Mood' were wafting across the night air as Roy approached the Nissan hut where the dances were held. As he stood in the shadows, he saw his mother emerge, laughing, with a dashing uniformed officer. Roy could hardly believe what he was seeing. The officer had his arm round Marion, who was nuzzling up against him. In a sort of trance, torn between anger, disbelief and sadness, Roy followed at a discreet distance till the two lovebirds reached the officers' quarters.

He watched them go inside. The light went on. After a few moments, it went off again. And a light went out in Roy's soul too. He hid in the bushes outside for 40 minutes, weeping. When his mother finally emerged, he sprinted round in a loop and intercepted her, pretending to believe her story that she was coming straight from the dance hall.

Sixty years on, the memory still caused him great distress.

'My dear mother had betrayed me! She'd betrayed my father too. For once, I actually felt sorry for him. I found out that the bastard she was cavorting with was called Major Morris. He must have turned her head. I couldn't let it go on. I had to get rid of him!'

I thought for a moment that he was about to give me a world exclusive on a murder for which he had not been tried. I could see the headlines in my mind's eye. *'I murdered the handsome Major. Serial killer reveals all to unknown Scots author.'*

The truth was that his rage at Major Morris led not to murder but to burglary. A week after discovering that his mum was having a fling, Roy broke into Catterick's military personnel records office. With gloved hands he removed certain files that were marked 'Confidential'.

'My plan was to put the papers and other incriminating items into the Major's quarters the next day. But I'll say this for the Army – they acted quickly. Too quickly, unfortunately. It took them years to deal with Hitler, but they dealt with me overnight.'

The day after the break-in, the teenage Roy was sitting in his room when he heard voices outside the door.

'It's routine, Mrs Hall. We're searching the entire residential area. Is this your boy's room?'

Roy was startled when two large military policemen entered. One of them said, 'If you don't mind standing up, son, this'll just take a minute.'

It took a little longer than that. One of the military policemen examined Roy's bookshelves whilst the other turned over his mattress.

'Jesus! Look at this!' said the first MP, pulling out the stolen Confidential file from a box under the bed. That was bad enough, but it was about to get much worse. In the box he also found assorted Nazi memorabilia, including a variety of swastikas made of metal and fabric. No sooner had the first military policeman found these than there was a whistle from the direction of Roy's bookshelves. The other MP was removing a thick tome from behind an encyclopaedia. It was a hardback book in a lurid cover that showed a photo of a bald man staring menacingly at the viewer. It was an evil stare, the kind that makes your flesh creep. Exactly the kind of stare, in fact, that we see in photos of Roy when he lets his guard drop and the mask of congeniality slips. It was, in short, the Stare of Death.

The man on the book cover was the role model on whom Roy based his own theories of the Man of Power and the Stare of Death. The military policeman read the book's title: '*The Great Beast* by Aleister Crowley.' He opened the title page and read out the following epigram: 'Do what thou wilt shall be the whole of the Law.' He turned to the inside flap of the dust jacket and read that this was 'The autobiography of the most evil man in the world. A self-confessed Satanist.'

The MP looked at Roy, asking, 'Are you a Satanist, son?'

Before Roy could answer, three photos that Roy had been using as bookmarks fell out. One was of Adolf Hitler. Another was of Doctor Goebbels, Hitler's propaganda minister.

The most enigmatic, perhaps, and certainly the rarest, was the third: a photo of the Nazi Reichstag where, inscribed in monumental letters above its giant doorframe – like a portal welcoming you to a new, darker world where evil reigned – was Adolf Hitler's personal logo: an intertwined A and H.

Those were of course Roy's initials before his name change. He kept a copy of that photo with him for the rest of his life. It was the only time he liked to think of himself as Archie Hall.

Thus Roy found himself confronted by two military policemen holding very incriminating evidence, including a book by 'the most evil man in the world' and photos of two other strong contenders for that dubious title. Hitler, Goebbels and Crowley could have won gold, silver and bronze in the Evil Olympics.

'You've got a lot of explaining to do, son,' said one of the military policemen, with a gift for understatement. Roy, to give himself time to think, began with his usual conversational gambit: 'But, Officer, there's a perfectly innocent explanation.'

'Oh, yes – and what would that be?'

After a beat, Roy said, 'I think it's important to know your enemy.' He was proud of his improvisational skills.

'I agree, son. That's why I think it's time we got to know you better,' said the burlier of the two MPs as they frog-marched him out for questioning. Marion looked on, choking back the tears.

'The problem,' Roy helpfully explained to me, 'was that I couldn't tell them the truth without betraying my mother. Without loyalty, what have we got? Nothing.'

'So what's the truth, Roy?' I asked. 'What *were* you doing with those Nazi photos and a book by Aleister Crowley?'

'Don't you see? I was going to plant them along with the confidential papers in the Major's quarters, make him look like a Nazi sympathiser and get him sent down for treason. But I ran out of time!'

I didn't believe that was the whole truth. I asked him for his true opinion of Hitler. Predictably he defended him as 'a Great Man, until he started turning people into lampshades'.

He trotted out the usual litany of Adolf's early achievements – he got Germany back on its feet, restored a sense of national pride, solved the unemployment problem, built the autobahns and designed the Volkswagen, which according to Roy was 'a really great wee car'. But even he had to admit that all that paled into insignificance when weighed against the death ovens.

I perceived that in praising Hitler's early career Roy was really talking about himself. After all, his own career had a certain charm, till he started turning people into corpses.

Under pressure he revealed that he was fascinated by Crowley's writings on how to impose one's will on others. He told me he'd learned from Crowley that 'the key was the stare. The unblinking hypnotic stare.'

Roy had realised – before the British Intelligence Services did – that Hitler had been heavily influenced by Crowley and the occult, and he surmised, correctly as it turned out, that Adolf had spent many hours in front of a mirror perfecting that hypnotic stare which would ultimately transform a nation of decent people into willing accomplices in genocide.

I had a sudden illumination. I asked him outright, 'So, Roy, tell me – did *you* practise your stare?'

After what seemed like an unconscionably long silence, he said, 'How the fuck did you know that?'

'A lucky guess,' I said. I didn't tell him that I'd spent years researching the Satanic origins of the Nazis. Unfortunately, the stare could only get you so far. The next step, whether your name was Adolf or Archie, tended to be murder.

Oddly, he admired Churchill and Hitler in equal measure. This apparent contradiction made sense when I recalled that Roy was schizoid and was waging war on himself.

For the time being, I left Adolf, the occult and that pesky genocide business aside and asked Roy how he was punished for his Catterick misdemeanours. 'The whole family was sent back to Glasgow,' he said. 'Naturally, this caused a breach with my father, who felt disgraced and humiliated. He would have felt a lot more disgraced and humiliated if he'd known the truth – that his wife had been shagging another man.'

Roy was sent for psychological testing. A degree of mental instability was diagnosed, with potential anti-social tendencies. It was recommended that he perform some public service to show that he could reintegrate himself with the community and become a useful member of society. Selflessly, Roy told them he'd like to do some work for charity.

As usual, he was a man of his word. He collected cash for the war wounded. He had of course decided that he was the war wounded, since he'd been traumatised by the business of Major Morris. The fraud he was about to perpetrate would therefore rest easy with his conscience, if he'd had one.

11

The Tin Man

As for you, my galvanised friend, you want a heart.

The Wizard of Oz to the Tin Man

COLLECTIONS FOR THE WAR wounded were organised by the altruistic Lady Pettigrew from her headquarters in Glasgow's city centre. As part of his rehabilitation, the 14-year-old Roy turned up in her office, well scrubbed, well dressed and oozing charm like pus from a suppurating wound.

He thanked her profusely for his Red Cross tin and his letter of accreditation. Knowing what we know now, giving Roy written authority to collect cash without imposing strict controls was about as sensible as giving a junkie the key to the cabinet containing the morphine.

As he put it, 'I had always known my artistic talents would come in handy.' He smiled wistfully. Recalling his first con trick brought back many fond memories.

It was time for the artist in him to get to work. He got hold of a tin that was the same size as the Red Cross tin. On his kitchen table, when his parents were out, he used a paint box and stencil to mark a red cross onto a white piece of paper, copying the original as faithfully as he could. With great fastidiousness, he glued the paper onto the tin can. When finished, he smiled at his handiwork.

He was now the proud possessor of two tins. In one of them, he would collect pennies for the war wounded: in the other he would collect pounds for himself. 'I had a tin for the tenements and a tin for the toffs,' he said with satisfaction. 'It was so simple, yet so elegant.'

Simplicity and elegance would become the hallmark of his work, even as the artist moved on to bigger and better canvases.

He went round the poorer areas of Glasgow's West End, such as Partick, collecting pennies and halfpennies in the legit Red Cross tin. Using his own handmade tin, he would collect in the more affluent areas, his favourite being Kelvin Court, a select residential area that was a veritable treasure trove of wealthy people and expensive *objets d'art*. The inhabitants of the Court liked the well-dressed and mannerly boy and gave generously, even apologising to him for only having small notes. With a smile, Roy would assure them, as they folded their crisp notes into the tin, that 'every little helps'.

The scam had various benefits. Apart from the instant cash it generated, he found that this was also a wonderful way of casing a place. He was already planning to expand his criminal empire by indulging in a little light burglary. The inhabitants of Kelvin Court would invite the charming young man into their homes rather than leaving him standing out in the cold whilst they fetched their money.

He started carrying a little notebook to record everything for future use. As soon as he left the flat he would write down all the salient details, eventually composing what he described as his 'Burglar's Bible'.

His earliest known literary effort consisted of the following:

Kelvin Court No. 37. Various interesting *objets d'art*, including small oil paintings and vases. Diamond brooch and pearl necklace on cabinet. Point of entry: small window in kitchen.

The fake can was always lighter because it was full of banknotes rather than coins. Roy extracted a profound truth from all of this, which he described as, 'To travel lightly is to travel well.'

Roy never did believe in anything heavy, whether on the physical plane or the philosophical one. For him, lightness was all.

He hated heavy clothes, like the coats he had to wear through the interminable Scottish winters. He avoided heavy people who, like his moralising father, embraced a burdensome and joyless creed. He had a suspicion of heavy industry, symbolised for him by the shipyards. He came to associate heaviness with servitude, like the heavy cuffs and chains with which he was manacled so often to officers of the law. In contrast, diamonds embodied the light, held the light, embraced the light. All his life, Roy sought the desirable lightness of being.

Whenever Roy the boy came back with his heavy can of pennies, Lady Pettigrew would be mightily impressed. Here was this lovely little boy going out in rain, hail or shine, with no thought of personal gain. He had quickly established himself as her favourite, a misunderstood urchin of the streets, a reformed Artful Dodger. Artful Dodger, yes: reformed, no.

As he handed her the can she would say, 'Another full can, Roy? It's so heavy! That's wonderful. But you can't go on like this. You'll wear yourself down. You go out in all weathers and always come back with a full tin.'

Roy said he owed it to the war wounded.

When she praised him further, he would modestly reply, 'It's all in a good cause, Lady Pettigrew. My contribution is very small. But I believe every little helps. I can honestly say that not a day goes by without me thinking fondly of the deserving poor.' He smiled. Lady Pettigrew smiled back, seduced as so many were by his charm.

With his tin-man profits supplemented by his takings as a burglar, he soon had enough stashed away to describe himself as a 'businessman'.

'What I did next,' he said, 'will amaze you.' He winked. 'You could say I had a very good war. Largely by being a very good whore.'

He chuckled, knowing he had whetted my appetite.

◊

Before he could tell me the astonishing truth about how he spent the remainder of his war years, it was that time again: the guard told us we were 15 minutes from the end of the interview.

Just enough time to get him a cup of tea and slip the banknote into the cigarette packet.

Roy was pleased that this time I didn't make a fuss.

The guard collected the lighter. Roy and I shook hands, and we both said we were looking forward to the next time. I headed for the train.

I bought a pack of cheap cigars at the station and a miniature of whisky in the catering compartment of the train. Whisky and cigars were my attempt to get inside Roy's head. I bought them because he liked them, not because I did. They were my writer's equivalent of a method actor getting into character by living the role. I also bought some Walker's shortbread, but this time it was because I liked it – a pathetic little gesture intended to demonstrate that I still had a will of my own.

As the train pulled out of York station, I chose not to dwell on the fact that by slipping the cash into the fag packet I had again capitulated to Roy's will. Exercising my right to denial and self-justification, I chose to accentuate the positive aspects of my mission. This project, I told myself, would be not just true crime but a meditation on true crime. I would write *In Cold Blood* with laughs.

I thought, *'Maybe Roy's right. Maybe only I can do his story justice and bring out its black comedy. Perhaps the New York Times will discreetly asterisk their review as "Funny as F***".'* There was no doubt that Roy was flattering me, showing me his most charming, most persuasive self – the self who could convince those in his circle that it was OK to kill.

Reminding myself that he was a vicious killer made me question the whole enterprise. The Stare Master was bending me to his will, just as Hitler made the Germans his willing companions in evil and Crowley the Great Beast got his acolytes to do the most outrageous things.

I decided I needed a second miniature to silence the nagging voice of doubt. The whisky and the heat would ensure that I'd be asleep by Carlisle.

12
Rough Diamond

The soul is placed in the body like a rough
diamond, and must be polished, or the lustre
of it will never appear.

Chinese proverb

I SPENT THE NEXT FEW weeks writing up my findings, trying to find the best vessel into which to pour the quicksilver of Roy's life. The BBC was considering a six-part or possibly even a ten-part drama, since the material was so rich. Already my appetite had been whetted for the promised revelations concerning his lurid wartime escapades. I could hardly wait.

I got hold of a new copy of a Nietzsche reader, which had extracts from all of the philosopher's major works. I also made copies of the Roy Rogers photos. These were supplemented, of course, by the cigars and the cigarette packet.

I travelled down to Full Sutton on a bright spring morning, an eager student ready to study at the feet of the master. I pushed any doubts I might have about glamorising a murderer to the back of my mind.

Roy embraced me like an old friend and professed himself delighted with the book and the photos. He had a green hardback lying on the table. Its cracked and worn spine bore the title *The Last of Mrs Cheyney*.

He lit up his cigar, courtesy of the lighter delivered by his friend the guard, and looked at the Roy Rogers photos.

He smiled at one showing me and the cowboy's famous horse Trigger, which had been lovingly preserved by a taxidermist.

'Which one of you is stuffed?' asked Roy, laughing like a drain at his own joke.

I smiled graciously.

In that schizoid way of his, he suddenly went from laughing hysterically to becoming silently morose as he continued staring at the photos of the iconic American cowboy.

'Are you OK, Roy? What's wrong?' I asked, like a dutiful son concerned for his dad's well-being.

He looked up at me with tears in his eyes.

'I let my mother down,' he said wistfully. 'I promised her I'd go to America. I never did, and now I never will. I always felt I'd end up in the USA. It would have suited me. It was the only place big enough for my talent.'

He started quoting from *The Arabian Nights* – a sure sign that he was digging deep into his heart, or whatever it is that a murderer has where his heart should be.

'Hear the tale of all the hardships that I suffered before I rose to my present state and became the lord of this mansion where we are now assembled.'

He looked wryly around the prison and sighed deeply.

'Look where I've ended up. Some fuckin' mansion, eh?'

I felt that if I didn't cheer him up the interview would go nowhere. I picked up one of the photos and declared that calling himself Roy after the famous cowboy was an inspired choice. His mood brightened. He told me that after christening himself Roy – a Baptism of Desire, we cradle Catholics would call it – he never looked back.

'My life's a rough diamond,' he said. 'Your job is to polish it.'

He reiterated that he did not expect to be paid anything and that he was doing it for what he insisted on grandiosely calling his 'legacy'. He was happy with the cash in the cigarette packets.

I told him I would do my best to do his story justice, even though he was a quicksilver character who was hard to pin down.

'Don't try to pin me down, son,' he said forcefully. 'I'm not a fucking butterfly.'

'But you seem to have lived several different lives. You're not just one person – you're a lot of people, Roy,' I opined. 'You just kept reinventing yourself.'

'Why shouldn't we reinvent ourselves, son?' he answered. 'After all, Scots are a nation of inventors, aren't we? We invented penicillin, the phone, television. But the most important thing to invent is yourself.'

He puffed magisterially on his cigar: 'See, son, most people never discover who they really are. They think the cards they are dealt at birth are the cards they have to stick with. I say throw the fucking things back into the pack till you get the hand you want. That's what I did.'

(*And look where it got you,* ' I found myself thinking.)

'We just need a little more confidence, son! That's what our sad wee thrawn nation lacks. Confidence. Style. Fearlessness.'

He would have made a great politician. His demagogic appeal was getting to me. If he kept pressing the nationalistic hot button, I'd be prepared to vote for him.

He continued: 'I tried to show Scotland the way forward. That's why the English punished me.'

(*Well, Roy, that and the fact that you murdered five people.*)

There you have it: Roy the Existentialist, the self-created man. 'The difference between me and ordinary people, son, is that they live in someone else's script. I write my own. I don't live my life in quotation marks.'

A large part of me believed that because he lived by his own rules he was more authentic than the rest of us. After all, I wanted to write my own script too. I was beginning to realise that in writing about his life and his beliefs I was also examining my own. In exploring the mind of a fantasist I was exploring the fantasist in my own soul.

As he spoke persuasively about the desirability of being the author of your own life, his aftershave kept wafting over to me, creating an uncomfortable feeling of excessive intimacy. I wondered if his victims had smelled that aftershave as he squeezed the life out of them. Was that cheap fragrance their last link to the sensual world? I don't know what aftershave he was wearing, but for aesthetic reasons I like to think it was Brut.

I went up to the tea bar, so that we could have an early cuppa. When I came back, he had reached a provocative conclusion.

'You know, son,' he said, 'you're like me in so many ways.'

'Really?' I replied, reminding myself that I had not as yet killed anyone.

'Yes,' he said nonchalantly. 'We both sit alone in a room for long stretches of time, talking to ourselves, telling ourselves stories. And we both lie for a living.'

Before I could respond, he continued, 'but I promised to tell you about my wartime adventures, didn't I? I will do so now, with no word of a lie. And you'll find that the truth really is stranger than fiction.'

He relaxed, took a deep puff on his cigar, and started talking.

◊

During those dark days when Britain stood alone against the might of the all-conquering Nazis, a Polish airman was billeted with the Hall family. Captain Jackobosky was 30 years old, stylish, confident and cultured. The 17-year-old Roy felt strongly drawn to this attractive man in uniform, with whom, given the lack of space in their modest home, he was to share a bed settee. Soon they were sharing bodily fluids too. The airman contributed to the Home Front by giving the young lad his first blowjob. In that age of rationing, the protein intake was greatly appreciated.

Thinking back to the business of Major Morris at Catterick, Roy reckoned that if having sexual relations with an officer was good enough for his mother, then it was certainly good enough for him. Admittedly his own love interest was a mere captain, but he was confident he could work his way up the ranks.

'I had found a new way of making contact with another human being,' he said, with uncharacteristic tact. 'I'd dabbled with girls, had a bit of a kiss and a cuddle here and there, but a man knew how to please a man better because he had the same equipment.'

Roy often made the sexual act sound like an exercise in practical mechanics, but then I suppose in many ways it is.

He was nevertheless at pains to point out that his relationship with the dashing freedom fighter was more than merely physical. They shared a patrician view of the world. And since all things earthbound and heavy were alien to Roy, he loved the very idea of flight.

Jackobosky was one of the many Poles who had come to Scotland to help the British fight the detested Nazis who had ravaged their homeland. Roy loved the Captain's thrilling tales of bravery and derring-do, seeing him as a real-life, more exotic version of Biggles – every young lad's favourite fictional flying ace. Captain Jackobosky was as good as it could possibly get for a pubescent young lad who was discovering his love of the same-sex experience. Jackobosky was Biggles with blowjobs.

There was apparently no penetrative sex, but as Roy was fond of putting it, 'We had a great time handling each other's joysticks!'

As in so much of Roy's life, there was an aesthetic as well as a physical dimension. Ever careful to establish his credentials as a true aesthete, he was at pains to point out that the dashing captain educated the 17 year old in the world of Art, and not just the art of the blowjob.

Whenever possible, given the restrictions of war, Jackobosky, in his immaculate uniform and highly polished flying boots, would take Roy to Glasgow's Kelvingrove Art Gallery, where Marion's campaign to instil in her son a love of great art was enormously enhanced by the fact that, thanks to the Polish captain, beautiful *objets d'art* would now and forever be associated in Roy's head with sexual gratification. Sex and culture seemed natural bedfellows.

The officer and his young beau shared a disdain for the values of the mob. The good captain was fond of discoursing on the true values of life, which by definition were aristocratic and contemptuous of the herd.

'You are an aristocrat of the spirit, my boy. Never forget that style maketh the man. Always dress to impress, always be immaculately turned out and always, *always* polish your footwear.' He would slap his highly polished knee-length boots to emphasise this last point, as he said, 'People always judge you by your shoes!'

Roy became enamoured of the Art Gallery's most celebrated painting, Salvador Dali's *Christ of St John of the Cross*, a magnificent portrait of the crucified Christ painted from a unique perspective. Roy's love of the painting had nothing to do with Christianity, and everything to do with the magnificent muscle definition of the subject. In short, the painting made him horny. He was delighted when I told him that on my first trip to California I had done all the tourist things, including a trip to the famous body-builders' paradise known as Muscle Beach, and learned that it was here that Dali found the man who modelled for Christ. His name was Russell Saunders, an actor and stuntman.

Roy salivated at the very mention of Muscle Beach: 'It sounds like my idea of Paradise,' he sighed. 'All those golden brown, well-oiled muscular young men showing off their magnificent bodies, so different from the milk-bottle torsos I grew up seeing on the cold beaches of Scotland.'

Blasphemous as it seemed to me, Roy was unapologetic about insisting he could not look at that painting without getting an erection. Now, knowing its background, he felt somehow vindicated. 'I'll bet that horny old goat Dali was getting his rocks off on that muscle definition too.'

It was an original, even persuasive take on what I had hitherto regarded somewhat simplistically as a masterpiece of religious art. I now had to mentally re-categorise it in the file marked 'homoerotic'.

Roy was introduced to that world by the Polish captain, about whom he always spoke with admiration and gratitude.

'You know, son,' he said, puffing expansively on his cigar, 'to this day there's nothing I like better than a stiff Pole.'

The Polish airman was no more than a happy prelude to the swelling act, and during those years when Roy's complex and ambivalent sexuality was defining itself there was a whole lot of swelling going on. Jackobosky eventually flew off into the sunset but not before he had whetted Roy's appetite for the sumptuous feast of the senses that was to follow.

As soon as he was old enough, Roy applied to join the Royal Navy. He was looking forward both to wearing the uniform and to spending a happy few years saying, 'Hello sailor!' with no fear of recrimination. These pleasures were denied him, however, because his Nazi obsession and penchant for Satanic literature that had been discovered at Catterick were on permanent file with the relevant authorities. Not even his apparent heroics as a Red Cross collector were enough to erase that dark stain on his record. He was deemed too mentally unstable for military service.

As a result, while his contemporaries were spending their youth fighting the Nazis, Roy was spending his ill-gotten gains from burglary and petty theft in the Central Hotel, pursuing the good life for which he always felt destined.

He was always welcome there, having ingratiated himself with the staff whilst his mother worked at the Malmaison. Besides, he always tipped well.

'The secret of life,' he said, 'is to tip well. With someone else's money, of course.'

Unfortunately, the blackouts marred the Messianic (or in his case Diabolic) view from the top floor.

One night he was finding consolation in a glass of champagne, whilst listening to the hotel's piano being played beautifully, not by the resident pianist but by a man he did not recognise, who kept catching his eye and winking at him.

The impromptu concert over, the man made a beeline for Roy's table, introduced himself as Vic Oliver, and asked the handsome young man if he could buy him a drink. Roy was flattered. He said yes.

'He seemed old to me at the time,' said Roy. 'He was only in his early 40s, but remember, I was just 17. So I always thought of him as Old Vic, just like the theatre. I never actually went to that theatre, but later on whenever people asked me if I'd ever been in the Old Vic, I could honestly answer yes.'

Roy did not immediately recognise the name Vic Oliver, even when the older man described himself as a well-known radio entertainer. A skilled musician whose schtick was to pretend to play the violin badly for comic effect, Vic starred in the popular BBC show *Hi, Gang!* and would achieve the distinction of being the first castaway on the perennially popular BBC radio show *Desert Island Discs*, where a celebrity is invited to choose his or her eight favourite records.

This was in the pre-television era, when the faces of many radio performers, even stars like Vic Oliver, remained unknown to the general public. When Roy asked about his accent, which was noticeably foreign, he revealed he had been born in Vienna and that his birth name was Victor Oliver von Samek.

It was Vic who was to impart to Roy his lifelong love of cigars. He offered the young man a Romeo and Juliet, lighting it up with a beautiful gold lighter whilst telling him conspiratorially that these cigars were his father-in-law's favourites. This information seemed superfluous till Vic leaned forward and revealed that his father-in-law was Winston Churchill.

In truth, relations between the musician and his illustrious father-in-law were always strained. Since Churchill had set up a magnificent intelligence-gathering network, it is highly unlikely that he would have remained unaware of the sexual shenanigans of the man who had stolen away his beloved daughter Sarah.

Vic's marriage ended in 1945, which meant that Winston got rid of Vic Oliver at roughly the same time as he got rid of Adolf Hitler. History can only speculate on which gave him the greater satisfaction.

Winston's antipathy towards his son-in-law is best expressed in an anecdote regarding a dinner party at which Vic was present. Churchill was asked for his opinion of Mussolini. Had the Italian dictator done anything admirable? Churchill took a large puff on his cigar and replied, glancing at Vic as he did so, 'Yes. He had the good sense to shoot his son-in-law!'

Within an hour of meeting each other, Roy and Vic were in bed together, as the latter taught him the joys of penetrative sex with a man. Roy had now graduated to full sex, having, as it were, passed the oral examination through the expert tutelage of the Polish officer.

After sex, Vic liked to hum 'Prelude to the Stars', the theme song of his radio show. In the morning, he said he could introduce Roy to some stars of stage and screen. The young man could keep the gold lighter if he agreed to come down to London for a few months, all expenses paid. Roy agreed enthusiastically.

'It was the first time I'd slept with a man,' said Roy nostalgically as he picked up the gold lighter. 'He gave me this as a present: 24-carat gold. It's been with me ever since.'

Within a week, the 17-year-old lad followed his mentor down to London, where, despite the Blitz, high society's gay elite frequently partied the night away above the darkened theatres of Shaftesbury

Avenue. Vic took him to all-male soirees in Ivor Novello's luxury flat overlooking Piccadilly Circus. It was a huge apartment with polished wooden floors, scattered rugs and a white grand piano in the corner.

Roy joined the ranks of the good-looking young men who were paid to act as waiters dressed only in thongs, their job being to satisfy the appetites – all the appetites – of the older men.

'I tasted the cream of London society,' said Roy. 'Literally!' He winked suggestively. It was not an image I particularly wished to dwell on.

The serving boys would flirt with the older men and for tips would perform sexual favours for the famous guests. Couples would drift off into bedrooms and toilets.

Discretion, Roy assured me, was of the utmost importance, because if outed the careers of these men would be over.

'But then again,' he added, 'these were not just men with friends in high places. They *were* the friends in high places.'

It was in these circles that he met Lord Robert ('Bob') Boothby, who was rumoured to be a lover of Ronnie Kray, the most notorious of all London gangsters. Boothby spent his life shuttling between high society and the criminal underworld. Like so many public figures who could not in those days afford to come out of the closet, he enjoyed living on the dangerous edge of things. He got a kick out of what Oscar Wilde called 'feasting with panthers'. When not consorting with the Krays, Boothby moved in exalted circles. He was a close friend of future Prime Minister Harold Macmillan and had been Private Secretary to Winston Churchill himself.

Roy claimed that it was through Boothby that he was invited to Somerset Maugham's villa on the French Riviera after the war – the famed Villa Mauresque. He went into great detail about swimming in the pool there and spending a weekend in the company of other young men whose physical perfection was matched only by the beautiful *objets d'art* with which they were surrounded.

This tale had a particular resonance for me, as I used to project myself as a hugely rich writer and tax exile in the Maugham mode. (I refer you to my earlier reference to Maria and the suntan lotion.) In some variations of the fantasy I had actually purchased the Villa

Mauresque. There was a particular poignant irony in the fact that Roy had actually been there. He'd come closer to living my dream than I had.

Yet he claimed that the post-war sexual adventures lacked the peculiar thrills of those wartime orgies which took place as the bombs fell, when the noise of energetic love-making was often drowned out by the sound of the air-raid siren. The prospect of imminent death lent added spice to the little death of orgasm.

Roy put it all in context for me, with some relish: 'Hitler often dropped his loads on London at the same time as the famous guests were dropping their loads on us.'

He continued, 'You have to understand, son, that things were shot off into the night which had nothing to do with the Germans. I suppose you would have to call it friendly fire. We turned the blackout to our advantage: when the lights went out, the pricks went in. On the stage, Terence Rattigan may have believed in separate tables, but in real life he was not much of a believer in separate beds.'

Rattigan, the handsome, charming, witty playwright, would chat up Roy whilst Ivor Novello gave an impromptu performance on the grand piano.

Roy saved his biggest revelation till last, nonchalantly dropping the bombshell (to use a metaphor apt for the Blitz) that it was here, in that gay wartime demi-monde, that he became the lover of Lord Mountbatten, Prince Philip's uncle.

I was stunned. I asked the obvious question.

'You mean – you mounted Mountbatten?'

'No,' Roy replied, ever a stickler for detail, 'Mountbatten mounted me. He believed it is better to give than to receive.'

He puffed reflectively on his cigar, savouring the memory.

'He was a generous soul, you see. He really was a loveable fellow. I could easily have fallen in love with him,' he added wistfully, 'but I realised he was just after me for my body. I contemplated having a tattoo on my arse saying "By Royal Appointment".' Wisely, he decided not to do so.

I found myself wondering what you call Mountbatten when he's rogering you? 'Louis' might be appropriate but seems a tad, if not a tadger, informal. 'Sir?' 'Your Royalness?'

I asked Roy what he called his royal lover. He answered frankly: 'Most of Mountbatten's gay friends called him "Mountbottom".'

I laughed in disbelief.

'Did *you* call him Mountbottom?' I asked.

'Of course not. That would have been disrespectful,' he replied. 'I called him the Queen.'

All this talk of sex seemed to have made Roy thirsty. He raised an imaginary cup. I stood up to go to the tea bar, but not before he had put the events he'd been discussing in historical and philosophical context.

'Funny how life works out, isn't it?' he said. 'During the war, if I'd got into the Navy as I'd hoped, I might have gone down on the high seas. Instead, I went down on Lord Mountbatten.'

13

Here's to you, Mrs Robertson

At your age I looked for hardship, danger,
horror and death, that I might feel the life in
me more intensely.
George Bernard Shaw, *Heartbreak House*

I CAME BACK WITH THE tea and a couple of biscuits. In the light
of Roy's recent revelations regarding oral sex, I resisted the
Cadbury's chocolate Flake on the grounds that it was too phallic.

'So, Roy, before you slept with Vic did you know you were
homosexual?'

'I'm not homosexual. I'm bisexual. So are you, son. We all are.'

For a second, I almost went along with him, thinking that to
disagree might disrupt his narrative flow. But I decided that it would
be a better policy to tell him what I really thought.

'I don't think so, Roy. I've only ever fancied women.'

'How quaint! You're in denial. Most men are. Thank God I'm
not. Liking men has certainly made life in prison so much more
interesting. A man has certain needs. Sexual needs . . .'

He looked at me suggestively, as if he were willing me to satisfy
those needs personally.

'You have sex in here?' I asked, too quickly, realising that I should
have tried to make it sound more like a question than an offer.

'Of course. Twice a week at least,' he replied. 'With two prison
officers. One male, one female.'

He said this so matter-of-factly I had difficulty processing the
information. I tried to envisage the logistics of a prisoner having
sex with a jailer. Where did they do it? In the cell? The showers? A

toilet cubicle? Nothing about Roy would surprise me. Or perhaps he was bluffing, trying to mess with my head.

I reminded myself that for many years he had been Britain's most successful confidence trickster. But subsequent revelations led me to believe he was telling the truth. He was a man with a voracious sexual appetite, and prison certainly seemed to have done nothing to diminish it.

As if reading my mind, he smiled and waved over at the prison officer in the corner, who nodded and smiled back. Was I imagining the warmth of that smile? Was that guard his lover? Or was the female guard who let us into the visiting area? Could both of them be his lovers?

'Sex with men is pure pleasure,' he said, smiling. 'It's the purest kind of sex there is. There's none of that nonsense about babies.'

'But babies are necessary for keeping the human race going, aren't they?' I said on behalf of heteros everywhere.

He shrugged. I decided this would be the moment when I turned to the delicate subject of his brother.

'Speaking of babies, Donald, your baby brother, must have been born when you were about 16.'

Roy's genial mood suddenly abated.

'He was not my brother! He was my *half* brother. He was born nine months after my mother's affair with Major Morris. My father had been trying to get her up the duff for years. Then along comes the Major and it's "wham-bam, thank you, ma'am".'

'You never liked Donald much, did you?' I asked, bravely.

'Like him? He was a useless small-time nothing. A loser. A pervert. He was no brother of mine! We were as different as chalk and cheese. He had no class. He was a waste of space. I used to bug the tits off him by calling him Morris Minor. I taunted him by saying, "I put the Roy in Rolls-Royce, but you put the Morris in Morris Minor."'

I decided I'd better leave the brother stuff alone for a while.

'So – when was the first time that you were arrested for a crime, Roy?'

'That,' he said, shaking his head ruefully, 'would be the unfortunate business of Mrs Robertson.'

◊

In 1945, the 21-year-old sophisticate returned to Glasgow from his London adventure. The war was over, and Roy bade a temporary goodbye to his upper-class acquaintances. He wanted to move in their circles some day, but with a little more dignity: 'Preferably not with a banknote for sexual services stuck between the cheeks of my arse.'

He came to believe that even that indignity was better than the joyless austerity of postwar Britain. Fortune favours the brave, he decided, especially when you give it a little nudge.

Big changes were taking place in the postwar world. Vic Oliver was divorced by Lady Sarah Churchill and Lord Mountbatten was given a new job, as Viceroy of India.

Roy claimed Mountbatten's new title of Viceroy was appropriate, since his Lordship had engaged in so much vice with Roy. He kept in touch with Mountbatten's inner circle and told me that 'Lord Louis, God bless him, remained adventurous on the sexual front. You could say that India just added more spice.'

I asked him to elaborate.

'It's common knowledge that Lady Mountbatten was shagging India's President Nehru. The English had been fucking India for years. Now it was a case of the Empire strikes back.'

It seems that with admirable zeal Lord Mountbatten partitioned his wife's sexual favours before partitioning India.

As I sat listening to Roy, I realised that two key elements had been omitted from earlier accounts of his life – namely, the humour and the politics.

Roy had penetrated the ruling class of Britain, literally and metaphorically. He knew their dirty little secrets. Journalistic accounts of his life have tended to concentrate on the blood and gore and missed the bigger picture, which is a perverse kind of social comedy. His story reveals the ruling class as not just venal but venereal. As a portrait of the British class system it's not just warts and all – it's genital warts and all.

His sexual mentors having left the arena, Roy had to move back in with his parents in Govan. His mother was worried that Mrs Robertson, the next-door neighbour, had not been seen for some time. Roy used his burglar's skills to climb along a window ledge and force open the latch from the outside. With his mother watching, he had to pretend it was beginner's luck.

Just as he was about ransack the place for valuables, his other neighbour, Mr McLaughlin, a tram driver, managed to force an entry. The two men went into the bedroom and found the unfortunate Mrs Robertson lying dead on the bed.

Mr McLaughlin was about to phone the police, but the ever resourceful Roy said they should inform the old lady's relatives first. This was a delaying tactic to enable him to pick the lock on a large bedside chest, which he claimed might contain correspondence that would reveal her next of kin.

Instead, crisply stacked in two cardboard shoeboxes at the bottom of the chest, he found two thousand pounds in cash.

Roy's first thought was that the relatives didn't deserve this, because they never visited the old lady. Others would make better use of the money. Others like himself, for example. He'd have to talk McLaughlin into it and cut him in, of course, since the tram driver had witnessed him making the discovery. McLaughlin needed some persuasion, but soon the silver-tongued Roy had him agreeing to split the loot down the middle. They then phoned the police.

As he looked at the corpse of Mrs Robertson, the ever-compassionate Roy remarked, 'Poor old soul. What a shame that her family wasn't with her at the end.'

'Still,' he thought, as he hid the money in the lining of his jacket, 'every cloud has a silver lining.'

Roy decided it would be a good idea for him and McLaughlin to tell the surviving relatives that they'd found the princely sum of one hundred pounds in a shoebox. The stratagem was brilliant, as ever. They were praised for their honesty. Mrs Robertson's son thanked him for being so trustworthy and gave him a present of a red leather-cased travelling carriage clock. For the rest of his life, sentimentalist that he was, Roy used it as his alarm clock whenever he'd to get up early to rob someone.

After the looting of Mrs Robertson's, it was party time. Roy got into the habit of dressing his adopted sister Violet, now in her early teens, in her best finery and taking her out to the cinema.

The movie that made an indelible impression on him at this time was *The Thief of Baghdad*. He and Violet went to see it several times at Glasgow's most luxurious cinema, the La Scala in Sauchiehall Street, where it was possible to dine as you watched. Characteristically, Roy made a recurring booking for the table and tipped well.

He could still quote a snatch of the film's dialogue to me, 50 years later.

'I am Abu the thief, son of Abu the thief, grandson of Abu the thief, most unfortunate of sons with a hunger that yearns day and night.'

He smiled briefly at the memory. 'What a great film! How exciting their lives were, compared to the lives of those around me.'

Note that he didn't say compared to his own life. By the age of 21, Roy had already had more adventures than most people pack into a lifetime. But he wanted more. Lots more.

'Then the bubble burst,' he said ruefully. His happiness was interrupted when two large policemen arrived at his mother's door and took him in for questioning.

'The tram driver went off the rails,' said Roy, spitting out some tobacco contemptuously. 'He was an amateur. He got drunk and cliped. Grassed me up. Said he felt guilty about old Mrs Robertson. He betrayed me. That is the one thing I will not forgive.'

Thus did Roy introduce one of his great themes. Like all paranoids, he was obsessed with betrayal.

'Was that your first spell in prison?'

'It should have been, but I had other plans. After all, it's well known that there's a very fine line between genius and madness.'

He winked and smiled that self-satisfied smile which suggested he knew something I didn't.

14

Aladdin Sane

Though this be madness, yet there is method
in it.

Shakespeare, *Hamlet*, Act 2, Scene 2

GIVEN HIS HISTORY OF mental instability, it was deemed necessary that before sentencing for the Robertson theft, Roy's mental state should be evaluated by two psychologists.

In a bare, cell-like room, he was confronted by a pair of white-coated experts, Doctors Davidson and Scanlon. Obsessed with cleanliness, Roy felt duty-bound to ask them how they got their coats so white. Did they use a special brand of washing powder? Was bleach employed? Did they have a unique method of drying?

Asking for laundry tips was a suitably eccentric opening gambit in Roy's game plan to establish himself as mad so he could be committed to a lunatic asylum and avoid a harsh prison regime. Though he was hamming it up for the doctors, he was a bona fide cleanliness fanatic. He would change his bedsheets several times a day. His fingernails were always well manicured. And there was that omnipresent, overpowering smell of aftershave.

Doctor Scanlon led the discussion. 'So, Archie, why did you steal Mrs Robertson's money?'

Roy looked at him with the stare I had come to know so well: a mixture of hurt and fury.

'My name is Roy.'

Doctor Davidson chimed in. 'Your birth certificate says you are Archibald Thomson Hall.'

There was a long pause before Roy spoke again. 'That is correct. I am Archie.'

Davidson and Scanlon looked at each other. They'd achieved a small victory. Their smug self-assurance increased as Roy continued, 'I am Archie the thief.'

Scanlon and Davidson permitted each other a small self-satisfied smile. The statement felt like a confession. But it wasn't. It was a quotation.

Roy continued, 'I am son of Archie the thief, grandson of Archie the thief. Most unfortunate of sons. With a hunger that yearns day and night.'

Scanlon's jaw dropped open. 'Pardon?'

Roy went on, 'This is the land of legend, where everything is possible when seen through the eyes of youth . . .'

He continued in that vein for some time, quoting his favourite chunks of dialogue from *The Thief of Baghdad*. By the simple device of replacing 'Abu' with 'Archie', he left the psychologists bamboozled.

Roy beamed with pride as he told me, 'Thanks to some amended movie dialogue, I avoided prison and found myself in Woodilee Home for the Mentally Disturbed. It wasn't the Central Hotel, but it was a fuck of a lot better than Barlinnie.'

In those days, Barlinnie was notorious as Glasgow's toughest prison. As previously noted, when it established its Special Unit to rehabilitate hardened criminals it became a breeding ground for media stars, celebrities, playwrights, poets and sculptors. In the golden years of the Special Unit, Barlinnie was like the Algonquin Round Table, with slopping out.

Back in the dark days of the 1940s, however, it was one of the most punitive prison regimes in the whole of the United Kingdom. Woodilee Home for the Mentally Disturbed, though no holiday camp, was much more user-friendly. It came under the aegis of Glasgow Corporation, whose somewhat depressing logo, the city's coat of arms, illustrated a downbeat rhyme that was drummed into the heads of Glasgow schoolkids:

Here's the tree that never grew, here's the bird that never flew, here's the bell that never rang, here's the fish that never swam.

The City Fathers, then as now, were firm believers in the power of negative thinking.

Basket-weaving was about as arduous as the Woodilee regime got.

'I made friends quickly with the basket cases,' said Roy, careful to avoid counting himself amongst their number.

'Friends like Charlie, who thought he was Napoleon. And Jim, who thought he was Jesus. Jim used to weave crosses instead of baskets, which was very brave of him. Charlie and Jim were typical of Woodilee's inmates. They had grandiose plans. Charlie kept saying how much he was looking forward to the Battle of Waterloo. I didn't have the heart to tell him not to be too optimistic.'

There was some renovation work going on at the hospital, and Roy, whose obsession with cleanliness inevitably led to him being put in charge of laundry duties, made a meticulous study of the workmen and their habits. He noted that at lunchtime they would take a break from their thirsty work, remove their paint-spattered overalls and go down to the local pub for a pint, leaving their caps and overalls in a heap in the corner beside their paint pots.

Having checked that the coast was clear, Roy carried a large bag from the laundry room and discreetly went over to the corner where they had left their stuff. He picked up a cap, an overall, a brush and a pot of paint and disappeared into the bushes. He re-emerged in a paint-spattered overall and cap, carrying a paint pot, brush and bag.

Striding jauntily up to the gate, he smiled at the guard and asked, 'Do ye have to be mad to work here?'

The guard laughed and replied, 'No, son, but it helps. How's the painting going?'

'Oh, a few more coats and we'll be there. I'm telling ye, this place is full of coats. White coats!'

Enjoying the banter, the guard joked, 'Aye, sometimes it's hard to tell the loonies from the doctors!'

Roy laughed as the man unlocked the gate. He walked round the leafy corner and continued a few hundred yards up the lane till he saw a thick clump of bushes. He darted in, took his own clothes out of the bag, and emerged like a young man enjoying a pleasant stroll.

He was free at last. He felt exhilarated. He would celebrate his new-found freedom by taking a paddle-steamer to Paradise.

15

The Lady Varnishes

When you visit Rothesay, you must visit the
gents' Victorian toilets on Rothesay pier. They
have been described as 'jewels in the
sanitarian's crown'. Ladies can be given a
guided tour at quiet times.

Beautiful Britain travel guide

ROY TOOK THE BOOKMARK out of *The Last of Mrs Cheyney*, the book that was lying in front of him. I was surprised and touched to see that the bookmark was a postcard – not just any postcard but one of Rothesay, a place dear to my heart. The beautiful picturesque town is the capital of the Isle of Bute, on the Firth of Clyde. I stared in fascination.

The postcard was old, dating from the '50s, I reckoned. Its colours were super-saturated. Those vivid and intense hues were the colours of childhood. The colours of memory. With its Technicolor gardens and impossibly blue sea, it looked like Paradise. And to Roy and me, it was.

I told him that Rothesay was my childhood Eden. My granny had a small flat there, the type known as a single end, where we holidayed every Easter and summer.

'You're right, son,' Roy said, staring at the postcard whilst running his finger lovingly over its intensely blue waves. 'It's the nearest Scotland has to Paradise. That's why I had to go there when I escaped from Woodilee. That's where I would go now if I could.'

The Isle of Bute, with its warm Gulf Stream currents and its palm trees, calls itself the Madeira of the North, though it is a safe bet that Madeira does not call itself the Bute of the South.

Roy became enamoured of Bute, naturally enough, when he heard it described as 'The Jewel of the Clyde'. The island was made for him: half of it is in the Scottish Highlands, the other half is in the Lowlands. Hence Bute is bipolar, like Roy himself. And like him it is capable of surprising you with moments of magnificence.

His eyes misted over with tears as we talked of Rothesay Castle, the Meadows, the steamships, and skiters, those large flat stones we both loved to skim across the waves.

'We all sink beneath the waves, son. We all end up at the bottom of the ocean, but some of us dance first. Dance across the waves, son. That's what I did. Before you sink, dance across the waves.'

The thing about your childhood paradise is that once you have eaten the apple of adulthood the door to Eden slams shut behind you. You are out of the garden and have to survive in the jungle. Yet no matter how many tropical islands you visit, no matter how many sun-kissed foreign strands, true joy is not really about hours of sunshine or the delights of duty-free: the place you love in childhood has a hold on your soul which remains unbreakable. The closest Roy and I ever became over the course of our very peculiar friendship was when we shared those childhood memories of Rothesay.

◊

Within a few hours of his escape from Woodilee, a smartly dressed Roy was boarding the *Waverley* paddle steamer bound for his beloved island.

On the deck, a kilted singer with his accordion band was giving a spirited rendition of 'The Day We Went to Rothesay, O', the lyrics of which went like this:

> One Hogmany at Glesca Fair, There was me, mysel' and sev'ral mair, We a' went off to hae a tear An' spend the nicht in Rothesay, O, [Chorus] A dirrum a doo a dum a day, A dirrum a doo a daddy O, A dirrum a doo a dum a day, The day we went to Rothesay, O.

A party of passengers sat listening, trying to solve the riddle that had perplexed so many before them. What exactly did 'dirrum a doo a daddy O' actually mean?

Roy saw a well-dressed lady who was about to light up a Russian cigarette, which she held with perfect poise in her cigarette holder. He moved forward to give her a light.

Those of you who have seen the film *An Affair To Remember*, a romance which begins on a boat, might like to think of the following exchange in those terms, with a few kilts, accordions and unintelligible Scottish dirges thrown in.

As Roy lit her cigarette, the Lady said, 'Beautiful lighter. Gold?'

'Twenty-four carat,' he replied, noticing her wedding ring.

'Beautiful ring,' he said. 'Gold?'

'Twenty-four carat,' she replied.

'We appear to have a great deal in common,' added Roy.

'So it seems,' replied the Lady. 'I'm sure we'll get along famously.'

They did. So much so that she invited him to dine with her at her hotel that evening.

'She was 15 years older than I was,' he told me. 'Married, of course, but let's not drag in irrelevant details. She was a lady of taste and refinement. She was on her way to see an actress friend in a show at the Winter Gardens.' The Winter Gardens, despite its name, entertained generations of holidaymakers over the summer months with a great range of Variety acts and talented performers.

The woman, whom Roy always referred to with chivalric tact as the Lady, was staying at the Glenburn, Rothesay's premier hotel.

'The Lady invited me there for dinner that night. That was how I discovered the stairway to heaven. I stared up at the hotel from the bottom of its steep stairs, which were beautifully lit with spotlights and fairylights. It all looked wildly romantic. To me, it was an enchanted castle. I was the handsome young prince about to breach its defences. I bounded up the stairs two and three at a time. I stopped at the top and looked down. The bay twinkled beneath me. I could see the silhouettes of islands I had yet to explore. I knew this was how I was meant to live.'

The candlelit dining area where he and the Lady enjoyed a delicious meal reminded him of the Malmaison.

'I came to think of the Glenburn as the Central by the Sea, and its restaurant as the Malmaison sur la Mer.'

The Lady poured champagne and asked him if he'd like wood pigeon or Loch Fyne kipper, caught and cured locally.

'I'm glad it's cured,' he joked. 'I never eat sick fish.'

'You're so funny, Roy!' laughed the Lady.

He couldn't have agreed more.

He asked her, 'Are we having dessert?'

'Oh, yes,' she said. 'But it's not on the menu.'

She smiled at him. He smiled back.

'I had a lot to smile about,' he said. 'She was stroking my balls under the table.'

I ask you, dear reader – who says romance is dead?

In the forthcoming biopic, we will no doubt dissolve from the ball-stroking incident to the bedroom. (*Low angle, under-the-table shot, please, Mr Director, sir. Hand-held, you say? Yes, that seems appropriate.*)

The Loch Fyne kipper was orgasmic in itself, but dessert consisted of a garden of fleshy delights that only the curvaceous contours of a mature woman's body can bestow. Roy had been with several men lately, but sooner or later everybody needs a bosom for a pillow, and he was no exception. As they lay in the Eiderdown Elysium of the Glenburn's king-sized bed (Roy, le Roi, would have settled for nothing less), the older woman decided to give her young lover an affair to remember indeed.

'It was one of the best nights of my life,' he said. 'I always think of it as The Lady Varnishes.'

I was confused. 'She vanished? What, in the middle of the night?'

"No, she *varnished* all through the night. We both did. She put a bottle of nail varnish on the bedside table, and as I was fucking her she told me to pick it up.

"'Slowly, Roy. More slowly. Take the varnish and paint a nail between each stroke."

'On each downward stroke I painted a different nail. I looked down at her jiggling breasts and I thought, "I love my life."

'Her breathing was getting heavier as she said, "Nice and slow, Roy, nice and slow." She started moaning loudly and came all over my cock as she rubbed her hard wee nipples with her mink stole.'

Roy smiled widely at the memory. He had painted not just her nails but a vivid word picture of the experience.

'It didn't end there. The next night, after the sex, we went to the cinema to see *Rebecca*, the Hitchcock classic starring Laurence Olivier and Joan Fontaine.'

'Did you like it?' I asked.

'I loved it! It had rich people and a devious servant. It was my kind of film.'

(*Of course. I should have realised.*)

Roy and his Lady discussed the film on their romantic stroll back to the Glenburn.

'Joan Fontaine's so beautiful, don't you think? So elegant,' said the Lady.

Roy saw an opportunity for gallantry.

'Not as elegant as you,' he smiled, looking at her manicured nails.

'I could feel myself getting hard as I said, "I love your fingernails."'

He kissed the back of her hand and got even harder as he thought of the sensual pleasures which awaited them when they got back to their hotel.

They had reached the Esplanade near the putting greens that ornament the lawns around the Winter Gardens. The greens are dominated by a large fountain, its multicoloured lights illuminating the spray in a dazzling cascade. As they approached, Roy asked his companion, 'Do you agree that Hall is a boring name? I've never liked it.'

'Well, it's not really you, is it, Roy?' she replied. 'You'd suit something more elegant.'

'Perhaps something French?' he asked.

'*Peut-etre.*'

Roy had been giving the matter much thought but had not as yet come up with a solution. It was the Lady who provided the moment of inspiration.

'What about Fontaine?' she said. 'That's French.'

'Of course,' he replied. 'French for fountain.'

'Yes! It perfectly captures your bubbly personality!'

Roy felt excited. 'I like the sound of that. Fontaine. Roy Fontaine.'

The Lady stopped and grabbed him firmly by the arm. 'Look, Roy, it's destiny!'

Coming into view in front of them was the beautifully illuminated fountain. Its colours changed in a heartbeat . . . red, yellow, blue, violet, orange. It was a chameleon, like Roy himself.

As they stared at it, a photographer approached. In the days before paparazzi, these were the photographers for the working classes who had gone 'doon the watter', the paparazzi for the proles. They worked for a company which took snapshots that you collected a day or two later from their offices near the pier. Punning on the fact that Rothesay was the capital of the Island of Bute, the company called itself 'Butey Snaps'. My own first boyish exposure to the lexical labyrinth of the pun was via Butey Snaps. They have a lot to answer for.

The photographer approached. 'Butey Snap, sir? For you and your lovely lady? A souvenir of your holiday on the Island of Bute?'

Roy was exulting in the moment.

'Certainly!' he said. As he and his Lady posed in front of the fountain, he pinned on his least insincere smile.

(Stirring music here, please, Herr Director. A terrible beauty is about to be born. The camera pops and we freeze-frame on a close shot of the Lady and the beaming Roy.)

I like to think that the Lady has kept that photograph in a frame. It's the photo of the birth of Roy Fontaine. Perhaps her children or her grandchildren wonder who that smiling, dapper man is, standing by her side in front of the fountain. Perhaps it's best they never know.

◊

In the harsh confines of the prison cell, Roy became maudlin at his memories of the Lady.

'She taught me so much about antiques, jewellery, upper-class manners, nail varnish and nookie. With her financial assistance, I laid low for a month in Rothesay. I contemplated burgling the Marquis of Bute, but she knew him and spoke so highly of him I decided not to. She went back to her husband. I went back to the asylum.'

'You went back?' I asked him, astonished. 'Why?'

'I'd done my homework. Under Scotland's Mental Health Act, if a lunatic stayed out of the asylum for more than 28 days, he could not be put back inside. So I returned on day 29, a free man. I took presents for Charlie and Jim. Wee nick-nacks, including some toy soldiers for Charlie and Rothesay rock for Jim, who blessed it and mumbled something about "upon this rock I will build my church".'

Roy decided it was time to set up in business for himself, re-investing his profits from petty burglary in 'Hall's Bric-A-Brac Emporium' in the Ibrox Road, Govan. One of his earliest victims was the Short family, a theatrical family of Variety artistes, who became famous under their stage name as the Logans. The boy, Jimmy Logan, was to become one of Scotland's best-known comedians, and his sister, Annie Ross, achieved international fame as a jazz singer.

One night when the family was out receiving an award for services to showbusiness, their house was ransacked. They were devastated. Mrs Short (aka Logan) had made the mistake of telling that lovely young man with the antiques shop in the Ibrox Road that the entire family would be out at the awards ceremony that night.

The Logans came home proudly clutching the award that was to join all their other treasures in the trophy cabinet – but sadly the cabinet, like the house itself, was bare.

Roy sympathised greatly with Mrs Short when she told him of her loss, saying he hoped that the police would recover the stolen goods soon. In this he could have been of some assistance, as the family's treasures were at that moment carefully stacked upstairs in his flat, awaiting transportation to a suitable 'fence' in London.

Roy got away with the Logan loot, but a few months later when various leads pointed to his shop 'the cops found that the stuff on my premises was hotter than a whore's G-string. I was sentenced to a year in Barlinnie. But just as one door closed another one opened. Destiny beckoned and revealed the way forward. My path in life was about to become clear.'

16

Buttlemania

The office of butler is thus one of very great trust in a household. Here, as elsewhere, honesty is the best policy.
Mrs Beeton's Book of Household Management

I N BARLINNIE, ROY MET the man who was to change his life. John Wooton would become Sancho Panza to Roy's Quixote, Watson to his Holmes.

Other inmates of the no-nonsense prison regarded Roy as effeminate, with his manicured nails, fastidious cleanliness and lashings of aftershave – or 'poof-juice' as they disparagingly described it.

If only those violent men had written down their prison experiences, they could have sold their memoirs to stage and screen as prolier-than-thou drama. Oh, now that I come to think about it, several of them did.

One of the most feared characters in the prison was Noddy from Newcastle, where men pride themselves on being macho. Noddy had gained his nickname from his fondness for headbutting his victims before pounding them to a pulp. This particular Geordie, who felt that to wear a sweater on a snowy day was a sign of weakness, had a nasty habit of attacking any inmate who looked at him the wrong way. He had already broken several noses, limbs and the occasional neck of his fellow prisoners, and Roy's policy was to give him a wide berth.

Unfortunately, one fateful day in the prison yard, the wind suddenly changed direction and the Geordie smelled aftershave the way a shark smells blood.

He tracked the source of the fragrance and went straight up to Roy, looking disgusted.

'Is that your poof-juice? Fook sek, ye smell like a whoor in distress.'

Roy gulped and saw that the prison guards were turning a blind eye. Maybe they didn't like poof-juice either. Maybe they thought Roy was a little too cocky and needed taken down a peg or two. Or maybe they just enjoyed seeing a con being battered. They were not about to be disappointed.

Roy awaited the first blow, staring intently at Noddy, trying not to show his fear. He knew this psycho Geordie's reputation. Trying to buy time, he said, 'Caring for your personal hygiene doesn't make you a poof!'

English comprehension wasn't Noddy's strong point. He grabbed Roy by the throat and put him in a headlock, screeching, 'Are you callin' me a poof?'

Choking, Roy tried to clarify the situation: 'No! *You're* calling *me* a poof!'

At that moment, a tall, elegant man stepped forward, adopting a boxer's stance.

'Why don't you pick on someone your own size?' he said to Noddy.

The other inmates murmured in admiration. Even the guards became more animated. They'd always seen Wooton as a quiet, gentle soul, but he suddenly looked like a man who knew how to handle himself, a man who wasn't afraid of a fight.

This was the first time anyone had stood up to the Geordie, who was hated and feared by everyone. It was all the more remarkable because Wooton was not defending himself, but intervening to protect a fellow prisoner.

Wooton was 12 years older than Roy, and well qualified in his role as his defender, having been South London Schools Boxing Champion in 1935 and Army Regimental Champ in 1946.

The Geordie didn't know any of that and unwisely called Wooton a 'soft Southern cunt'.

That was a big mistake. Wooton danced round him, landing punches everywhere, treating his opponent as a punchbag. Five minutes later, Noddy was lying on the concrete of the prison yard, screaming like a child. He was now missing several teeth. His lip was cut and swollen, and blood gushed from his broken nose. The other prisoners cheered like kids seeing the schoolyard bully getting his comeuppance.

Finally the guards intervened, dragging the Geordie off to the prison hospital and telling Wooton, with a wink, that he'd be put in solitary, unless of course he'd be interested in joining the prison boxing team. He chose the latter.

Roy told me, 'I knew I had a friend for life. A man in whom I had complete trust.'

He thanked Wooton profusely, and the two had a cup of tea together, over which the Englishman told him that he was doing time for attempted theft from a country house. Wooton had tried to steal some *objets d'art* whilst posing as a butler.

'Sadly, I didn't have the acting skills to sustain it. The Lord of the Manor noticed what he called my "peculiar walk". He saw that I walked in unnaturally short steps, something I'd picked up over the years from the prisoner's exercise yard. It's called "prisoner's walk". M'lud recognised it from his days in the army. He called the police at once.'

Roy was not deterred. He immediately saw the genius of this business plan: 'As a butler, you don't need to go in the window. You go in the front door! That's brilliant!'

'Exactly,' replied Wooton. 'It's nice work if you can get it.'

Roy would dedicate many years of his life to getting it.

'How can I find out about butlering?' he asked.

'It's not butlering. It's buttling,' replied Wooton. 'To buttle. With two Ts. The butler was in charge of the wine. He used to be known as the yeoman of the buttery.'

Roy looked blank. 'What's butter got to do with it?'

'Nothing. The buttery was where the wine was stored, in large casks called butts.'

Given Roy's sexual predilections, any job with a 'butt' in it was bound to be appealing. He would later pithily refer to himself as 'the man who put the butt in buttling'.

Wooton gave him a reference book on the subject, the immortal

Roberts' Guide for Butlers and Other Household Staff.

I commend this work to your attention. It is as endearing and eccentric as its author's name suggests. He was Robert Roberts, a name as comically repetitive as Humbert Humbert in *Lolita* or Major Major in *Catch 22*, with the important proviso that those characters were fictitious.

Robert Roberts was a black American manservant who wrote the guide in 1827, as a book of advice for 'my young friends Joseph and David', who were thinking 'about entering into gentlemen's service'.

It's a measure of the guide's usefulness that it is still in print today. It has chapter titles like:

> Brushing and folding gentlemen's clothes
> Directions for cleaning mahogany furniture
> Italian varnish, most superb for furniture
> A great secret to mix Mustard
> To preserve the brightness of fire-arms.

For Roy, one of the most fascinating things about the book is the fact that it was written by an American. Roy always liked Americans. He found that *Roberts' Guide* was more useful than its British equivalents. It gave the aspiring butler handy practical tips whilst remaining free of the excessive class snobbery that in Roy's view poisoned the well of social interaction in Britain.

The book also had useful tips on the great questions of life and death. Obviously worried that his young friends Joseph and David might succumb to the demon drink whilst handling all that claret and fine wine, Robert Roberts gave them invaluable advice, in an astonishingly prescient nineteenth-century anticipation of late twentieth-century aversion therapy.

In a chapter endearingly entitled 'To reform those that are given to drink', Roberts says:

> Put, in a sufficient quantity of rum, brandy, gin, or whatever liquor the person is in the habit of drinking, three large live eels, which leave until quite dead. Give this liquor unawares to

those you wish to reform, and they will get so disgusted against
it, that, though they formerly liked it, they will now have quite
an aversion to it afterwards; this I have seen tried and have the
good effect on the person who drank it.

For those wishing to avoid society's opprobrium on the drink front
but not wanting to go all the way with the dead eels, there is a
compromise solution in Roberts' very next chapter, entitled 'To
prevent the breath from smelling after drink'. He helpfully
recommends that you 'chew a bit of the root of iris-troglotida, and
no person can discover by your breath whether you have been
drinking or not'. All of you at home with a spare bit of iris-troglotida
lying around would do well to remember that.

Drink was to play a significant part in Roy's bloodiest crimes.
Could three dead eels have changed all that? Sadly, we'll never
know.

He told me that discovering the Roberts book on buttling was
one of the most rewarding and transformative experiences of his
life, both spiritually and materially. It took pride of place on the
shelves in his cell. *Roberts' Guide* was a link to the lost elegance of his
mother. Here was her sense of taste and decorum writ large.

Of course a career as a butler would not have appealed half as
much to Roy if he had believed for a moment that he was actually
going to *serve* these people in any real sense. No, his life's motto could
have been the same as James Joyce's: '*Non Serviam*. I will not serve.'

I told him that, and he asked if he could borrow my pencil to write
it down. I lent him the pencil, which of course I would not have done
knowing what I know now. In my defence, I should point out that we
were at this point still in the honeymoon period of our relationship.

I dictated the whole quote from memory, while he meticulously
transcribed it. It was seared into my heart: I used to have it on my
wall during my wilderness years in the bedsit. Roy put it up on the
wall of his cell.

It is the manifesto for artists, anarchists and independent spirits
everywhere. To that list we can now add at least one murderer.

Non Serviam. I will not serve that in which I no longer believe, whether it calls itself my home, my fatherland, or my church: and I will try to express myself in some mode of life or art as freely as I can and as wholly as I can, using for my defence the only arms I allow myself to use – silence, exile, and cunning.

Roy, of course, had no intention of serving his alleged lords and masters. He would do a magnificent impersonation of a servant, but in reality he would be a fifth columnist, a spy in their household, and buttling would be his cover.

◊

Long nights of monastic study followed his decision to make the part of the butler his greatest-ever performance. He was determined it would be a scene-stealing, eye-catching role that he would be capable of playing for the rest of his life.

He spent every available moment lying on his cell bed, reading *Roberts'* and other assorted guides to buttling. Often he would forget the time. The grille would slide open and the guard would tell him to put his light out and get some shut-eye, because slopping out was at 6 a.m.

He learned the duties of the butler off by heart. Whilst cooking spuds, he would rehearse in the prison kitchen, laying out the plates on a table as if they were the best silver service. He rehearsed from memory.

'The butler is responsible for the household plate. Each night he has to make sure it is carefully locked away.'

Roy smiled to himself as he thought, 'This is obviously the job for me.'

It was common for him to be interrupted in the midst of such reveries. Sometimes when he was lost in fantasy in the kitchen, the warden would have to intervene with: 'Fontaine! What the hell are you doing? Can you no' smell burning?'

Roy would snap out of it and rush over to switch off the cooker before the potatoes were incinerated.

He told me that the very thought of sleeping beside the silverware gave him an erection. In the prison kitchen, he would pick up an old tin plate and start polishing it lovingly, lost in fantasy as he thought of the possibilities suggested by the guide.

> In the morning the Butler will clear away the more precious items, such as silver ornaments from the drawing room. When the family is away from home he might have to deposit the most valuable items in a place of safety.

The place of safety Roy had in mind was his own bank vault. He had found his vocation. He had experienced his epiphany. Not since that apple fell on Newton's head or Archimedes had that bath has a man's purpose been so startlingly revealed.

His path was now clear. He would devote the bulk of his life to treading that path with the devotion of a hero of his beloved *Arabian Nights* on his way to Mecca.

'It was essential that I familiarise myself with the world of my future employers,' he said. 'Fortunately, the prison library had a dusty copy of *Burke's Peerage*. No doubt it was placed there to teach us respect for our so-called Lords and Masters. It taught me everything I needed to know!'

Burke's Peerage, Baronetage and Knightage, to give it its full title, has, for over 175 years, recorded the genealogies of the UK and Ireland's titled and landed families. It is often referred to as the Bible of the aristocracy. It certainly proved of much more use to Roy than that other Bible with its vengeful God.

He and Wooton got into a daily routine in the prison library. Roy would take down the heavy copy of *Burke's Peerage* from the shelf and sit at a table opposite his friend, who would open the book and ask questions like, 'What is Lord Moxton's coat of arms?'

Roy often brought his dislike of the aristocracy into his mocking answers.

'It's the big deer-type thing . . . on its back legs.'

'Roy! Be serious!' answered Wooton.

'OK, if you insist! It's an argent heraldic antelope.'

'Good,' replied Wooton. 'This is your Bible!' He prodded the hard cover of the book with his finger. 'What colours are emblazoned upon his coat of arms? And what do they signify?'

Roy had studied hard. He answered quickly.

'Red and gold, signifying generosity and elevation of mind, and blue, signifying that his ancestors were murderous conniving bastards who got all their wealth by robbing poor folk like us.'

'Roy! Behave yourself!'

'OK. Blue, signifying, would you believe, loyalty and truth.'

'And what is the motto of the Moxton family?'

'*Vincit Veritas.*'

'Which means?'

'Truth prevails. If you believe that you'll believe anything. They're a bunch of lying cunts!'

Wooton continued, unperturbed.

'Of which clubs is Lord Moxton a member?'

'White's and Saint James.'

'Excellent, Mr Fontaine,' said Wooton affecting a posh accent. 'When can you take up the appointment?'

◊

Roy and Wooton were released within a month of each other in 1951. The elegant Englishman met Marion Hall on the day of Roy's release, and they took an instant liking to each another. Roy encouraged the relationship, reckoning his friend would make a much better father than the one he actually had. It was a sentiment in which Marion increasingly concurred.

She believed her son's crimes to be no more than his exuberant high spirits and intelligence looking for a proper channel of expression. She felt pleased that the friend he had made in prison had all the attributes of a gentleman, albeit a gentleman thief.

In Wooton's presence she felt like an artist again, a true bohemian like all those wonderful free-spirited women Shaw and H.G. Wells wrote about. Shaw had written fondly of rogues and vagabonds, and Marion shared his enthusiasm. Wooton lived on the fringes of the law, and he appealed to the vagabond in her soul. His very presence seemed to bring out her inner Maisie. She felt she should stick with her husband for the time being and see how things developed with Wooton.

Roy devoted himself wholeheartedly to securing excellent references as a butler. This proved much easier than it otherwise might have done, since he wrote them himself.

He briefly moved back in with his parents whilst he explored his new-found literary gifts. Marion blamed his criminal past on his father's failure to encourage the boy's creativity. Roy promised them that he was now a reformed character who was seeking to put the impeccable manners his mother had taught him into a lifetime of service as a butler.

By the light of a bedside lamp, he wrote his own references on quality embossed paper that he had stolen from swanky hotels. Beside him was the upper-class gossip sheet *The Lady*, its adverts for 'Domestic Servants' circled. He would write: 'To whom it may concern: Mr Roy Fontaine served in my employ as Butler for four years and he performed his duties with great diligence and efficiency. I recommend him highly and with total confidence. [signed] Lord Mandeville.'

This stratagem was to prove highly successful. It was astonishing how few employers actually checked references. Roy covered himself by saying the author of the reference was 'travelling'.

He made himself very attractive to prospective employers. He was a confident, sophisticated and immaculately turned-out young man who could discourse knowledgeably on such matters as antiques, diamonds and paintings. He always stressed in job interviews that he'd be firm with the servants. That played well. He had been inspired, as ever, by the wise words of Robert Roberts on the delicate art of how servants should address their Master: 'You must know that it is a very impertinent thing to strive to force a conversation on your superiors . . .'

Roberts has this advice for the Master himself when dealing with servants: 'Avoid all approaches towards familiarity, which . . . soon breaks the neck of obedience.'

But there were some things for which neither *Roberts' Guide* nor *Burke's Peerage* could prepare you, as Roy found out when he went for an interview with prospective employer Lady Amelia Ampleforth.

Immaculately dressed, Roy stood before the very patrician Lady

Ampleforth, who was reading his letter of reference through her bifocals.

'Lord Mandeville writes you a glowing reference, Mr Fontaine, in his beautiful copperplate hand. How is his tennis these days?'

This was a question Roy had not been expecting, but he met it with his usual aplomb.

'Oh, much as ever, ma'am. His backhand still needs a little work.'

Lady Ampleforth stared at him intently over her glasses.

'Really? That's extraordinary, considering he's blind! I don't know who you are, Mr Fontaine, or what your game is, but if you do not leave at once I'll call the police!'

Roy bowed and headed for the door, making a mental note to do more research in future. Pride dictated that he make some sort of reply, so before exiting he turned and said, 'Blind, ma'am? No wonder he has a problem with his backhand!'

He exited, and left the estate, cursing his bad luck.

He was more successful in his next interview, securing the butler's job with Lord Penrose at a castle in the north of Scotland – but, as Roy said with some bitterness, 'it wasn't a butler he wanted, it was a slave.'

On the first day of his new job, he found himself sweating profusely, in full butler's livery, as he pushed a large heavy object that resembled a lawnmower. Lord Penrose stood to the side, barking orders: 'Fontaine – the lines are not straight! Get it right!'

Roy was marking out the white lines on his Lordship's tennis court.

Panting for breath, he asked, 'Are you sure this is part of my duties, sir?'

'Your duties are what I say they are,' replied the unsympathetic Lord.

'Of course, sir,' said Roy, affecting meekness whilst mentally reminding himself to 'rob this bastard some day'.

As he pushed his heavy load, he clenched his teeth and cursed under his breath: 'It didnae say anything about this in the fucking book I read.'

He told me that 'having heard another butler post was available elsewhere, I left immediately, borrowing a few precious items that I felt would never be missed. I did leave a resignation note of sorts.'

On the morning of Roy's sudden departure, Lord Penrose found himself staring in a state of shock at his tennis court. His jaw dropped as he saw Roy's parting message written in two large white letters in the middle of the tennis court. It said simply: 'FU'.

Three months later, Lord Penrose's castle was looted.

◊

As Roy concluded his story with a knowing wink, the guard told us our time was up. He collected the lighter from Roy, who shook my hand warmly before giving me *The Last of Mrs Cheyney*.

'Check out the opening paragraph, son,' he added. 'It's how I've lived my life.'

I opened the book and read it out loud:

> The gospel of hospitality, according to Mrs Cheyney, was simplified to a simple commandment, but must be obeyed. One must be entertaining. The cardinal sin was to be dull.

I smiled and told him I was looking forward to reading it.

'It started life as a hugely successful West End play,' he said. 'It was so successful that it was made into a hit movie three times, starring Norma Shearer, Joan Crawford and Greer Garson respectively. My favourite was the one starring Joan Crawford.'

I browsed through the book on the train home. It was prefaced with a sexy still from the movie showing Joan Crawford and her prospective prey in the bedroom. The blurb was suggestive:

> On a fast boat to England, Joan Crawford (as Fay Cheyney) finds herself in wealthy Frank Morgan (as Lord Kelton)'s stateroom bed. Turns out, Ms Crawford is part of a gang of jewel thieves. Things get complicated when Crawford is increasingly attracted to dashing Robert Montgomery (as Lord Dilling), who thinks he knows Charles the butler (Mr William Powell) from somewhere . . .

Jewels, sex and devious servants. Is it any wonder Roy loved it?

When I went to bed that night I read the first few chapters. I suddenly felt uneasy, as I realised that the other pair of hands that had cradled this book had cruelly extinguished human life. I felt I should be wearing rubber gloves to protect me from contamination. I put the book down and drifted into an uneasy sleep. I would not have slept at all had I known what awaited me the next morning.

17

Scarface

I think scars are sexy because it means you made a mistake that led to a mess.

Angelina Jolie

I WAS AWAKENED THE FOLLOWING morning by a loud ringing on my doorbell. I groggily dragged myself out of bed and went downstairs in my dressing gown, thinking it must be the postman.

Instead, I was confronted by a small, barrel-chested man who had a large scar on his face. The scar resembled the forward slash on a computer keyboard and ran from his earlobe to the corner of his mouth. It was whiter than the rest of his face and at first, in my sleepy state, I thought it was some sort of body piercing.

As shock raised my level of awareness, I realised that the mutilation was not self-inflicted or voluntary, but the work of a hostile hand.

'Paul Pender,' he said, staring at me menacingly. I didn't know if that was a question, a statement or a threat. I recalled Roy saying that he had friends on the outside who owed him favours. Suddenly terrified, I found myself wondering 'Why me?'

Had the twenty-pound note in the cigarette packet not been enough? Had Roy expected fifty? Had I inadvertently called him Archie? No matter. I was preparing myself for the worst.

'Yes,' I answered, my voice sounding strangely falsetto as I resisted the impulse to scream. Maybe he was really after Becky Farr. She was just around the corner. I could give him her address. No, that would have been ignoble and unforgivable. Even a TV critic deserved better than that. I decided to take my punishment like a man.

He had his hands behind his back, holding some large object that I naturally assumed to be a chainsaw.

As he drew his hands forward, I took a step back, flinched and instinctively closed my eyes, wondering if he'd start with the limbs or go for the straight decapitation.

When I opened my eyes, he was handing me a basket of fruit.

'Ah'm Joe,' he said. 'This is fae Roy.'

I took the basket, delighted with the gift and with the fact that my head was still attached to the rest of my body.

'Thanks, Joe!' I said.

Scarface's mood changed in an instant. 'Ma name's no' Joe!' he spat, edging menacingly towards me as he fixed me with a psychotic stare worthy of Roy himself.

'But you just said it was . . .' I grovelled, instinctively stepping back, trying to get out of range of the razor-sharp blade that he undoubtedly had secreted upon his person.

'Ma name's TOE!' he shouted, foaming at the mouth like a rabid dog. The veins on his neck started swelling like they were about to burst.

'Toe! Like on yir fuckin' foot!'

'Oh, I see. Toe!' I said, as if it were a common name. 'My mistake. Sorry . . . Toe.'

'It's OK,' he said in the spirit of compromise, wiping the angry spit from his chin. 'It's no the first time it's happened.'

Subsequent research amongst Glasgow's criminal demi-monde (or Scottish playwrights, as they were otherwise known) revealed that Wee Toe had just been released from prison. He had earned his nickname by cutting off the little toe of a rival gang member a few years earlier. This happened during Glasgow's reign as Europe's City of Culture in 1990. For a brief shining moment, culture vultures were hoping that Glasgow might witness a new type of white-collar intellectual crime – a turf war over, say, the right to distribute tickets to Peter Brook's *Mahabharata*. Sadly, though, Glaswegian crime remained as sleazy, lowlife and drugs-related as ever, and Wee Toe's crime was no exception.

Gangsters, like the rest of us, need heroes. Toe had modelled his actions on those of the legendary Big Toe, the notorious Billy 'Toe'

Elliot, who should not in any circumstances be confused with Billy Elliot the charming young ballet dancer in the hit movie of that name. For avoidance of doubt, let's call that Billy Elliot 'Ballet Elliot'. He won't be featuring in this sordid tale.

Unlike his hero Big Toe, Wee Toe had not actually killed his victim. He had merely cut off the poor man's wee toe and left him to bleed, so that his victim would limp his way through life.

Billy 'Big Toe' Elliot, on the other hand (or should that be the other foot?), had not only cut off his victim's big toe but had allegedly stuffed it in the poor fellow's mouth before killing him. Big Toe thought big.

I thanked Wee Toe, turned the basket towards him and offered him any fruit he fancied. He looked pained, and I regretted saying it as soon as I realised that 'have any fruit you fancy' was most likely a phrase he'd heard many times in prison, either as victim or predator.

Wee Toe looked at the fruit, grunted his refusal, turned and walked off, mumbling something to himself. I might have guessed he'd pass on the fruit: he had carnivore written all over him.

I tried to be philosophical. Although I was alarmed that Wee Toe now knew my home address, I was grateful that at least he was not Big Toe. I made a mental note not to fall out with Roy. Sadly, it proved to be a resolution I would not be able to keep.

18

The Crown Jewels

Uneasy lies the head that wears the crown.
Shakespeare, *Henry IV: Part II*, Act 3, Scene 1

ROY SPENT A GREAT deal of time between our meetings polishing his bon mots for maximum effect. He was, of course, a compulsive liar, so I took everything he said with a pinch of salt, or a large Siberian saltmine. On the train, en route to our next encounter, the disquieting questions resurfaced. Was I deliberately flattering him? Was I in danger of glamorising a cold-blooded killer? I pushed such doubts to the back of my mind and concentrated on the interview.

My years of solitary confinement in a bedsit had given me a fair degree of empathy with Roy's situation. After all, writers and prisoners have a great deal in common. We spend our time alone in a room fantasising, having grandiose dreams to compensate for our drab reality.

Against the hypnotic hum of the train I put together a brief checklist of 'Rules for Writers, Criminals and Other Vagabonds'.

Writers, criminals, and other vagabonds, I concluded, should:

1) Be dangerous.
2) Challenge authority.
3) Live by their own rules.

In short, to quote William Blake (as Roy and I often did), both the writer and the criminal believe that 'I must create my own system, or else be enslaved by another man's.'

When I arrived at Full Sutton, Roy was keen to continue his story.

'I found fulfilment when I secured my next position in 900 beautiful acres of Stirlingshire with Lord and Lady Warren-Connel. My employers thought my references were impeccable. Of course they were. I'd written them myself.'

The Warren-Connels lived on rich farmland near the picturesque Scottish village of Balfron. Here, in marked contrast to his time with Lord Penrose, Roy began to really enjoy his duties.

'I had the not-so-onerous task of cleaning Her Ladyship's jewellery. This meant steeping them in gin and watching them become even more sparkling. Aladdin in his cave never had it this good.'

The Warren-Connels were scions of a shipbuilding dynasty, which reminded Roy of how fortunate he was not to be working with those troglodytes who wasted their lives slaving away under the hulking shells of the great ships in the yards.

In his butler's quarters, he would stare in rapture at a glass of gin inside which a diamond brooch glittered and winked at him. His modus operandi was simple yet extraordinarily effective. As he described it, 'I would record details of the smaller diamonds – the ones at the end of the brooch. Shape, size and cut would be noted. People never look at the small diamonds – they concentrate on the big ones in the middle. I'd had some experience of this whilst resetting jewellery in my shop.'

He would measure the smaller diamonds using a set of jewellers' pincers and send the details to his bent contact in London's Hatton Gardens, the centre of the UK's diamond trade. His contact would make glass replicas. Roy would do the swap, replacing the smaller diamonds with the replicas.

Another example of his dedication to his butler's duties is the fact that he made a habit of opening any letter to his employers that he deemed of interest. He would boil a kettle, steam open the envelope and enjoy a cup of tea whilst he read the contents.

One letter in particular excited him: 'With a father who worked in the Post Office, I had a lifelong interest in the mail. I followed my normal practice of steaming open anything that piqued my curiosity. This one was a bit special. The crest said St James's Palace.'

He took the large, gold-embossed card out of the envelope and read it with mounting excitement.

> The Lord Chamberlain lets it be known that Lord and Lady Warren-Connel are commanded by His Majesty the King to attend the Royal Garden Party at the Palace of Holyrood House on the 15 June. A special windscreen sticker is enclosed for your use. Please give this to your chauffeur.

Lord and Lady Warren-Connel were already booked on a flight to the Bahamas, but Roy thought that trifling detail was no excuse for turning down the Royals' generous invitation. All he had to do was borrow two items for the day. The first was his employers' Bentley. The second was John Wooton.

The morning of the Garden Party found Wooton, in his immaculately tailored chauffeur's uniform, waiting beside the Bentley in the driveway of the Warren- Connels' country house. Roy emerged in full formal dress complete with top hat and flower in his buttonhole, looking every inch the aristocratic gent. Wooton whistled through his teeth in admiration as he opened the door of the car.

'Your carriage awaits, my lord. May I say you look like a real toff? I doubt that the real Lord Warren-Connel ever looked this good.'

'I only hope I haven't overdone it,' replied Roy, with uncharacteristic modesty.

'No, you look like the Lord of the Manor. To the manor born, you might say.'

Roy didn't laugh. He made the jokes. He liked to think of Wooton as the straight man.

They set off on their pilgrimage to Edinburgh, a pleasant and scenic journey of about one hour. The Bentley drove majestically through leafy country lanes, Roy savouring the rich smell of its plush leather interior. It was, he thought, the aroma of wealth. He'd like to get used to it.

When the limo reached the more populous outskirts of Edinburgh, the magnificent car attracted a great deal of attention from passers-by. Roy waved his hand regally at them, like the king he felt himself to be. Especially today. He was, after all, having lunch at the Palace.

As they approached the Royal Mile, at the foot of which sits the Palace of Holyrood, he gave Wooton the sticker to put on the windscreen.

'This is great practice for when I get a real job as a chauffeur, Roy. Thanks for the references. You write brilliant letters.'

'That's the least I can do for you, John,' said Roy with rare sincerity. 'Do unto others as you would do unto yourself, as somebody once remarked.'

'Just think,' said Wooton, 'you're about to meet royalty. It's a special day. A day to remember!'

Wooton was unaware of the fact that Roy, only a few years earlier, had been intimate with Prince Philip's uncle.

'I wasn't intimidated by royalty,' he told me. 'In royal company I was hardly going to touch the forelock when I'd already touched the foreskin. Still, the King had been ill and this might be my last chance to meet him. The little princesses would be there too. And of course I knew there would be lots of jewellery.'

As the Bentley inched its way majestically up the Royal Mile, Roy asked Wooton to pull over. He had spotted something that required further investigation – a shop bearing the simple sign 'Mowbray House Antiques'.

With his highly developed antennae for such things, Roy had seen gorgeous gems winking at him like potential lovers. It seemed like an invitation, and today, after all, was dedicated to accepting invitations graciously.

Within minutes, Roy was staring into the window of the antiques shop. He decided that now, whilst he was in full formal dress, would be a good time to make the owner's acquaintance. He entered and saw a Bohemian-looking older woman standing behind the counter. She was the shop's only occupant.

Roy smiled and doffed his top hat to her as a mark of respect. It helped that he was dressed so formally. He was already in character.

'Good day, madam. May I compliment you on your exquisite taste? Quite the most breathtaking display of *objets d'art* I have seen. And of course in the Diplomatic Corps I've been all over the world.'

'Really?' she replied, impressed. 'I like a gentleman who is capable of discernment.'

The two of them were already getting on famously. He introduced himself as Lord Warren-Connel, and she revealed that she was Esta Henry, the proprietor of this fine establishment.

He asked if he might possibly see a selection of items, as it was Lady Warren-Connel's birthday soon.

Esta opened her safe and took out a beautifully ornate diamond ring.

'When she opened the safe, I almost fainted with excitement. She told me that Queen Mary was a regular visitor to the shop. One entire wall was covered with cheques signed by all the crowned heads of Europe.'

Roy told her he was about to meet the King and brandished the gold-embossed invitation as proof. He always insisted that props are essential for the criminal mastermind.

'From that moment on,' he said, 'she was putty in my hands.'

His instant rapport with Esta is yet another reminder that though the tabloids inevitably describe him as the Monster Butler, the Killer Butler, or the Evil Butler, for the greater part of his life he was perceived by those who came into contact with him as the Charming Butler.

Rare particles, according to subatomic physics, have charm. As do rare people. Charm is often mistaken for warmth. It is in fact the opposite. When I think of charm, I think of Yeats' line: 'as cold and passionate as the dawn'. One of the reasons Roy and I hit it off was that his veins and mine were filled from the same Arctic source. It's a wonder our blood flowed at all.

Esta Henry was fascinating in her own right. She had flown to King Farouk's Egypt to negotiate face to face with him for the sale of the Egyptian crown jewels. She was a larger-than-life character who found in Roy's outsize personality a kind of mirror image of her own. There is no doubt that she regarded him in some ways as a kindred spirit.

Later, after he robbed her, she would visit him in prison and give him money to help him get off to a good start on his release, even though he'd been what she'd described as 'a naughty boy'. She told one interviewer that it was difficult to find anyone quite as amusing as Roy. That's charm of a very high order.

For the time being, though, he bid Esta a fond farewell. He had a king to meet.

The Bentley arrived at the foot of the Royal Mile, where a special barrier had been erected. A white-gloved policeman came over and looked approvingly at the car's occupants and at the sticker on the windscreen.

'Can I see your invitation, sir?' he said. 'It's only a formality.'

Roy affected a perfectly modulated cut-glass aristocratic accent as he handed over the embossed invite.

'Of course, officer. I'm afraid Lady Warren-Connel is indisposed. Ingested some dust on the polo field. She has requested that I pass on her best wishes to the King.'

'That's very kind of her, sir.' The policeman saluted. 'Enjoy your day!'

The barrier was lifted. They drove through as Roy observed, 'Cops don't treat you like that in Govan.'

Wooton was impressed with his friend's chameleon-like qualities. 'You're some man with the accents, Roy. I nearly cracked up when you said, "She has requested that I pass on her best wishes to the King."'

Roy smiled. He always liked to keep his audience happy. It was his duty as a star.

The limo parked in the VIP car park in the Palace grounds. Wooton played his part impeccably, opening the door deferentially to his 'master'. Throughout his criminal career, the quality of Roy's performance, like that of any talented and charismatic leading man, tended to bring out the best in his supporting players, who inevitably raised the level of their performance.

'Sorry you can't come with me, John. But you know how shittily we upper-class types treat our servants!'

'That's OK, my lord. I'll enjoy some smokes and get a suntan! Good luck!'

Roy showed his invitation card to an official at the gate and entered the grounds of the palace, which nestles in scenic splendour at the foot of Edinburgh's imposing volcanic hill, Arthur's Seat. Roy looked up at the brooding hill and felt inspired by the spirit of Arthur, the once and future king. He felt like saluting it, one king to another.

Well-dressed members of the aristocracy were parading around the colourful marquees that had been erected at regular intervals. Roy doffed his top hat to the elegant ladies as he stared open-mouthed at their glittering jewels. He gazed longingly at a dazzling necklace around one lady's neck.

'It took all my willpower not to tear it from her neck and do a runner,' he remembered wistfully. He struck up a conversation instead.

'Beautiful day!' he said, in his best upper-class accent.

'Isn't it just!' she replied jauntily.

'I hope it keeps up for the Glorious 12th,' opined Roy, referring to the opening day of the grouse-shooting season on 12 August. 'One abhors shooting in the rain. Dampens both the spirits and the sport!'

'Oh, they say the shooting will be good this year.'

Roy didn't respond. He was too busy fixating on her neck, like an axe man calculating which angle would give the cleanest cut.

'If you'll permit me being so bold, that is a very fine necklace. Nineteenth century, by the look of it. Ruby, isn't it? Beautiful how it catches the light. May I hazard a guess that it's a rose cut?'

'My word! That's it exactly! Are you a connoisseur of rubies?'

'Gemstones are a kind of hobby of mine,' he said, without a word of a lie.

'Have you seen the beautiful golden arrows on display?' she said. 'They have the most exquisite sapphires set into them.'

Roy was fascinated.

'Really? Where would I find them?'

'Through the refreshments tent. There's a special exhibition by the Royal Society of Archers.'

'Sounds fascinating. I'll pop in. Good day to you, madam.'

He doffed his top hat to her.

'Good day.'

A moment later, the lady's husband came out of the refreshments tent with a couple of glasses of champagne. She took one, saying, 'What a charming man! I forgot to ask his name.'

Roy walked through the refreshments tent, where a liveried royal manservant was walking around with a silver tray holding dainty cucumber sandwiches and chilled champagne.

Taking a sandwich and a glass of champers, he strolled nonchalantly through the tent, smiling at his fellow guests.

He entered the display tent where a large photo beside a display case showed the King at the centre of a group of men who were dressed ceremonially in what looked to Roy like amateur theatrical versions of Robin Hood outfits. The caption said 'The Royal Society of Archers – Ceremonial Guard of Honour to the King'.

Throughout the marquee, in display cases and on tables, were photos showing the history of the society, along with various exhibits – a bow, a quiver and, in pride of place, a small box containing three arrows made of gold, with sapphires inlaid.

Roy gazed in rapture at the display. Suddenly he became aware of a couple standing beside him. The husband, Lord such-and-such, remarked that, 'It seems a bit odd having a bodyguard with bows and arrows in this day and age – don't you think?'

He turned to Roy for approval.

'You're absolutely right,' said Roy, 'what with all these criminals going about! It would need more than a bow and arrow to stop them, if you ask me!'

Suddenly a shout went up in the tent and the liveried Chief Barker appeared, looking more like Dickens' Mr Pickwick than any inhabitant of the twentieth century. He announced, in his stentorian town-crier voice, 'My Lords, Ladies and Gentlemen. The King and Queen and the Princesses Elizabeth and Margaret will receive you now if you would kindly make your way out to the garden and form an orderly line.'

The guests shuffled out, Roy holding back till the end. As he exited, he passed very close to the table with the golden arrows.

In the palace gardens, the guests lined up for royalty. King George VI, his Queen and the two princesses walked along the line, chatting with them.

The royal party reached Roy, and the King shook hands with

him. A stickler for etiquette, Roy bowed and said simply, 'Your Royal Highness.'

The King smiled his practised smile and moved on. Embarrassed by the stammer he spent his life conquering, he was a man of few words. Next on the royal conveyor belt was the Queen, who on her daughter Elizabeth's coronation a few years later would become the much-loved Queen Mother – everyone's favourite royal. She shook Roy's hand with a smile that looked more spontaneous than that of her husband. Having dutifully bowed, scraped and uttered a suitably deferential 'Ma'am', Roy could not resist one further comment. 'Your Royal Highness,' he said, bowing to Her Majesty, 'may I be so bold as to say how much I admire your tiara? It's quite the most beautiful I've seen.'

The Queen smiled graciously and said, 'Why – thank you. Yes, we are rather fond of it.'

She moved on, and he shook the hands of the young princesses Elizabeth and Margaret. 'If only my mother could have seen me chatting with the royals,' he said. 'It was a long way from Govan Cross! What I really wanted to do was to grab the Queen's tiara and run, but I realised that you got beheaded for less. Besides, I'd already handled the crown jewels!'

'Really?" I said, mystified. He winked, and stared at me with a cheeky grin, making a squeezing motion with his hand.

It was only then that I realised he was making an obscure reference to Lord Mountbatten's testicles.

When I asked him if he liked the royals, he shrugged.

'They're a fairly entertaining bunch of sexual degenerates,' he said. 'I enjoy the spectacle of monarchy – all that pomp and circumstance. Although with Mountbottom it was more pump than pomp.'

I told him that the records indicate that the three golden arrows were stolen on the day of the Royal Garden Party. He feigned surprise, winked and said, 'Really? I'm sure there's a perfectly innocent explanation.'

The Warren-Connels never found out that they had been invited to the Royal Garden Party, but Roy's rural idyll was shattered a few weeks later when two police officers arrived on his doorstep and informed him that their colleagues in Glasgow had made them aware of Roy's criminal record. They would have to inform his employers.

Roy claimed he was trying to turn over a new leaf, but he knew that once word got out about his criminal past his life on the Warren-Connel estate would become untenable.

'Besides,' he told me, 'I liked my employers so much I had lost the urge to rob them. I decided it was time for fresh pastures.'

He regretfully took his leave of them and picked up where he had left off with John Wooton. Roy could not forget the very special Aladdin's Cave he had discovered on the morning of the Royal Garden Party. It was time to pay Esta Henry a return visit.

19

Deep in the Heart of Torquay

Oh, give me land, lots of land, under starry
skies above. Don't fence me in.
Cole Porter song sung by Roy Rogers in the
movie *Don't Fence Me In*

HAVING DECIDED TO ROB the spirited old lady, Roy initially asked Wooton to play the principal role of a rich Texan visiting her antiques shop, on the grounds that Esta had met Roy already in the guise of Lord Warren-Connel. Wooton said he didn't have the nerve to carry it off.

Roy was secretly pleased. There were always dangers when you cast a supporting player as the leading man. It risked ruining the intended victim's suspension of disbelief and could imperil the whole project.

He knew in his heart that Wooton was a character actor, while Roy was the archetypal leading man who could play a huge variety of roles. He'd already performed the role of 'His Lordship' in front of Esta, but like any ambitious and talented actor he wanted to increase his range. An even more colourful character was about to emerge.

As a worshipper at the shrine of Roy Rogers, he felt that it was time he asserted his own claim to be King of the Cowboys. He told Wooton that for his next role he needed to get hold of a Stetson. A local theatrical supplier obliged. So it was Roy, not Wooton, who ended up wearing a false moustache and goatee beard, a Stetson and some cowboy boots. He went into the little shop on the Royal Mile with a swagger and a smile as big as Texas. He was carrying a large briefcase.

The writer Robert Musil said that 'truth wears many garments'. So in his colourful career did Roy. Esta didn't for one second connect the top-hatted aristocratic lord she had met with the brash Stetson-wearing Texan who lost no time in introducing himself: 'Howdy, ma'am! Two things you got a lot of here in Scotchland: rain and history. Ah love your history.'

He asked to see a Georgian carriage clock that he knew from his previous visit was kept in the safe. As she opened the safe to fetch it, Wooton phoned as planned from the phone box across the street to ask her a whole series of pre-arranged questions.

She had to go into the side room of the shop to answer the phone. As she did so, Roy emptied the contents of the safe into the briefcase. As he was about to exit, he noticed that he'd missed a few smaller items of jewellery. He swept them into the Stetson and placed the hat firmly back on his head.

While Wooton was still bamboozling poor Esta with questions, Roy discreetly left the shop and got into the getaway car that was parked just outside, giving Wooton the thumbs-up. The tall Englishman joined him and they drove off into the sunset with their precious cargo.

It was as simple as that. As they sped down the southbound motorway, Wooton smiled at Roy the Singing Cowboy as the latter launched into a spontaneous chorus of 'This is where the Cowboy Rides Away'.

'My heart is sinking like the setting sun, setting on the things I wish I'd done. It's time to say goodbye to yesterday. This is where the cowboy rides away.'

Twenty miles outside of Edinburgh, they pulled into a side road beside a field, where Roy changed into his civilian clothes. They briefly examined their haul. It was extraordinary. It included a silver Georgian tea service, a platinum evening watch that had once been the property of the Prince of Wales, a Fabergé snuffbox that had belonged to the Duchess of Kent and a significant portion of the Hungarian crown jewels.

For reasons best known to himself, Roy decided to put his false moustache and goatee beard into a spare jewel box and secrete it down a rabbit hole. Dear Doctor Freud, I'm sure rabbit holes have some deep psychological significance (go ask Alice!) but it's beyond me.

The happy pair visited Roy's family, where he fulfilled his prophecy of turning his sister Violet into a princess by adorning her with precious jewels. He gave her gifts of earrings and a brooch, telling her not to wear them for a while, 'till they are fully paid for'.

He told his family that he was a legitimate antiques dealer. Roy was delighted to see that more than the jewels were glittering that day. Every time his mother looked at Wooton he saw her eyes sparkle. Wooton had a twinkle too.

After this brief encounter, the partners in crime headed south to sell their haul to a bent dealer in Torquay, a quiet town that nestles by the sea in the south of England.

One of the town's main claims to fame is the Torquay hotel that was the inspiration for *Fawlty Towers*, the hilarious situation comedy starring former Monty Python star John Cleese as Basil Fawlty, the bad-tempered hotelier – of whom more anon.

There were some grand hotels in Torquay, very different from Fawlty Towers. Roy and Wooton walked into one of the best of them – the Imperial Hotel. The two dapper gents felt they deserved a celebratory meal. Though no longer in costume, Roy was still in character as the rich Texan oilman. He'd have made a great JR in *Dallas*.

He liked to inhabit his roles, and it often took him a while to resurface from the deep ocean bed of his performance. Coming up too fast gave him the psychological equivalent of the bends: if he came out of a role too quickly he would forget who he was for a time. Even if it was only for a few minutes, it was terrifying, like a victim of Alzheimer's whose identity has come loose from its moorings.

When Roy strode into the Imperial Hotel, he still had his deep Texan drawl. He had wanted to wear his Stetson, but Wooton managed to dissuade him, on the wise grounds that the cowboy hat was the instantly recognisable symbol of the Esta Henry heist.

Wooton would have preferred that Roy drop the Texan pretence completely, especially when they walked into the middle of a reception organised by Torquay's Lord Mayor and were introduced to a guest who happened to be the Chief Constable for Devon and Cornwall!

Wooton was almost paralysed by fear, but this was exactly the kind of dangerous situation in which Roy revelled. 'It made me feel more alive,' he said.

Having concluded some business with their bent dealer en route, Roy now had plenty of cash to flash around. He started regaling his fellow guests with tales of 'the good ole USA', claiming his ancestors were from Torquay and that he'd come back to look for his roots.

He told the Mayor that he was so taken with the town that he'd like to make an investment in its future. The English gentleman accompanying him was, he said, his financial advisor. The Mayor was so impressed that he invited them to the charity ball reception and asked Roy if he'd be prepared to say a few words. He said he would be happy to do so.

This was still a time of postwar reconstruction, and Americans, particularly rich Americans, were most welcome.

'Besides,' he told me with a wink, 'I've always loved big balls!'

As Roy entered the grand ballroom, the band, on the instruction of the Lord Mayor, struck up a chorus of 'The Star-Spangled Banner'. Roy accepted their applause graciously as the Mayor introduced him: 'Ladies and gentlemen, please be upstanding for Wilbur Waterman the Third!'

Roy savoured the warm applause and made a speech in which he claimed that his great-grandfather was from Torquay and that he had decided to make a charitable donation to the town. He modestly held up a hand to forestall the applause.

'Ah am touched by the generosity of y'all in inviting me to this dinner,' he drawled. 'And in appreciation, Ah'd like to say a few words. Y'all should know that Torquay reminds me a lot of Texas. Sure, you're by the sea and we're in the desert, and we have oil and you don't, and you have a pier and we don't, and you drive on the wrong side of the road . . . and so on. But despite these superficial differences what we have in common is a big heart.'

This was met by enthusiastic applause.

Roy was starting to have fun.

'And speaking of big hearts, as Ah look around at the waistlines of y'all – you, my Lord Mayor and your lovely Rubenesque wife, and many of you dignitaries and other fat cats – Ah feel secure in saying, as we move on to the creamy dessert on top of all those rich sauces, that a massive coronary is just a heartbeat away! So, Ah have decided to donate a million dollars to heart research in your local hospitals here in Torquay. What the hell, I won't miss it,' he said. 'Ah'm worth a coupla billion.'

This was met by thunderous applause. At a signal from the Lord Mayor, the band struck up another round of 'The Star Spangled Banner'.

It was later noticed that the Mayor's gold chain of office had vanished.

'Great days,' said Roy nostalgically. 'Great days indeed.'

Before we moved on, I wanted to get to the bottom of the Esta Henry robbery. I had read several accounts of it and no two were the same. The basic facts were consistent, but details, sometimes significant details, were different in the various accounts. Was Roy embellishing them, I wondered? I suspected that he was adding rococo elements as the mood took him. In a different version of the Esta scam, for example, it was Roy's accomplice who went into the shop and wore the Stetson.

I asked him what the truth was. He smiled and said, 'Leave them guessing, that's what I've always said, son. You don't need to put your story in a straitjacket. Believe me, I know a thing or two about jackets that tie up the back. Give yourself some wiggle room. Whether you're a writer or a jewel thief, you must appreciate the need for a good polish.'

'Are you saying, Roy, that each time you tell a story, it goes through a new draft, just as I do different drafts when I write a script?'

'Something like that, yes.' He leaned forward and whispered, 'The reason for the alternative version is that John agreed to take the rap for the robbery, because we knew he'd get a far lighter sentence than I would. God bless him. I got off with a lesser charge of receiving stolen goods. He pretended he'd worn the hat and false beard and moustache, and Esta went along with it, because she liked me so much. She was a wonderful lady. She must have realised that a performance like that was simply not within John's range. He was shite at accents for a start.'

I replied, 'If I'm writing your story, I have to know what's true and what's not.'

'I'm telling you the truth,' he said vehemently. 'My legacy's important to me.'

His legacy? He was beginning to sound like a retiring US President establishing a foundation. What would Roy's be known as? The Fontaine Foundation for Misunderstood Murderers? Compassionate Killers, Inc?

'So you really were the Texan in the Stetson?' I asked.

'Ah sure as hell was, boy!' he said, affecting a flawless Texan accent. He then winked at me and added, 'But keep it under your hat!'

20

The Man Who Knew Too Much

> If you bring off adequate preservation of your
> personal myth, nothing much else in life
> matters. It is not what happens to people
> that is significant, but what they think
> happens to them.
>
> Anthony Powell, *Books Do Furnish a Room*

AFTER THE TEXAN SCAM, Roy took a lease on a luxury flat in London and started frequenting an upmarket hotel where a drunken waiter told him that there was a fortune in the safe. Unfortunately, the premises were guarded by a large Alsatian. Roy made it his business to befriend the dog, bringing it regular supplies of meat and assorted doggie treats.

He enlisted the help of a safe-blower. Late one night they sneaked into the hotel whilst the night porter was asleep. Roy patted the dog and gave it meat laced with sleeping pills. Soon the dog was fast asleep too. They blew open the safe and escaped with the haul.

Roy took a little holiday in Jersey, where he posed as a successful businessman and befriended a wealthy and lonely widow. To his delight he discovered she was off to visit friends in America. He said he'd see her when she got back. He burgled her instead.

He returned to London with his ill-gotten gains. Unknown to him, the safe-blower accomplice had got drunk and given the game away. When Roy got back to his London flat, two policemen were waiting for him.

'Betrayed once again!' he said bitterly, still smarting from the pain of it 40 years later.

He was sent to Parkhurst, on the Isle of Wight, which he hated with a passion. It was a tough regime that was known for good reason as 'Britain's Alcatraz'. From the moment he entered it, Roy was determined to escape.

Using only kitchen utensils, he and another inmate, whose nickname was Bo-Bo, managed to tunnel through a wall behind the kitchen stores. Roy's heart leapt when he got a glimpse of daylight. He knew that out there was the sea, his beloved sea with its promise of freedom. He didn't have a plan for crossing the water as yet, but there were plenty of boats about and he'd find a way. Roy always found a way.

Bo-Bo was excited too. So excited, in fact, that as he chiselled away at the last brick he punctured a gas pipe.

'My initial reaction was *we're fucked*!' said Roy.

'So near and yet so far. I did my best to lag it up with some rags, but I wasn't sure that I'd stopped the gas flow. We planned to escape the next day.'

Next morning there was an almighty explosion in the kitchen. A prisoner had discarded a cigarette butt, and Roy's dreams of freedom literally went up in smoke. The prisoner was injured, the kitchen was closed down for weeks and an inquest began to find out who was responsible.

Walls have ears, and prison walls have mouths too, and very talkative ones at that. Bo-Bo had discussed his exploits with his cellmate, who grassed on him and Roy.

'Ironically, it worked to my benefit,' said Roy. The authorities decided he was an agent provocateur, a stirrer of discontent, a lightning rod for trouble, capable of imposing his will on weaker individuals and of leading normally mild-mannered prisoners like Bo-Bo into bad ways, in that Pied Piper way of his.

Like a parasite being transferred to a more benevolent host, he was moved to the more user-friendly regime at Nottingham. There he became a fan of popular Governor Bill Perry.

'He was a good man,' said Roy. 'He was very decent to all the cons under his charge. He didn't try to punish me for my escape attempt at Parkhurst. Instead, he said he saw great potential in me and appointed me the prison's librarian.'

Roy was a genuine book-lover, and this was his dream job. He made up a reading programme for himself, and with the Governor's permission ordered books for the library. His particular passion was for books on etiquette and geology. Of the latter, he said, 'I was particularly interested in the section on precious stones.'

In jail, he also made a detailed study of antiques, history, politics, philosophy and finance, so that he could discourse knowledgeably on all of them. He could mix comfortably in any company. He was seen as well educated and highly intelligent, in the fine Scottish tradition of the 'lad o' pairts' – a youth from a humble background who is considered talented or promising. In other circumstances he could have been a captain of industry or a successful politician.

'It's amazing,' he told me, 'what you can pick up in the prison library. There are no distractions, you see.'

He did a great deal of research on fine wines. Knowing that parole boards look favourably on prisoners who are seen to be genuinely seeking gainful employment on their release, he applied to a few catering colleges to study courses leading to a qualification as a sommelier. The parole board, used to cons applying for mundane manual jobs like plumbing and joinery, found this both exotic and impressive.

They were also impressed by the fact that Roy had written to Lord Rank, the supremo of the Rank Organisation, who dominated British film distribution in the '50s and '60s, asking if there were any job opportunities. The organisation's famous logo showed a very muscular young man in crotch-hugging briefs hitting a gong with a large mallet. The ideal job, Roy thought (though he didn't say this in his job application), would be oiling that muscle man's torso. In conversation, Roy would puckishly refer to the logo as 'the half-naked man with the massive dong'.

After months of diligent study and voracious reading, Roy became an expert on fine wines without actually being able to taste them. I told him this reminded me of blind Homer imagining the sea as 'wine-dark'. Roy was flattered and pointed out that he often gave the Governor advice on his wine cellar.

He also became an expert on etiquette. 'I could've written "A

Snob's Guide to Society" by the time I was finished at Nottingham,'
he said. 'I used to advise the Governor on such matters as the
proper way to address a public official in correspondence.'

From this point on, whichever prison he was in, his reputation as
an expert on the labyrinthine and arcane ways of the British class
system would inevitably lead the Governor to seek his help on the
epistolary front.

1963 was a watershed year for Roy. Two momentous events
occurred. First was a new ruling that long-term prisoners who had
served two-thirds of their sentence could be released. On hearing
that he would be one of them, Roy did something that no other
prisoner did: he ordered a suit from Harrods.

In early 1963, another event occurred, which to most people
feels like a tsunami but which in Roy's case caused hardly a ripple
on the surface of his life.

His father died.

Governor Perry called Roy to his room and told him that, as he
was a model prisoner, he had decided to let him out on an
unsupervised weekend parole pass to go to his father's funeral in
Glasgow.

The Governor pointed out that in doing this he was putting
himself on the line. 'If you do a runner, it will make me look like an
idiot. If you don't come back, I will withdraw all privileges for your
fellow prisoners and you will be a very unpopular man for a long
time to come.'

Roy promised he would honour the conditions of the parole and
return on schedule.

'It was out of a sense of loyalty to the Governor that I vowed to
stick to my word – though I was severely tempted to do a runner to
Dublin.'

When he attended the funeral, he spent less time mourning his
father than he did celebrating the fact that his mother and Wooton
had grown closer. His brother Donald was also in attendance. Roy
was disgusted to discover that he had been arrested for 'pestering',
as it was delicately described, a young girl in a local cinema. 'That
little fucker brought shame on the family,' he said, with no hint of
irony, as if his own record were blameless.

I have often speculated on why Roy hated Donald so much. It was sibling rivalry of Cain and Abel proportions, and it was certainly not reciprocated. Donald was in awe of his glamorous big brother's criminal sang-froid and desperately sought his approval. The real problem was that in Roy's head Donald embodied the principle of betrayal. He was convinced the boy was the son of Major Morris: from the moment poor little Don popped out of Marion's womb, he symbolised her betrayal of Roy and his father.

John Lennon was once asked if he felt the Beatles were supermen. He replied, 'I do sometimes – until I look at Ringo.' When Roy looked at Donald, he was reminded that he was not an Arab adventurer, a Sultan, a Sinbad or a Pharaoh. He was just wee Archie Hall from Govan. His brother represented everything he hated and feared in himself.

Donald's second-rateness made Roy question his own greatness.

'Am I just a small-time criminal like him? A nobody?' he would ask himself. He could not allow himself to believe that. He refused to doubt his own genius. He wanted his brother out of his life.

Roy stood out at his father's graveside as being better dressed than his relatives: his cousins and uncles were either unemployed or working in the shipyards. His accent was more refined and Anglified than theirs, but it was still recognisably Scottish. He told them that he was 'in business' in London, which was true. He simply neglected to mention that his business was crime.

After the purvey, he walked with Wooton along the Govan Road, through the slums where he was raised. The mocking voices of his childhood echoed in his head with cries of 'Erchie! Erchie!' In the background were the silhouettes of the great shipyard cranes, pointing at the sky like the bony fingers of old men.

As they passed the Fairfield's building, Roy nodded towards Neptune. He felt they still had a deal, even though the trip to America was a long time a-coming. He looked through the shipyard gates and realised that some of the men slaving away in there had been at school with him. He found himself thinking how different his life was from theirs.

Ironically, even though he would be returning to prison in a few hours he felt more free than if he'd spent his life, as they had, behind the shipyard gates. He felt proud that he'd never been and never would be a wage slave, like those men he was watching as they performed their honest toil in blood, sweat and tears. They were enslaved by another man's system. He would never allow himself to be.

Turning to Wooton, he said, 'Behold the dignity of labour. They'll be peeing or shitting in the trough any minute.'

Wooton, used to Roy's rants against the herd, was itching to give him some good news. When he finally got the chance to talk, he told Roy that he and Marion were planning to get married. Roy was delighted, saying that he couldn't wish for a better stepfather. And so, in that topsy-turvy world that Roy inhabited, the day of his father's funeral became one of the happiest days of his life.

Wooton revealed that he and Marion had enjoyed a few discreet weekends in Dunoon, on the beloved Firth of Clyde. Unlike Rothesay, Dunoon doesn't loom large in my personal cosmology. The great Scottish stand-up comedian Billy Connolly sang a song entitled 'Why don't they come back to Dunoon?' in which he joked that a newspaper had a competition in which the first prize was a week in Dunoon and the second prize was a fortnight in Dunoon.

The town got a bad press during the Cold War years, when it was a base for American nuclear submarines. This scarce does it justice, and I am assured that now the imminent threat of nuclear annihilation has abated it makes a very pleasant weekend retreat.

In the midst of his mother being matched and his father dispatched, Roy hatched a plan to make the weekend even better. He called the Lady with whom he had enjoyed the fleshy paradise of Rothesay. She escaped from her husband long enough to enjoy a long afternoon in bed with Roy at the Central Hotel, where he re-acquainted himself with every nook and cranny of her voluptuous flesh. For old times' sake they reprised the nail-painting delights of the Lady Varnishes routine.

As they were making love, knowing that he would be returning to England in a few hours, Roy felt a patriotic wave of affection for his native land. Caressing her full breasts and enjoying her moist furrow, he burst into an impromptu chorus of 'For these are my mountains (and this is my glen)' – a nationalistic dirge sung by kilted entertainers the Alexander Brothers. Its potency as a romantic ballad had hitherto gone unnoticed. Those of you seeking suitable songs for getting down and dirty with that special person in your life should perhaps give the Alexander Brothers a chance.

After a refreshing session of sensual delight, he was ideally placed to catch the late train south. That was the beauty of his beloved Central Hotel: you were always only minutes away from jumping on a train to freedom.

Still in patriotic mode, before he boarded he bought some miniatures of Glenfiddich scotch and a tin of Walker's shortbread for his cellmates.

'I deliberately timed my trip so that I would arrive one minute before the expiry of my two-day pass,' he said.

To his fellow prisoners, he was a hero for not doing a runner.

For acts of loyalty such as those, as well as for his natural charisma, Roy was very popular in prison, where his nickname of 'Roy the Boy' related to his boyish charm and appetite for life, regardless of his biological age.

He survived in prison with the help of contraband and the physical charms of the steady parade of young men whose sexual favours he enjoyed. In return, he regaled them with exciting tales of his adventures and tips on how to carry out Roy-style scams on their release.

He often embellished the truth, of course. He told one young admirer that, 'I said to the judge – you have no respect for humanity and you will go to hell for ever.'

'Did you really say that?' asked the admirer.

'No – of course not,' replied Roy. 'What do you think I am – a fucking idiot?'

When he was released from Nottingham, Roy immediately answered an ad in *The Times* for a butler, and his glowing references, self-penned, got him the job. He pretended he'd been abroad since his last period of service.

'I moved on several times,' he said. 'My guiding principle was simple: the richer the better. I gained great insights into the peculiar ways of the ruling class. I discovered that the gentry are thieves like me: the only difference is that they robbed and plundered hundreds of years ago and have bought themselves respectability.'

His new employer asked him if he'd mind serving breakfast to himself and his male friends – who liked to sit on the sun terrace in the nude. Roy said he'd be comfortable with that, if those were the Master's wishes. In full formal dress, he found himself handing to several nude men copies of the London *Times* and the *Daily Telegraph*, which conveniently covered their private parts. The extroverts preferred the smaller-format tabloids.

He was, as he put it, 'finding out the naked truth about the ruling class'.

He inevitably found the sexual habits of the upper classes much more flexible than those of the lower orders. One employer, on welcoming several couples to his weekend retreat, told Roy to leave the guests' shoes outside the rooms in the morning and gave him a list of who was swapping partners with whom.

He had been buttling for a few months when he met Phyllis Nye, a cook. He suggested to her that they should offer their services together. In reality, this was to give him extra cover. They advertised in *The Times* and found employment in Hastings, with an elderly gentleman from the USA.

'That was no good,' said Roy. 'The old boy was American, and I liked him too much to rob him. The Yanks are far better employers than the English. They're not stuck-up, class-ridden perverts.'

The American gent's wife gave him jewels to clean. 'I didn't even think about making copies,' Roy said sportingly. 'Instead I just steeped them in gin and marvelled at their beauty.'

Roy and Phyllis found a job with another employer, a diplomat whom he did not like. That made his job easier. There was no moral dilemma. In Roy's view, this man deserved to be robbed, and he gleefully obliged, switching real gems for glass copies made by his bent contact in London.

Roy was now fleecing the rich, but that wasn't good enough: he wanted to fleece the super-rich. He felt he was moving closer to his goal when he secured a job with Sir George Aylwen, a former Lord Mayor of London. Many of Aylwen's friends and associates were fabulously wealthy property developers who'd built powerful relationships with the Lord Mayor in order to help them develop prime London real estate. As Roy astutely foresaw, the Aylwens would prove to be a useful stepping stone to the richest of the rich.

Sir George and Lady Aylwen had a luxury apartment in London's swanky Mayfair. Lady Aylwen, according to Roy, was extremely accommodating. There were flowers to greet his arrival. As their relationship blossomed, she took to inviting him to her boudoir on the pretence that she needed him to light a cigarette for her.

It was more a case of 'come on, baby, light my fire'. As soon as Roy entered the bedroom, she would pull him on top of her to stoke the flames of passion. Surprisingly, he did not enjoy these encounters.

'She liked to bite, slap and scratch. I'd come out of her room looking like I'd just gone ten rounds with Mick McManus,' he said, referring to a popular wrestler of the era.

In all my firefighter father's warnings about the dangers of smoking in bed, he said nothing about being bitten and scratched by a sado-masochistic aristocrat.

Later, when Roy was arrested and convicted of jewel theft, Lady Aylwen wrote a play about a crooked butler called 'Hardcastle'. It was never published, to the regret of the publicity-craving Roy. 'I'm not surprised she put the word "Hard" in the title,' he laughed. 'That's how she liked me to give it to her: hard and rough.'

He felt uncomfortable with his amorous aristo. He preferred men, and he thought that the rough treatment she meted out in bed was above and beyond the call of duty. He became more intent than ever on landing a bigger fish.

His chance came when he read a newspaper report about Sir Charles Clore's butler having taken an overdose of drugs. This suggested that Sir Charles, one of the United Kingdom's richest men, might be a demanding taskmaster, but it was an opportunity Roy could not afford to miss.

Clore knew the Aylwens, and Roy asked Lady Aylwen for a reference. She sportingly obliged, writing that she'd been more than satisfied with his services. She certainly had.

When he went to the interview, he noted that Sir Charles' residence was replete with Picassos and an abundance of treasures that would have made Aladdin salivate – including a Fabergé egg that alone was worth half a million pounds at 1963 prices.

Impressive as ever in interview, Roy got the job. Again Phyllis Nye accompanied him, totally unaware of his nefarious schemes. He quickly devised a master plan for robbing his new home. His plan was thwarted, however, just a few weeks into his new tenure. After pouring a glass of water for a dinner guest, Roy put it down in the centre of the polished table instead of taking it back to the serving table as strict etiquette demanded. The suspicions of his new boss were aroused. Sir Charles said to a friend, 'He's no more a butler than I am. He had one eye on the port and another on the silver plate.' In fact, Roy told me that he had indeed been distracted by the diamond necklace adorning one of the guests.

Clore had Roy investigated by a zealous private detective who contacted previous employers. They checked and double-checked and discovered that various precious articles had disappeared. Roy was summoned to the library, where Sir Charles informed him that his services were being dispensed with.

'May I ask why, sir?' asked the shocked Roy. Sir Charles read from the private detective's report: 'Because you are a thief, a burglar, a receiver of stolen goods and a sexual deviant.'

After a short pause, Roy asked, 'Is that all, sir?'

Sir Charles passed the report on to the police. They arrested Roy before he could cover his tracks, but not before he had done some detective work of his own. He felt he had recognised a young blonde woman who often shared the ageing Clore's bed. He discovered she was none other than Mandy Rice-Davies, one of the expensive young call girls at the centre of the sex scandal that would soon rock the Conservative government.

'I believe that's why Clore really wanted rid of me,' Roy said. 'I was the man who knew too much.'

As a result of the facts uncovered by Clore's detective, Roy was sentenced in January 1964 to ten years' preventative detention at the high-security prison at Blundeston in Suffolk. The presiding judge said, 'In works of fiction, the butler-crook is a well-known figure. Those of us old enough to remember the play *The Last of Mrs Cheyney* will know that these sorts of figures are surrounded by an aura of glamour. But you, who have emulated that butler, have proved yourself a dangerous criminal. You are a man of obvious intelligence who made up his mind to prey on society.'

Phyllis Nye was found to be not guilty on all counts. The judge told her, 'You have been fooled by a very, very clever crook.'

Before he left the court, Roy took the time to thank the judge for likening him to Mrs Cheyney, one of his favourite fictional characters. He quoted her views on the gospel of hospitality and recommended that the judge try to catch the Joan Crawford film, which in his opinion was the best of the three versions made from the book. Roy would be happy to lend him the book if he wished.

The judge declined his generous offer.

'I got ten years!' Roy said indignantly. 'The ruling class punished me for knowing their dirty little secrets. I got ten years for crimes against property when child molesters were only getting three. They sent me to a high-security prison that was meant to be impossible to escape from! Still,' he said smiling, 'I've always liked a challenge.'

21

The Great Escape

A robin redbreast in a cage puts all heaven in
a rage.

William Blake, *Auguries of Innocence*

BLUNDESTON PRISON, NEAR LOWESTOFT in Sussex, was a state-of-the art high-security prison that stood in 90 acres of inhospitable land made even less welcoming by the permanently chill wind blowing in from the North Sea. It cost half a million pounds to build and had CCTV cameras throughout. It was one of the first places in the country to have such surveillance everywhere.

Everywhere, that is, except in the prison kitchens – a fact that Roy was quick to note. No one had ever escaped, and it was confidently assumed that no one ever would. Roy had other ideas.

He naturally sought a job in the kitchen, as that was traditionally where security was weakest in any prison. He got the job, which surprised him, given that 'the last time I'd been in a prison kitchen I'd blown it up'.

'I was lucky,' he said. 'The prison authorities were either very forgiving or kept crap records. I discovered it was the latter. They knew I'd made an escape attempt at Parkhurst, but the stupid cunts didn't bother checking out the details.'

He explained the importance of the kitchen from the point of view of the aspiring escapologist.

'Whenever I found myself in a new prison, the first thing I would do was check if there were any kitchen smells. Now why do you think I did that, son?' he asked, staring at me intently in a sorcerer-

and-apprentice kind of way. Sadly I failed to come up with an answer. He sighed as if to say I'd never be more than a very junior member of the criminal club, and explained, 'If there are no kitchen smells, that means the place has big ventilators. And big ventilators usually go out through the roof. Which means that if they're big enough you can go out through the roof too.'

From his cell, he could see a rooftop skylight. He decided from its placement that it must be for the ventilator shaft. Further investigation revealed that the ventilator itself was located in a locked cupboard behind the kitchens. Resourceful as ever in the criminal arts, he used baking dough to make a copy of the lock, from which he made a makeshift key in the metalwork class that the authorities had helpfully provided for his rehabilitation.

Needing help with his master plan, he befriended George O'Neill, a prisoner with the reputation of being a good escapee. Together they worked out the details. When the coast was clear, Roy got into the cupboard, from which he could see the small window above. Using a long piece of string to judge the angles, he calculated the window's circumference and cut it out on a piece of newspaper. George held up the paper and Roy successfully crawled through it. They were elated. The skylight at the top of the ventilator shaft was big enough for them to climb through.

Roy decided that they should make their escape on a day when several English FA Cup ties were being played. He reckoned many of the guards would switch over their closed-circuit TVs to watch the football.

A bent friend on the outside agreed to leave a getaway car at a safe distance. Roy enlisted another inmate, an expert driver named Don Whittaker. These were the three who would endeavour to make the Great Escape.

Roy pumped them up by telling them that if they succeeded they'd be in the history books, the first prisoners ever to escape from a high-security prison in the United Kingdom. He was building his legacy once again.

He told them it was essential that all three of them be put on kitchen duties on the night of the escape. When this proved impossible, Roy intercepted the prisoner who was taking the list to the Governor's office, bribed him with some cigarettes and replaced the names with his own, O'Neill's and Whittaker's.

The evening before the planned escape they loosened the screws of the ventilator shaft. Unfortunately, there was a high wind that night, and they spent sleepless hours listening to the cover rattling. The prison staff didn't realise its significance. Next evening, the three went as planned through the kitchen cupboard, up the shaft and out onto the roof.

They froze as they heard a loud piercing whistle. The voices of the guards below shouted, 'Stop them!'

'We're done for!' said George. 'They've spotted us!'

'No,' whispered Roy encouragingly. 'They're watching the football!'

Unusually for a Glasgow lad, Roy had little interest in football, but that night it became his favourite sport.

The three made it to the prison yard, which was surrounded by a perimeter fence. They took a long plank of wood and used it as a gangplank. Before they went up, Roy took out a pepper pot and sprinkled all three of them.

'It'll put the dogs off the scent,' he said.

They were almost undone immediately. Don Whittaker trapped his foot on the barbed wire on top of the fence and cut it badly. He was bleeding heavily. 'Go on without me!' he said as he dropped over the wall and lay in agony. 'I'll just hold you back, lads.'

Roy would not hear of it. They were in this together. He told George to help him prop Don up, and the unlikely group hobbled off into the night as ominous storm clouds rolled in from the North Sea.

Their prospects of success suffered another potentially fatal blow as torrential rain began to fall. They knew they would be soaked to the skin by the time they got to the getaway car, but at least it would provide very welcome shelter. When they reached the appointed spot, however, their spirits sank as deep as their shoes in the mud. The car was nowhere to be seen.

Roy's face became as angry as the sky.

'That devious fucker didn't leave us the car!' he said. 'And I paid him a fuckin' fortune!'

George voiced the opinion that Roy's accomplice must have taken the money and run, confident that they wouldn't escape.

'I'd been betrayed again,' Roy told me, the old anger rekindling. 'The other two wanted to give up, but I said no, we couldn't let ourselves down now that we had got this far. I told them if we crossed the river we still had a chance.'

The three of them could hear the angry waters of the swollen river Waveney in the distance. It normally meandered peacefully between Norfolk and Suffolk. Tonight, however, it was a terrifying torrent.

This was one of those moments when Roy's qualities of loyalty and leadership were on full display. He had already stuck by his injured pal: now he gave his accomplices a stirring Three Musketeers speech about one for all and all for one. He said the cops would assume they had made their escape by road. He chose not to emphasise that the cops would never believe anyone could be mad enough to try to cross the river on a night like tonight, because frankly the odds of survival were minimal. But Roy was so desperate not to go back inside he was prepared to risk it.

'It was a case of Victory or Death!' he said.

He was, consciously or otherwise, echoing the words of Hitler, his early hero and mentor. 'Give me victory or give me death' was the Fuhrer's catchphrase, which he sold big-time to the Germans. For those of you too young to remember, he got death.

'So you talked them into risking it?' I asked.

'I did indeed,' he said, with the self-satisfied smile of a man who is used to having his will prevail. His persuasive skills were all the more remarkable considering that George and Don revealed they couldn't swim.

'That's OK,' said Roy. 'Neither can I.'

That was a big fat lie, but a brilliant one: it cemented team spirit. Doctor Goebbels would have been proud of him.

Roy was in fact a very strong swimmer, having spent much of his adolescence in the public baths, working himself into a lather, often literally, over the torsos of young men. He claimed to have done anatomically challenging things with those young men and soap on a rope. In between all the other kinds of new strokes he was learning at the baths, he became adept at the breaststroke and the crawl.

As the three escapees contemplated the swirling waters in the distance, Roy painted a depressing picture of an ignominious return to the cells and the hell of solitary confinement. Even a watery grave had to be better than that. By the time he had finished, his land-lubbing pals were convinced.

They continued through marshland in the torrential rain. Suddenly they heard the ominous wail of the prison siren. 'The scream's up!' said Whittaker.

'The helicopters will be out soon!' added George, knowing that the RAF base at Lowescroft was close by.

'No,' said Roy, 'they won't want to go up in this storm. We can use that to our advantage.'

They heard the distant barking of dogs, which focused their minds wonderfully. Hobbling as fast as they could, they managed to reach the riverbank. The Waveney was in full spate. 'We'll never get across that,' said Don.

'Yes we will,' replied Roy. He wasn't entirely convinced, but the adrenalin was pumping through him. It was a long time since he'd felt so alive.

He led them along the riverbank. Through the thick curtain of rain they saw an allotment. Roy spotted a couple of shovels and said, 'We'll take these.' The other two looked confused. 'Paddles,' he added helpfully.

As the barking got closer, they walked along, desperately hoping to find a boat. Instead they found a small wooden landing platform moored to the bank, intended to help occupants of small boats disembark.

'This'll have to do,' said Roy. 'We can use it as raft!'

The other two were not convinced, but Roy persisted.

'All we have to do is stay afloat till we get to the other side.'

The other two remained rooted to the spot. The barking of the dogs got louder.

'It's either this or years in solitary,' Roy shouted through the storm. 'They'll never forgive us for escaping. They'll make an example of us!'

He was right. The authorities would not look kindly on men who had dared to breach Blundeston's supposedly impregnable defences.

The prison authorities, like the gods, are not mocked.

He stepped on board the raft and held out his hand. After a moment's hesitation the other two jumped aboard and Roy untied the makeshift raft from its mooring, setting them loose on the swirling water.

They paddled furiously with the shovels, trying to stop the raft from spinning out of control.

'I felt like one of the boys on the raft in *Coral Island*,' said Roy proudly, his eyes lighting up at the memory of it. 'That was one of my favourite books as a kid. Now I wasn't just reading about such adventures. I was living them!'

They floated past the Waveney Cricket Club, which was having a reception that night after the cricket match. The balcony of the clubhouse overlooked the river. Two drunken cricketers spotted them and realised from their attire that the men on the raft were escaped prisoners.

'We'd been seen!' said Roy. He remembered the schoolboy story of the Sun and the Wind, so he stopped paddling for a moment to smile and wave at them. They smiled and waved back, raising their glasses, shouting, 'Good luck, lads! You can do it!'

Thirty years later, Roy remembered them with a smile. He took pride in never grassing on a colleague, and he felt eternally grateful to them for not calling the cops.

'What good sports they were,' he said. 'I saw cricketers in a more sympathetic light after that. We could see in the distance the beams of the helicopters from the Lowescroft RAF base. We rowed with extra strength when we realised that they were moving away from us, searching the roads and lanes. They obviously didn't believe anyone would be mad enough to be on the river that night.'

Roy was mad enough to do anything, as he demonstrated time and time again throughout his career. He had the reports of psychiatrists to prove it.

Five miles downriver, they managed to reach the opposite bank and jump off the raft. They punched the air in triumph and gave each other wet hugs of joyful relief. Roy suggested that they each throw an article of clothing into the river to make it look like they'd drowned, but the other two were too cold and wet to do so. He went ahead anyway and took his shirt off. He dumped it in the river, hoping it would be found and identified. The idea of faking his own death had always appealed to him. He had, in a sense, already killed off Archie Hall.

Freezing, he led them towards the dark silhouette of a farm. The farmer and his wife were sleeping. The escapees managed to break into a room and steal some dry clothes. Unfortunately, the only available getaway vehicle was a tractor attached to a cart filled with manure.

'It'll have to do,' said Roy. He knew the police would be looking for three men, so he and the injured Don covered themselves with manure while George drove, avoiding roadblocks till they reached another farm where they washed, changed their clothes and stole a proper car.

Roy was shocked at being covered in manure. For one so scrupulously clean and used to smelling fragrant it was traumatising. 'I'd found myself in the shit several times in my life,' he said, 'but this was the first time it was literal.'

The trio drove north, heading for Glasgow, where Roy knew a corrupt bookie who would look after them and supply them with everything they needed. They drove through the night via various side roads and arrived in the early morning. They dumped the car in the River Clyde at Dalmuir.

Accompanied by their bookie friend, the three celebrated Britain's most daring escape with a champagne supper – where else but in the Central Hotel?

Roy regaled them with nostalgic tales of how his mother used to work there. 'It was here,' he said proudly, 'that I started to learn my craft.' In an impeccable French accent, he ordered the best wine and had a knowledgeable discussion with the wine waiter. His companions were impressed.

The bookie told them that a rival of his, who had a large estate in Perthshire in the north of Scotland, had a house full of cash and valuables that was just waiting to be burgled. A few days later, the three attempted to do just that. But Roy had forgotten the important truth preached by Baden-Powell, presumably whilst he was scouting for boys: 'Be prepared'.

They disabled the main alarm before entering but had not

realised that there was a secondary alarm linked to the local police station. They were ransacking the house when they heard the police car approaching: George and Don managed to reach their getaway car, but Roy was upstairs, and any delay could have been fatal. They drove off, leaving him to his own devices.

He scampered down the drainpipe, experiencing a brief nostalgic pang for his days as a cat burglar, and proceeded to make his escape on foot. He realised he'd been lucky: the police car was pursuing the other two in the getaway car.

He saw a hotel in the distance and made a beeline for it, associating it, as he always did, with sanctuary. He saw that it had outlying chalets and broke into one of them. He was lucky yet again, finding jewellery, clothes that fitted him, some cash and a handsome attaché case. He re-emerged dressed as a businessman, confidently walked down the hotel driveway and caught a bus into the city.

He cunningly asked the driver for a return fare. When the bus was boarded by a policeman looking for the burglars, Roy sat puffing confidently on his cigar, reading the *Daily Telegraph* that he'd stolen from the chalet for just such an eventuality. The cop was about to question Roy when the driver intervened, telling the policeman, 'He's OK – he's just bought a return ticket.' The cop disembarked and waved the bus on.

'It works every time,' Roy told me. 'No one ever thinks that a man on the run would buy a return.'

He headed back down to London, where he returned to the luxurious Dorchester Hotel. He thought he deserved some pampering after his recent adventures. From the Dorchester he had easy access to London's West End and the good things of life – such as men, women, theatre, gourmet meals and Turkish baths. The baths in Russell Square were a particular favourite.

As he passed a police station not far from the hotel, he saw his own face beaming out at him from a Wanted poster. He was shocked. There were much better photos of him that they could have used, ones which would have made him look much more handsome. He consoled himself with the thought that he might benefit from the fact that it wasn't a very good likeness.

22

The Fugitive

'Free to hide in lonely desperation, to
change his identity, to toil at many jobs . . .
free to run before the relentless pursuit of
the police.'
Intro to the 1960s TV show *The Fugitive*

DECIDING HE NEEDED TO get away from it all, Roy went down
to Cornwall. He was intent on resting and recharging his
batteries, but when he took one look at the local jewellers he
couldn't resist paying them a visit. He immediately enlisted
Wooton's services.

Dressed in his Savile Row suit, he entered the shop. 'I had already
planted my accomplice and we went through the "My lord"
routine,' he said.

He browsed for a few minutes, till Wooton came in and said,
'Lord Menzies-Jones! Haven't seen you since the Burma Campaign.'
They had a quick chat before Wooton exited to the getaway car.
Roy, now firmly established in the minds of the shop's staff as a
peer of the realm, started examining very rare gems. He said he
could not really appreciate them unless he saw them in natural
light. 'May I?' he said, gesturing towards the door.

'Of course, my lord,' said the deferential sales assistant. It was
simple. Roy walked out of the door with the precious gems and
jumped straight into the getaway car. Unfortunately, a police car
was nearby and the driver saw them speeding off. They gave chase
through the narrow streets of Falmouth.

Wooton, an expert driver, managed to shake them off by driving more dangerously than the cops were prepared to do. He dropped Roy back at his hotel. The two decided they'd be less recognisable if they split up and Wooton made his escape separately.

In the hotel, Roy passed two chambermaids and gave them a friendly 'hello'.

'I was casting out my line and hoping that one of those two pretty little fish would bite. I was still pumped up after the robbery and the car chase, and I needed some recreational nookie to help me unwind.'

One of the maids responded with a warm and encouraging 'Hello, sir!'

The other looked stunned. She had recognised him from a photo in the newspaper as 'The Mastermind behind the Great Escape'. He could tell from her reaction that she knew who he was. When the maids went downstairs, he crept to the top of the staircase. He heard her tell the concierge to phone the police. There was nothing else for it. He jumped out of the window and the chase was on again.

He hailed a taxi. To explain away his dishevelled state, he told the driver that his wife had been in a car crash and had been rushed to hospital in Plymouth. The taxi was flagged down by a police officer looking for two men – Roy and Wooton. The driver told the officer that he was rushing his passenger to hospital. The policeman offered him a police escort. Roy pretended to be delighted.

They arrived at the hospital and Roy realised he'd have to do yet another runner. Saying he was going to the Enquiry Desk, he slipped round the corner and jumped out of the window, thinking he was on the ground floor – but the hospital was on a hill and he was one floor up.

He tumbled downhill and sprained his ankle. Knowing the policeman would be after him in a few minutes, he hobbled towards a rubbish bin. He opened it only to find it was full of stinking, rotting vegetables. He had no choice but to climb in and pull the rotten vegetables over him. He had to hide there for hours. He could hear the police outside looking for him. When night fell, he emerged and made his way to the train station. Stinking to high heaven, he got the train back to London.

Any passenger unfortunate enough to sit in his smelly compartment soon got up and left, gagging. First manure, now rotten vegetables. The fastidious man who had an obsession with cleanliness was beginning to feel he had sacrificed enough for his art. He was tiring of life as a fugitive.

A few months after the rotten-vegetables debacle, he bumped into a young woman named Margaret in a hotel bar and started up a conversation with her. He soon realised he had found the perfect cover for a man on the run. She was pregnant and had left her disapproving parents in Ireland.

'I knew the cops would never be looking for a man with a wife and kid,' he said. He proposed they live together and placed an advert for his services as a butler in *The Lady* magazine, securing a post in Warwickshire. He faked references for Margaret saying that she was an experienced and highly accomplished cook. They were fired when it emerged that her culinary talents stretched to double eggs and chips. She also had a disturbing habit of throwing away shoes left outside bedroom doors.

Margaret had her baby in December of 1965. Roy noted with wry amusement that the registrar of births was a Mr Butler.

Margaret had no idea that Roy was on the run. One night they were watching an episode of the TV series *The Fugitive*. The hugely popular show was about a man convicted of killing his wife. He was on the run, trying to prove his innocence as he searched for 'the one-armed man' who had actually committed the crime.

'How would you feel if I was on the run?' Roy asked Margaret.

'I'd feel no different about you,' she said.

'Good,' he replied, 'because I'm the most wanted man in Britain.'

After a brief pause, during which the imperturbable Margaret processed this astonishing piece of information, she replied, 'I don't care if you're wanted, as long as you want me.'

They toasted each other's health with a glass of malt.

'Margaret didn't ask questions, so she never did find out where all the cash came from to give the kid the best possible start in life,' Roy told me proudly.

'It came from one of my best-ever performances. At last I was the hero from *The Arabian Nights* that I'd always wanted to be. It was the role I was born to play.' He proceeded to tell me the mind-boggling tale of Sheik Medinah.

23

Sheik your Money Maker

I'm the Sheik of Araby, your love belongs to
   me . . .
You'll rule this world with me, I'm the Sheik
   of Araby.
'The Sheik Of Araby' – popular song of the 1920s

Every great singer has his signature song and every great criminal
has his signature crime. McCartney has 'Yesterday', Lennon has
'Imagine', Sinatra has 'My Way', and Roy has Sheik Medinah.

Roy's signature crime was one in which his qualities as a con
artist, a burglar and a fantasist came together in perfect harmony,
so that at long last his dream self and his real self became one, like
a photo coming into perfect focus. Finally he could become the
Sultan he had always felt himself to be. For Roy, this wasn't acting.
This was just being himself – albeit the self he had been in a
previous life.

He ordered an Arab robe from a London theatrical costume-
hire shop, telling the sales assistant he was mounting a stage revival
of Valentino's *The Sheik*. With a stolen credit card, he purchased 12
large expensive suitcases, which he and Wooton filled with bricks
and newspapers. He daubed his hands and face with tincture of
iodine, staining his skin brown, and made the hotel reservation
under the name Sheik Medinah. He ordered a Rolls-Royce for the
day and paid for it too with the stolen credit card.

In full Arab dress, he rehearsed in front of a mirror. He smiled,
bowed and held his hands in a praying motion as he said to his
reflection, 'Greetings, O mighty Sultan!'

Wooton, who was watching the performance, added in appreciation, 'Allah be praised!'

When they arrived at the Dorchester in the chauffeur-driven Rolls, the hotel staff fell over themselves in supplication, eager to carry the heavy suitcases up to his palatial suite. Roy gave them a suitably generous tip.

The Sheik looked at the gems for sale in the Dorchester's own jewellery shop. 'Mere trinkets!' he said dismissively in his best Arabian accent. He instructed the hotel manager to do better. The manager, sensing a fat commission, phoned round various Hatton Garden jewellers. Within a few hours several arrived with their most precious gems.

Sheik Medinah instructed them to come to his suite. One dealer went to shake his hand, but the Sheik pulled back, saying, 'No! I must not touch the Infidel.'

'Of course,' Roy told me, 'the real reason was that I didn't want the dye to rub off.'

The Sheik said that as the feast of Ramadan was approaching and he was in the presence of impure Infidels, 'To honour Allah, I must cleanse my sacred parts. Mercifully, the toilet facilities are facing Mecca.'

He went into the bathroom and ran a bath. Steam was rising as he instructed the dealers to bring the gems through for his inspection. Used to the eccentric ways of rich Arabs, they did so.

The dealers sat in the main room, dreaming of large commissions. After a suitable interval, when the Sheik showed no sign of emerging, one of the dealers knocked discreetly on the bathroom door. There was no reply. He alerted the others, who feared the Sheik might have had a heart attack and drowned. Hotel staff were called. They forced the door open. The bathroom was full of steam. When it cleared, they saw a pile of Arab robes lying on the floor. He had exited through an adjoining room.

Dressed in the smart suit he had worn under his robes, Roy was at that moment walking triumphantly through Covent Garden, the proud possessor of a tidy fortune in precious jewels. The haul was worth over a million pounds.

With his new-found wealth, Roy ensconced himself, Margaret and the baby in a comfortable detached house in Paddock's Wood, near Tunbridge Wells in Kent, the county which is known as 'the Garden of England'. The garden could now boast its very own serpent.

He cultivated a bourgeois lifestyle and played the role of the well-off country gent with gusto. He bought a Jaguar that he drove on a forged licence, since he'd never actually bothered with the tedious business of sitting a driving test. Driving licences were for ordinary people. He became a member of the local country club and joined the local Conservative club 'to meet the right kind of people. People I could rob.'

This was a happy time in his life. He was ecstatic when he was invited to be best man at the wedding of his mother and John Wooton.

'I couldn't have asked for a better stepfather,' he said. 'Stepfather and partner in crime – what more could a man ask?'

The only fly in the ointment was when his brother Donald, just out of prison for petty theft, turned up at the wedding. When he found out that Roy was going on holiday for a fortnight to Weston-Super-Mare, he wanted to come along too, but his big brother wouldn't hear of it.

Two days after Roy arrived in the seaside town, the police received an anonymous tip-off that he was hiding out there – Roy Fontaine, the brains behind the Great Escape, one of the most wanted men in Britain. It was not yet known that he was also Sheik Medinah.

He was arrested in a dawn raid and sentenced on various charges of theft and fraud at the Central Criminal Court. The judge had already scribbled '15 years' against a formidable list of convictions for theft and fraud. When asked if he had anything to say in his defence, Roy made a typically ingenious plea.

'In this court, a judge of Your Lordship's great experience and eminence will, over the years, have heard many a man plead for mercy. I will make no such plea. I am not a mere product of my upbringing and unfortunate social origins. I had a loving mother who ensured I had a wide-ranging education and a father who enforced discipline. I stand before you today as a man who makes no excuses for himself or for his crimes. My Lord, if you see fit to impose a firm sentence – do so! I will take it like a man!'

A tearful lady in the public gallery started clapping. The ermine-robed judge crossed out the figure '15' and replaced it with a '10'.

Despite this small triumph, the doors of Parkhurst clanged shut behind him once again. He advised Margaret that since he could no longer provide for her or her daughter she'd be better off emigrating. She put the child up for adoption and moved to Canada.

'I was back in the prison I hated, after two glorious years of freedom,' he said bitterly.

He remained convinced that his brother was the informant.

'All because Donald cliped to the cops. The treacherous wee bastard.'

◊

I felt a break was called for, so I suggested coffee. Roy nodded vacantly and stared at me in an eerie fashion, like a man remembering a murder.

24

Harem Scare 'Em

There was an old fellow of Lyme
Who lived with three wives at a time
When asked 'Why the third?'
He replied, 'One's absurd;
And bigamy, sir, is a crime.'

Popular limerick

I went to fetch the coffee and slipped the twenty-pound note into the cigarette packet with well-rehearsed dexterity. I had become blasé about the prison rituals. The format was well established: I would duly perform the cash-into-fag-packet sleight of hand with the effortless ease of a professional conjuror. A few more visits and I'd be pulling eggs out of the guards' ears.

When I came back and sat down at our little Formica table, Roy revealed that he knew more about me than he'd been letting on. He said, out of nowhere, 'Tell me about *Beautiful Lies*.'

That was the title of a TV drama I'd written that had been broadcast a few months earlier. It dealt with an encounter between George Orwell and H.G. Wells during the Second World War. I had no idea Roy knew of its existence. He was obviously building a file on me, just as I was on him.

'It's a TV play of mine,' I said.

'*Beautiful Lies* is a great title,' he said. 'You should copyright it.'

I told him you cannot copyright a title.

He brightened and said, 'Excellent! Then I'll use it for my autobiography!'

The suggestion got under my skin, as it was meant to. He was playing another of his mind games on me.

I rose to the bait.

'Roy, you'll blow your credibility if you put the word "lies" in the title,' I said.

He puffed on his cigar and nodded sagely.

'Relax, son, I was only winding you up. I'm not really going to call it *Beautiful Lies*. I want my autobiography to be as honest as possible. But it is a great title.'

After that, the atmosphere started to improve. He laughed when I told him *Beautiful Lies* was originally called *Anticipations* (after the H.G. Wells book of that name) and that I was asked to change the title when the female production staff told me they hated answering the phone because when they said 'Anticipations' it sounded like they were plying their trade in a massage parlour.

He decided to provoke me again: 'I've spent my life telling beautiful lies, but that's what you do too, isn't it, son? You make up stories. You tell lies for a living. That makes you some sort of hoor, doesn't it?' he said, favouring the Glaswegian pronunciation of 'whore'.

I defended myself by saying that all art was a kind of beautiful lie. I had walked into his trap.

'Ugly or beautiful, son, a hoor is still a hoor!'

Now he was really bugging me, undermining my sense of moral superiority.

I found myself saying, 'Art is the lie that tells the truth. That's what Picasso said.'

He thought about that for a moment, savouring the thought as he would savour a good cigar.

'Picasso was just like me,' he said: 'A horny old goat who loved to fuck.'

This may have been oversimplifying the greatest artist of the century, but, like so much Roy said, it had a kernel of truth which was both hard and painful, like the coin in the Christmas pudding.

I was uncomfortable with our discussion of artists as beautiful liars and upmarket whores. I changed the topic by asking him what it felt like when he was sent back to Parkhurst.

'I was a good boy second time around,' he said. 'As an escapee and a high-security prisoner I met more interesting people. I was now part of a very special elite. Many of my fellow high-security prisoners were spies: there was Peter Kroger and Paddy Meehan, who were linked to MI5. They taught me how valuable Government secrets are. That information was to come in handy later.'

Roy the snob enjoyed his new VIP status. Having escaped from high-security Blundeston, he was regarded as something of a hero by his fellow cons.

'After a few years of quiet contemplation, memorising *Who's Who*, studying *Burke's Peerage* and working hard in the kitchen, I was deemed such a good boy that they transferred me to Hull, which was a kinder, gentler institution. I was almost happy there.'

To his delight, Hull was now run by Bill Perry, known and liked by Roy from his time in Nottingham. It was in Hull that romance blossomed, after a fashion, when a handsome young villain called David Wright came into Roy's cell and asked for some advice about precious gems – specifically, how to go about stealing them on his release.

'We operated a kind of barter system,' said Roy. 'I gave David tips on how to steal jewels, and he gave me his arse.'

Before you could say 'Get your precious rocks off!', the two men were lovers. Roy blamed many of his subsequent woes on his susceptibility to this young man's stunning good looks. He claimed Wright's beauty was the snowball that started the avalanche of his own slide into murder and mayhem.

As far as his young friend's physical attractions were concerned, Roy wasn't exaggerating. Curiously enough, he rarely did. He embellished here and there, re-arranging the furniture of his inner life when he got bored, in search of his own personal feng shui, but his reality was so preposterous, so much larger than life, that exaggeration was normally unnecessary. Photos reveal that Wright was indeed as handsome as Roy claimed, with the masculine good looks of a matinee idol.

'I was always too vulnerable to the pleasures of the flesh,' said Roy, wistfully. He regarded himself as first and foremost an aesthete, more susceptible to beauty than to wealth. He always said money was merely a means to an end. The end often belonged to a beautiful young man such as David Wright. When he became entangled with Roy, Wright condemned himself to the ranks of the beautiful and damned.

In the early days of their romance, they were at it like rabbits. Their enthusiastic coupling became a case of *coitus interruptus* when Roy was transferred to Preston and sent out on parole to work in the kitchens at Whittingham Mental Hospital.

'Strangely, I felt at home there,' he said.

Given that he'd been declared insane several times in his life it didn't seem that strange to me, but I let him continue.

'Ever since my early stint at Woodilee, I've felt comfortable amongst basket cases. I felt more at ease in the asylum than in the hostel where I had to spend several days a week as a kind of halfway house. The hostel was a flea-ridden dump. I vowed I'd find some way of avoiding staying there.'

He started studying for his City and Guild exams in catering. As he put it, 'I wanted to be the *best* butler possible.' He was a method actor, and it was important to get the details right: 'I was determined never to make a mistake like the water jug again.'

His efforts were appreciated. Soon he was promoted and put in charge of the hospital stores.

It was there that he met Mary Coggle, a cleaner who dreamed of the bright lights of London. Mary herself had a colourful background, like so many of the characters who became involved with Roy. It's as if they saw in him some sort of dream self, the kind of person they would like to be: flamboyant, debonair and charismatic. He was the charming rogue who thought much bigger than they did and offered them a bigger, brighter, more exciting life.

With Mary, it was lust at first sight. Within an hour of meeting, they found a private room where, according to Roy 'she put away her mop and cleaning fluids and cleaned out my fluids instead. She was good. It didn't take me long to get rid of my muck.'

Roy always did have a way with words.

Mary had grown up in Belfast, where she'd popped out no fewer than nine children as her own personal contribution to making the Catholic Church truly universal. The Church in Ireland, ever keen on hearing the pitter-patter of tiny Catholic feet, had outlawed condoms. Mary had been married twice but both marriages had collapsed under the weight of nappies and domestic duties.

She believed that having done her bit for motherhood she was entitled to have a little fun. She took herself over to England and settled at first in the unfashionable northern fastness of Preston, which she used as her temporary base, like an encamped army planning its march on London.

She has been reduced to the role of a bit player in Roy's drama, a modest candle beside his blazing furnace, but we should pause for a moment and give the woman her due. She had received an award for bravery when she risked her own life to save some children from drowning. It was her very fearlessness that would ultimately prove her undoing.

For the time being, though, all was sweetness and light. She had met the man who would show her the way to the big life she craved.

No matter how apparently innocuous the activity Roy was engaged in, he would find an ingenious way of turning it into a criminal enterprise. He started to steal supplies from the hospital stores and sell them on to a local shop run by a widow with two teenage kids. Her name was Hazel Patterson.

He had met her at the local RAF club where he'd gone looking for a pilot in the sexy tradition of his Polish airman. He quickly switched allegiance from air to sea when he found out that Hazel was chairwoman of the local branch of the Chorley Sea Cadets. To impress her, he launched into his repertoire of sea-faring poetry, going into what he called his 'Masefield Mode'.

Hazel was amazed that he could quote the whole of 'Cargoes' by heart. Like so many other women, she quickly fell for his silver-tongued charm. He had her at 'Quinquereme'.

She became his lover, and he suggested that when he had served his time he might move into the flat above her shop. She was delighted, taking this to be evidence of his firm desire for commitment. It was in fact evidence of his firm desire to rob her.

The stage was now set for his romance with Hazel to blossom. He bought her a large bouquet of flowers and asked if she would like to get engaged. She was thrilled. Of course, she might not have been if she'd known that the flowers were purchased with money he had stolen from the cash register in her store. He always was very generous with other people's money.

He told her he regretted the bad behaviour that had got him into trouble in the past and was now determined to mend his ways. She bought it hook, line and sinker, like a good Chorley Sea Cadet.

They got engaged, with Roy supplying a huge sparkler after working a scam in a hotel using another variation on the 'My lord' routine. He had let the staff at the hotel know that he was Lord Travers and was having a quiet weekend with Lady Travers.

Wooton then arrived as a uniformed chauffeur and asked for 'His Lordship' at reception, thereby confirming his fake identity.

'His Lordship' then called the best jeweller in the area and said he would like to buy a diamond ring for her Ladyship and that a chauffeur would be dispatched immediately.

Wooton drove in a hired Rolls to collect the jeweller, who was summoned to His Lordship's room, where the dealer was vouchsafed a mere glimpse of 'Her Ladyship' wearing a facepack just as she disappeared into the bedroom. In reality, 'Lady Travers' was Mary Coggle in her first supporting role.

'Lord Travers' took the dealer's jewellery and said that as his wife was too shy to be seen in her facepack he'd show her the jewels in the bedroom. They left through an adjoining door. By the time the dealer went to look for them, they had disappeared.

That was how Roy had come into possession of the huge sparkler he gave Hazel as her engagement ring. She was delighted, of course, not knowing that the engagement ring was, as Roy put it, 'hotter than a sumo wrestler's jockstrap'.

When he had finally served his time on parole and was officially a free man again, Hazel organised a party in Preston to celebrate his release. He turned up late for it. He'd been in London at the Tutankhamun exhibition, with a dual purpose: to satisfy his Arab fantasies and to case the joint with a view to relieving it of its priceless treasures. He'd seen all the 'Egyptian Mummy' movies as a kid. Now he wanted to star in one of them.

He decided the museum security was too tight and abandoned the plan, but the exhibition was to have one unexpected benefit: it was there that he met a tall, elegant woman named Ruth Holmes, who believed his story that he was an antiques dealer with a particular interest in Egyptology. He had read a great deal over the years on the history and culture of Ancient Egypt. Having as a boy seen an Egyptian tomb in Kelvingrove Art Gallery, he had convinced himself that he was the reincarnation of a pharaoh.

At the London exhibition he bought a poster of Tutankhamun that was to take pride of place on the walls of the prisons he would subsequently inhabit. He regarded the poster as a memento of a better life, albeit a previous one: a life where his greatness was acknowledged and he was worshipped as a god.

Ruth was entranced by this articulate, handsome, well-dressed and charming man who could speak so eloquently about the beautiful, exotic and infinitely mysterious culture of Ancient Egypt.

That night he took her for an expensive meal. She invited him back to her sumptuous apartment in Knightsbridge, where the relationship quickly became physical. He told her that though he often had to go up north on business, he looked forward to seeing more of her in London. She was delighted. For a year he led a double life, leaving Hazel every weekend for 'business in London'.

He was in fact doing the business in London with Ruth, having driven down from Preston in his Jaguar. He eventually presented Ruth with an engagement ring – stolen, of course. He led the high life with her, a life of love-making and going to glitzy parties.

Ruth had a well-paid job in a fashion house. She thought Roy was a loveable rogue, so different from the boring men she normally met. She reckoned that he just needed the love of a good woman. Roy, on the other hand, felt that he needed the love of several good women, and some bad men too.

Craving a share in a luxury London pad, he married Ruth Holmes in September of 1972. There was a delicious irony in the fact that Roy, the criminal mastermind, married a woman who shared her surname with the world's most famous fictional detective. Holmes was the perfect cover for Roy's Moriarty.

He was delighted with his peripatetic lifestyle, constantly on the move between Preston and London. 'A moving target is harder to hit,' he said sagely.

It was a lifestyle that dovetailed perfectly with his harem. He told me that he was having sex with Ruth, Hazel, Mary and the male chef from the hospital.

'I was a Sultan – why shouldn't I have a harem? Ruth was just my number one wife. Hazel and Mary completed my golden triangle. Three women are ideal. You can rotate them, like crops or squads of football players. Let boring suburban men be happy with a life of monogamy – or monotony, as I prefer to call it!'

He switched on one of his most sincere expressions and added, 'Never trust any word with mono in it, son.'

He sat back and puffed on his cigar, a man meditating upon a profound truth. 'Two of my least favourite words,' he continued, 'begin with mono. Monogamy and monotheism.'

He took another meditative puff and added, 'Make that three words. Add monorail. I hate that fucking word too.'

Intrigued, I asked him to elaborate.

'Well, it's obvious that monogamous or, to put it more accurately, monotonous relationships are totally at odds with the way we men are wired – to sow our wild oats over any field we fancy instead of sprinkling them only in the one field for the rest of our lives. Monogamous relationships are so obviously absurd and such a fucking waste of time that I don't even need to talk about them. Monogamy's like living in a street full of restaurants and dining in the same one every night. Of course you're going to want to taste the food in the place across the road. Even if it looks a bit more downmarket than the place you're used to. Even if it's fast food. Sometimes you feel like fuckin' fast food. If you don't try it, you'll never know just how tasty it might be.'

He took a deep puff whilst he considered the next stage of his argument.

'Then there's monotheism – the belief in one God. Fuck sake, as far as I'm concerned that's one God too many. You know how I feel about the Christian God – that angry old man who's always smiting his enemies. The Gods of all the other religions are just as bad, claiming they have some sort of monopoly – there's that mono again – on truth.'

'What about the monorail, Roy?' I asked, ever the attentive acolyte. 'That sounds like a strange one.'

'The monorail? Most people spend their lives on the monorail, son. Round and round they go. Round and round in circles, day in, day out, year in, year out – always the same predictable routine. Till they are so fucking bored they feel like throwing themselves off. Fuck that. I've lived my life on the rollercoaster, son. That's the only way to live. Sure it can terrify you, it can make you nauseous, but it's always exciting. The rollercoaster makes you feel alive. The monorail makes you feel dead. That was always my problem with marriage. That's everybody's problem with marriage, if they're honest. It's a monorail. By adding a few women – and men – into the mix, I tried to convert it into a rollercoaster.'

Hazel was happy on the monorail with Roy above the shop in Preston, but she began to wonder why her fiancé kept putting the phone down whenever she entered the room. She was about to find out.

Under pressure from his mother, Roy agreed to let Donald work in the shop. He had never been able to pin the Weston-Super-Mare tip-off definitively on his brother, so he agreed, largely to keep Marion happy.

Once more, where Donald was concerned, things very quickly started to go wrong. He stole a tuba from the local Salvation Army.

Roy described this as 'possibly the stupidest act in the entire history of crime. Can you imagine trying to resell a stolen Salvation Army tuba? There's no demand for it, and everybody thinks you're a heartless cunt for stealing it in the first place. Besides, have you ever tried to carry a tuba? It's not like a harmonica – you can't just stick it in your back pocket and look inconspicuous. Stupid cunt. He was a fuckin' disgrace to the family!'

Roy's cup of joy was certainly not full and running over when two policemen came to the store to question Donald about the theft. Roy was there with Hazel, whom he introduced to the policemen as his fiancée. To his horror, one of the officers recognised him.

'I met you at a charity ball in London,' said the cop, in a friendly tone. He glanced quizzically at Hazel, as he added, 'You were with your wife. A tall blonde woman.'

This naturally came as a shock to Roy's short, dark-haired

fiancée, who was stacking boxes of Rice Krispies at the time. In an instant she felt her life go snap, crackle, and pop. Her legs buckled and she had to sit down.

'There's a perfectly innocent explanation,' said Roy, wondering how on earth he could wriggle out of this one. Before he could think of anything, the cops accused him of bigamy, and Roy saw a chink of light. He pointed out that he was not in fact married to Hazel – they were 'only engaged'. Even the police had to agree that he was therefore 'not quite a bigamist'. Though he was behaving like a heartless scoundrel, he had committed no crime and could not therefore be arrested.

Instead, they charged Donald with the theft of the tuba, professing themselves satisfied with arresting only the younger of the Hall brothers, although in truth they felt they had missed the whale and caught the sprat.

Roy was left with a lot of explaining to do. He assured the traumatised Hazel that the marriage to Ruth was only a marriage of convenience and that he would commence divorce proceedings immediately. It's a measure of Roy's powers of persuasion and Hazel's desperation to believe the best of him that she allowed him to go on living with her. Meanwhile her children, in particular her son Colin, were building up a loathing for Roy and the way he manipulated their mother's emotions.

He did eventually divorce Ruth – or more accurately persuaded her to divorce him – in September of 1973, when he would find himself back in prison for reasons we will come to later. I asked him if he was sad about divorcing her. He shook his head and said, 'No, I was getting bored.' Domesticity was obviously not his scene, even when he tried to spice it up by turning the monorail into a rollercoaster.

He would not be the first Sultan to find that the pressures involved in running a harem diminished the pleasure of the performance.

'I craved a man again,' he confided, stroking the shaft of his cigar suggestively. 'I'd had enough of women and their impossible demands.'

Yes, I reflected, women kept making such impossible demands

– like their partner telling them the truth, for example, or not having a couple of other women on the side. Or actually buying the ring rather than stealing it.

Roy grew more animated as he said, 'Yes, I craved a man. I craved excitement. I found both in the Affair of the Cabinet Papers.'

25

From Russia with Love

I am here not as the accused, but as the
accuser of capitalism, dripping in blood from
head to feet.

Red Clydesider John Maclean, defending
himself at his trial in 1918

OY'S MOOD BRIGHTENED WHEN he left behind the miserable
world of the marital monorail and started telling me about
his bizarre role in the adventure he called the 'Affair of the
Cabinet Papers'.

We were back on Planet Roy – a world of political intrigue,
subterfuge, ruling-class duplicity and gay liaisons in sumptuous
hotels, all of which this new adventure had in abundance.

He introduced the topic with a joke that had become popular
during the Profumo affair, which brought down the Conservative
Government of the early 1960s. John Profumo was a high-flying
government minister, a member of the British Cabinet, who became
embroiled in a sex scandal involving two young call girls, Christine
Keeler and Mandy Rice-Davies. You may recall that Roy claimed to
have spotted the latter in Sir Charles Clore's boudoir. Busy girl.

The 49-year-old Profumo was accused of having sex with Ms
Keeler, who was 19 at the time. She was allegedly dividing her
sexual favours between Profumo and a certain Commander Ivanov,
who, you won't be surprised to learn, was a Soviet spy. The scandal
became the subject of the successful British film entitled, in the
imaginative way of such things, *Scandal*.

Roy told me his joke: 'During the Profumo affair, they used to say that being a politician was like being a carpenter.'

He looked at me expectantly.

'You're supposed to ask why,' he said impatiently.

'Why *is* a politician like a carpenter, Roy?'

'One loose screw and the whole cabinet falls apart.'

He slapped his thigh, laughing uproariously.

The tale he went on to tell confirmed once again that he had an uncanny instinct for being in the right place at the time – especially when shenanigans involving the ruling class were involved.

On a visit to London he had gone to one of his favourite watering holes – the American bar of the Savoy. There he met a handsome young man who was carrying an expensive-looking attaché case. They laughed and joked over cocktails, and Roy, now the older man (he was nearly 50), gave the young fellow an expensive cigar, lighting it with his 24-carat-gold lighter.

'I wanted sex, pure sex, to celebrate the moment,' said Roy, forcefully. 'I've always been a bit of a romantic,' he added poignantly.

The routine of older man, cigar and lighter worked for him just as it had for Vic Oliver so many years earlier. Soon Roy and the young fellow were romping in the feathered luxury of a king-sized hotel bed.

Roy's motives went beyond mere lust.

'The attaché case had caught my eye,' he explained. 'I'd never seen one before which was monogrammed "ER II" – the monogram of Her Majesty the Queen.

'I felt I deserved it,' said Roy, 'given that I'd spent so many years of my life detained at her pleasure. Possessing the young man wasn't enough. I had to possess the case too.'

In the wee small hours of the morning, he tiptoed out of the bedroom with the attaché case while the young man slept, exhausted by the energetic joys of casual sex. As Roy put it, 'I left him well and truly fucked.'

When he got home, he realised that he had hit the jackpot. With pounding heart he discovered that it contained top-secret files marked 'For the Prime Minister's office only'.

The papers had been prepared by a secret Government think tank for a briefing of the British Cabinet. They revealed much valuable information on global economics, security, foreign policy and the world oil situation, which the Government did not want to fall into the wrong hands.

As a true patriot, Roy anonymously phoned up the Home Office the next morning, revealing that he had the papers. He sportingly offered to give them back to the Government – at a price. He said he had put himself in harm's way by possessing such incendiary material and that he should be compensated for his trouble. The Home Office not surprisingly saw it differently and refused to cooperate, accusing him of blackmail. Roy accused them of hypocrisy. 'Let's face it,' he told them, 'politics and blackmail are practically synonymous!' They were not persuaded by this argument.

Shocked by their inflexibility, he fell back onto Plan B, which involved selling the papers to the Russians. Ever anxious to cast himself as the hero of his own drama, he decided he was no longer merely a British patriot but a caring citizen of the planet, altruistically committed to the cause of the oppressed proletariat.

He would now play the role of a hero in the proud tradition of Red Clydeside – the radical left-wing tradition that had dominated the shipbuilding yards of Glasgow where he had grown up. The tradition stretched from the turn of the century till the 1970s, when Jimmy Reid, the communist shop steward, became a popular hero in Scotland and was elected Rector of Glasgow University.

Your dedicated author was an undergraduate wandering through that very Grove of Academe at the time, and in the spirit of that anarchic era, when hair was long and time was short, I had a healthy distrust of authority. I can still hear Reid's rasping voice echoing around the debating chamber during his investiture speech as he warned the student body that the State was encouraging us to join the rat race. He rolled his r's in his defiant Glaswegian brogue as he reminded us 'You a-r-r-r-e not r-r-r-rats!'

Roy remembered his mother telling him stories of an earlier Clydesider who was also a champion of the people – John Maclean, a local schoolteacher who, shocked at the conditions in which his pupils lived, joined the Communist Party and fought for the dictatorship of the proletariat. As a girl, Marion had met John

Maclean. She was always sympathetic to radical left-wing politicians, having been schooled in the Fabian socialism of her hero George Bernard Shaw. She told her son that the English ruling class imprisoned Maclean, whilst the Russians, for all their faults, honoured him.

Lenin made Maclean his first Russian consul abroad, and even named a street in Leningrad after him – *Maklin Prospekt*. This was particularly exciting for young Roy, since he was born in Maclean Street in Glasgow. He felt a special bond of destiny with Maclean, a presentiment of greatness.

Always impressed by high achievers, Roy was proud that a Scotsman of lowly origins very similar to his own had achieved global fame. While the English ruling class vilified Maclean and tortured him by force-feeding during his hunger strike in Aberdeen's Peterhead Prison, the Russians put him on their postage stamps.

Having grown up in Govan with a politically aware mother, Roy was very familiar with the history of the Red Clydesiders, who represented Communism with a Glaswegian face. He told himself that what he was about to do was in that proud tradition.

Casting himself as a noble working-class hero, he strode proudly into the Russian Consulate in London's Brompton Road. By way of establishing a bond, he told the woman who initially interviewed him that his mother knew John Maclean and that he was a great admirer of Maclean's work. He also said he had some documents that would be of interest to them.

All of this took place under the Orwellian stare of a large portrait of Lenin and various other hirsute Russian ideologues. The woman wrote down everything he said and asked him to come upstairs to meet her senior officer.

This fellow sported a pencil moustache, which was deemed less intimidating than the thicker Stalinesque variety that the State guidelines recommended for KGB agents 'who are intent on extracting a signed confession'.

The senior officer took Roy into a private room and consulted his female colleague's notes. He asked Roy what the significance was of his mentioning the singer-songwriter of 'American Pie'. Was Roy speaking in code? Did the reference to America in the song's title suggest that he was perhaps seeking employment as a double agent?

'What the fuck are you talking about?' asked Roy, completely baffled. 'American Pie?'

The song was a big hit at the time. Then the penny, or perhaps the rouble, dropped.

'That was *Don* McLean, ya fuckin' numpty! I'm talking about *John* Maclean, the heroic Red Clydesider!'

The confusion was cleared up, but only after Roy realised that the name John Maclean meant much more to him than it did to these alleged Communists. In fact, they told him that there were plans, as part of the reforms that would eventually become known as *perestroika* and *glasnost*, to rename Leningrad's *Maklin Prospekt*. That name was deemed too redolent of the old Stalinist regime, they said. They wanted a name that would reach out to the world in a friendly spirit of co-existence. Its proposed new name, which could hardly have been more insulting to Roy, who was still in proud Red Clydesider mode, was English Avenue. Sadly, English Avenue it became and English Avenue it remains today.

This perceived grievance made Roy negotiate more aggressively as they discussed the purchase price of the Cabinet papers. Much haggling took place.

'I asked them not to talk in roubles,' said Roy. 'Fuck sake, what use were roubles to me? You could only spend them in Russia, and I had no plans to go to one of the few countries in the world that's colder than fucking Scotland!'

They mentioned a price. 'It still didn't sound like a fair price to me, so I told them I'd think about it and get back to them soon. Of course, like an amateur I had forgotten that MI5 had the place bugged . . .'

He returned to Hazel, whom he had persuaded to sell her shop and open a joint account, so that he now had access to her funds. She was keen to settle down with him once and for all, and she did all that he asked. She should have known by now that it was always dangerous to give him what he wanted.

He got a job as a butler at a manor house in Warwickshire, and she went with him as a cook. Grimshaw Hall, owned by Mr Angelo Southall, dated from the sixteenth century and was set in 300 rambling acres, with its own swimming pool, sauna and collection of vintage Rolls-Royces and Lamborghinis. It was Roy's kind of place.

He and Hazel had been there for just two weeks when the doorbell rang. When he opened the door, his jaw dropped. He did not announce the guests, thereby violating one of the fundamental duties of a butler. His employer Mr Southall heard some commotion at the door and shouted, 'Roy, who's that?'

Roy replied, 'It's for me, sir.'

'Yes, but who is it, darn you?'

Roy took a deep breath before announcing as matter-of-factly as he could, 'It's MI5, sir.'

The three large gentlemen who confronted Roy told him that they'd tear Grimshaw Hall apart if he didn't reveal the location of the Cabinet papers. He knew he couldn't mess them around. There weren't many people whom Roy met who were more ruthless than himself, but these chaps really meant business.

He led them downstairs to the wine cellar, where the attaché case was hidden under a wine rack. Sensing that he probably wouldn't be laughing again anytime soon, Roy smiled wanly and quipped, 'It was a very good year for secrets.'

While he was in custody awaiting trial, he received a visit from a Commander Wilson of MI5, who knew of Roy's intimacy with influential members of the ruling class, including Lords Mountbatten and Boothby – as well as Churchill's son-in-law Vic Oliver. The Commander suspected that Roy might have been garnering state secrets via pillow talk and passing them on to the Russians.

'Tell me everything you know about the Russians,' he demanded.

To which Roy pithily replied, 'I believe they live in Eastern Europe.'

Before Commander Wilson could register a response, Roy continued, 'How many years are you going to give me for nicking a poxy fucking briefcase? If the Government fucks with me, I will fuck with them. I have deposited with several friends and my legal representatives details of my sexual liaisons with Lord Mountbatten, Lord Boothby and Vic Oliver. In the event of anything untoward happening to me, these are to be sent to various newspapers, along with a vivid description of the sexual shenanigans currently taking place between government ministers and male prostitutes in a swanky gay club off Park Lane. The club is very popular with prominent members of Ted Heath's Conservative Government, which, as you will be aware, Commander, is at this moment running the country under the banner of restoring wholesome family values.'

This gave the Commander much food for thought.

Roy rammed home his advantage by stressing that 'these revelations will make the Profumo affair look like a vicar's tea party. Or maybe a vicars and tarts tea party.'

It was a high-risk stratagem, but it worked. When Roy was sentenced to four years in prison, senior law officers and policemen were astonished. Most of them had assumed that for contravening the Official Secrets Act he would go down for at least ten. Nevertheless, even with his reduced sentence, he would be 52 when he got out.

Having his 50th birthday in jail distressed him greatly. In 1975, halfway through Roy's sentence, John Wooton visited him with the shattering news that Marion had died. Roy was devastated, but because of his escape record the prison authorities would only allow him to attend the funeral if he was handcuffed to a police officer. He thought this would be too great a humiliation for his family and a desecration of his beloved mother's memory. He regretfully decided he could not attend under those conditions.

I asked him as gently as I could if something snapped in him when his mother died.

He reacted angrily.

'Of course it did. She was my mother! She was the most important person in my life. You'd have to be a monster not to love your mother!'

He wiped away an apparently genuine tear.

She was the only person he ever truly loved. She rooted him to the world of right and wrong, albeit loosely defined. While she was alive, his moral code forbade crimes of violence.

All that was about to change.

Sinbad had lost his moral compass and was about to sail into dark and stormy seas.

26

Blood Sports

All men kill the thing they love.
Oscar Wilde, 'The Ballad of Reading Gaol'

THE GUARD ANNOUNCED THAT visiting time was almost over. Roy
smiled and shook hands as usual at the end of the session.
On the way back to Glasgow, I was again assailed by doubts
about the nature of my enterprise. I knew our next meeting
would bring us to his first murder, and I feared I was going to
find the details distressing. I asked myself if I was helping to
legitimise his heinous crimes. I also felt guilty about continuing
to smuggle cash in to him.

I thought of my father and asked myself what he would make of
my actions. When your dad has medals for bravery, you want to be
brave too. Next time when Roy wanted me to slip the cash to him,
I hoped I would have the guts to say no.

But a few weeks later, my desire to avoid confrontation triumphed.
I suppressed my doubts and on my next visit it was business as
usual.

◊

On his release in 1977, aged 53, Roy had been sentenced to a total
of 42 years in jail for non-violent crimes. If he had died at that
point, he would have been remembered as a loveable rogue, a real-
life Raffles – which is how he saw himself.

As he put it: 'If a person's worth knowing, they're worth robbing.
If you can't beat them, rob them. From the beginning I had a noble

ambition, and made a conscious career choice: I would steal beautiful jewellery from rich people.'

The first two-thirds of his life would have made an entertaining Ealing comedy, but now, as the subject matter darkened, his biopic would suggest a different studio – Hammer House of Horror.

On his release, Roy went briefly back to sponging off Hazel for all she was worth. When her well ran dry, he decided to move on. Having bled her of her profits and placed tremendous strain on her relations with her own family, he sought pastures new. He told her he was going to work on the oil rigs off the north coast of Scotland. In reality he had answered an advertisement for the post of butler to the widow Lady Margaret (aka Peggy) Hudson in the Scottish Borders.

Lady Hudson was the 74-year-old widow of junior Conservative minister Sir Austin Hudson. She lived in Kirtleton House, a 200-year-old rambling mansion in Dumfriesshire, one of Scotland's most scenic shires. It was there that she interviewed Roy in May of 1977.

He told her he wanted to settle in the countryside and that his dream was to put enough money aside to open an olde worlde country inn.

Lady Hudson was impressed by his ambition, his knowledge of fine wines and his suggestion that he catalogue her library, an area in which he had a certain expertise. Unbeknown to her, he had catalogued several prison libraries. The interview was going swimmingly until Lady Hudson said that 'written references are never enough. I'll have to speak to your former employer.'

She looked at the employer's name. He was a certain Major Wooton.

'I do not know Major Wooton personally, but he sounds a decent sort,' she opined. Roy agreed, having lovingly crafted a whole biography for the fictitious Major, which included distinguished war service and an advisory role in Churchill's War Cabinet.

Roy was caught unawares when she requested the good Major's telephone number.

'I'll call him today,' she said.

This was a potentially big problem for Roy, since Wooton, now resident in Lytham St Anne's in the north-west of England, did not actually have a telephone. Many of the Englishman's prison colleagues had been trapped by having their phones bugged, and that was not a risk he was prepared to take. Wooton had decided it was much safer to use the call box at the bottom of his street, and Roy had used that phone often when visiting. That was the number he had given Lady Hudson, confident that in the rarefied world of buttling, references were seldom checked. Now Roy was in the Scottish Borders and the phone box was two hundred and fifty miles away. Worse, Wooton was on holiday, so Roy couldn't ask him to take the call.

As ever, he improvised. 'I'm afraid the Major will not be there today, ma'am. He's addressing a regimental dinner. You'll get him at home tomorrow – preferably between 7 p.m. and 7.30 p.m.'

Lady Hudson made a note of this and said she would give Roy her decision regarding the post after she had spoken to the Major.

'I thanked her, walked down her gravel path and ran like fuck to the train station.'

Next day, an exhausted Roy was standing in a state of nervous tension at the phone box. An old lady was inside. It was just before 7 p.m. He'd been waiting for at least twenty minutes. Her dog, a little Jack Russell, was tied up to an adjacent lamp post. It was a bitterly cold night. Roy thought that maybe she wasn't really talking to anyone, perhaps she was just keeping herself warm. If she didn't get out of there soon, he'd die of hypothermia. Maybe the dog would too. Lady Hudson would call at any second. His anxiety level was starting to go off the Richter scale. Direct action was urgently required.

He untied the dog and tried to shoo it away. It wouldn't budge. He contemplated shoving it away with his foot, but he liked animals too much, and, besides, Jack Russells can be vicious little tykes. Maybe a gentle lob into the bushes? No, he came up with a better plan. He snapped off a small branch of a nearby tree and threw it as far as he could, shouting, 'Fetch!'

The dog gave chase, disappearing into the bushes. The old woman was oblivious to all this. She still had her back to the action. He opened the door of the phone box and put his finger down on the receiver, cutting her off as he said, 'Madam, your dog is in grave danger. He has run off into the bushes! There are vicious foxes around. You'd better get him back as quickly as possible.' The old woman, looking shocked and confused, hobbled out to look for her four-legged friend, who eventually emerged, stick in mouth.

No sooner was Roy in the box than the phone rang. It was Lady Hudson. He took a deep breath and calmed himself, like an actor about to go onstage. In his best Guardsman's voice, he intoned, 'Yes, madam, this is Major Wooton speaking.'

The 'Major' went on to give Roy a glowing reference, saying he was 'one of the best chaps you could ever want in service. He served with me in Burma. Fontaine is honest, hard-working and intelligent, good with guests and staff, and well prepared for any household emergency. He also knows a thing or two about fine wines. I cannot recommend him highly enough.'

So far, so good. Roy was pleased with his performance. But the hard-to-please Lady Hudson threw him another curveball.

'May I speak to the Lady of the House?' she said. 'I always like to speak to the Lady of the House before employing staff.'

'Fuck me,' said Roy to your loyal scribe, 'I didn't see that one coming. I said that unfortunately my good lady wife was out addressing the Women's Institute. Lady Hudson said she'd call back tomorrow. I didn't want to go through this farce all over again – so I said, "Hold on, my wife has just come in."'

'I then gave myself a glowing reference in the voice of an upper-class woman. I modelled my vocal style on Dame Edith Evans playing Lady Bracknell in a film version of *The Importance of Being Earnest*.'

To prove that he had lost none of his old skills, he then gave me a demonstration, intoning, 'A handbag! A handbag!' with the perfectly judged pitch and enunciation of an upper-class woman of a certain era.

Lady Hudson was satisfied. She thanked the Major's wife for her time. Roy put the phone down and breathed a huge sigh of relief. He knew he'd got the job.

◊

He fell in love with Kirtleton House. He had his own flat and access to the swimming pool. When Lady Hudson was away, he led the good life, *la dolce vita*, in the Scottish Borders, entertaining young men in the pool, playing fun games with loofahs and soap on a rope.

He spent a good deal of his time chatting up potential paddling playmates in the local pub, where his favourite drink was Bacardi and Coke. In such situations, he would refer to it as a 'Bacardi and Cock'. He often put some cash into the charity collection can at the bar, remembering fondly how such cans had helped launch him on his illustrious career. He felt it was important to give something back.

Meanwhile he exercised quiet authority over the staff at Kirtleton House and placed intelligent, well-informed orders for her Ladyship's wine cellar.

'I was the perfect butler to Lady Hudson,' said Roy with characteristic humility. 'At least I would have been if I hadn't been planning to rob her of everything she possessed.'

Not long after taking up the job, he was given a ride from the station by a woman he met as he was coming off the train. When he told her he was going to Kirtleton House, she said she was heading there too. She turned out to be Lady Hudson's best friend. She believed that Roy, with his sophisticated manners and his refined accent, was a friend of the family. When she found out he was only the butler, she stopped the car and told him to get out and walk.

Roy was incensed. 'I hated that stuck-up bitch,' he said. He vowed revenge.

A few weeks later, he stole a valuable brooch of hers at one of Lady Hudson's dinner parties.

'If I saw a piece of jewellery I fancied, I'd chuck it under the bed. These people were so rich they'd never remember when they last had it. If they did remember, I'd find it under the bed and be a hero. Otherwise, I'd sell it.'

Sweet as things were at this time, Roy needed hearts as well as diamonds in the great card game of life. He still corresponded with David Wright, his handsome young lover from Hull.

Roy sighed when he mentioned him. 'I was about to make a

huge mistake,' he said, shaking his head.

'The sacrifices we make in our search for nookie,' he added, with the authoritative air of a wise old philosopher, like Confucius with a hard-on.

'The dictates of the heart,' I added, trying to be empathetic.

'No, son,' he replied. 'The heartaches of the dick.'

He sighed at the memory.

'Everything goes pear-shaped when you start thinking with your cock. Wright wanted a holiday, and I wanted his arse. With Lady Hudson's permission, I invited him up for the weekend. She met him as she walked her dogs. Their tails started wagging as soon as they saw him. Before I knew what was happening, she offered him a part-time job as a gardener! That wasn't really part of my plan, but at least I'd have regular nookie. We picked up where we'd left off in prison. I was happy for a while, but then it all went to hell in a fucking handcart.'

Wright, like Roy, was bisexual and soon formed an attachment to Jeannie, a local woman. Roy noticed that a valuable ring had gone missing whilst Lady Hudson was away for the weekend. He was furious when he bumped into Jeannie in the local pub and saw it on her finger. He told her it was stolen by Wright and that it must be returned immediately. Reluctantly, she did so.

That night he and Wright had a blazing row. Roy said he was planning a big heist that would relieve Lady Hudson of all her worldly goods. He talked about the stolen ring and said, 'You're risking all that for a trinket? A trinket for a tart? Wise up, son. That's not how a professional goes about his business.'

Wright stormed off to the pub in a huff. He hadn't returned by the time Roy went to bed.

In the wee small hours of the morning, Roy was awakened by a loud bang. He opened his eyes, startled and still half asleep, only to find himself gazing down the warm barrel of a recently discharged .22 rifle which was pointed at his head. A bullet had missed his face by inches. It was now lodged in the headboard.

'If I'd placed the pillow three inches higher, my brains would've been splattered all over the headboard! I tried to jump out of bed, but the mad fucker walloped me in the face with the butt of the rifle! He nearly broke my cheekbone! There was blood everywhere.

I had a big gash just beneath my eye. For a minute I thought he'd knocked my eye out. Then the big fuckin' wean started greetin' [the big kid started crying, for those of you not privy to the richness of the Scottish dialect].'

'He was greetin'! Can you believe it? After he'd tried to kill me! He said we should try not to have rows. Aye, I thought to myself, and while we're at it we should try not to blow each other's brains out! But I had already decided that if any brains were going to be blown out around here, they wouldn't be mine!'

Roy took the gun gently from Wright and put it down by the side of the bed. He saw clearly now that his assailant had been drinking heavily. Despite the fact that he had narrowly avoided death and was having difficulty stanching the blood pouring from his wounded face, he told the younger man that everything would be all right if they acted quickly. They had to: Lady Hudson would be returning the following day.

Roy fetched some Polyfilla, the sticky paste that he used for small household repairs, and filled the hole in the wall behind the headboard. He did the same with the headboard itself, concealing the hole with Polyfilla and some brown boot polish. Robert Roberts had written lyrically about the many imaginative uses of boot polish, though even he stopped short of recommending it to cover up bullet holes.

After getting Wright to help him turn over the bloodstained mattress, Roy went to the gunroom and put the gun back in its rack. When he returned to the bedroom, Wright was asleep on the mattress.

'Sleeping off the drink,' said Roy venomously. 'During our big row earlier, he'd threatened to blackmail me, saying he'd expose me if I didn't share everything 50/50 with him. He wanted half of the entire proceeds of the clean-out I was planning. I thought his threat had just been bravado. Now I knew he was capable of anything – even murder. I asked myself what Roy Rogers would have done if someone had tried to kill him. He'd have left him dying in the dust.'

Roy puffed on his cigar in rapid breaths, as his anger started to flare up again like a recurring toothache. 'No one had ever betrayed me as he had. He would do so again, unless I stopped him!'

During that long sleepless night Roy devised his plan as calmly and coolly as he devised his scams. But this was of a different order.

He was now a man bent on murder.

The next day, he and Wright went about their business as usual. Lady Hudson's dogs needed a steady supply of fresh rabbits, and it was the job of Roy and his friend to provide them.

'The mistress's dogs are hungry,' he said to Wright. 'We'd better bag a few bunnies.'

Roy remembered his partner's naivety with scorn. 'The stupid bastard didn't suspect a thing. It was as if the night before had never happened.'

They went to the gunroom and chose their weapons. Roy deliberately took the rifle with which Wright had tried to kill him.

Each gun held six bullets. Within an hour, Wright had fired off his six shots and potted three rabbits. He asked Roy why he wasn't shooting: Roy claimed it was because the rabbits so far had only been babies – he wanted to pot a bigger bunny.

Roy told him the big rabbits were on the other side of the hill just past the ruins of the estate's old castle. But first, said Roy, they should take a rest and have a smoke. The rest he had in mind for his young friend was of the eternal variety.

They walked towards the castle ruins and Wright sat down for a smoke. Roy handed him his beautiful gold lighter, which the young man had always admired. Roy had told him earlier in their romance that he would give it to him when they settled down together.

'I didn't really mean it,' he told me, 'but it was a good way of getting some bonus nookie.' Ever the aesthete, Roy had compassionately decided that his victim should commune with beauty just before he died, and the lighter was a thing of beauty.

They were on the banks of the Pokeskine Sike burn. It was an ugly name, and it was about to witness some very ugly deeds. Roy looked at the ruins just before he pointed the gun at Wright's head. Perhaps in some part of himself he sensed that soon his own life would lie in ruins, his dreams of opulence and the good life over, his stairway to heaven crumbling all around him.

Wright rolled a cigarette and lit it up. He turned to hand back the lighter, only to see the gun pointing at his head. His face hardly had time to register terror before Roy pulled the trigger.

'He stood up and looked like he was trying to say something. I couldn't believe it! I thought I'd missed! Then blood gurgled from his mouth, and he fell back, twitching. I unloaded another five bullets into him – mostly into his chest. I paused between each shot, hoping the twitching would stop, but it didn't – not until I'd fired the last bullet. He fell amidst a bunch of ferns. I could see the whole area around him turning red.'

'What were you thinking at that moment?' I asked quietly, hoping for some deep spiritual insight into the mind of a first-time killer.

'I was thinking, *Those bloody ferns are going to be a fucking problem.*'

It was macabre for me to reflect that Wright had died clutching the lighter which lay in front of me now. I had used it to light his killer's cigar.

Roy saw me looking at it and said wistfully, 'This lighter has served me so well.'

'Burn with a hard, gem-like flame,' I murmured as a throwaway remark, trying to take my mind off the murder he had just described.

Roy pounced on this and asked me to repeat it. I explained that it was a quote from the writer and philosopher Walter Pater, who said we should live as Epicurean pleasure-seekers, with no thought of tomorrow.

He asked me to quote it in full. I did. This was easy for me, as I had written out the full quote during my wilderness years in London and stuck it on a cork board in my bedsit. I used to dream on a daily basis of burning with a hard, gem-like flame even as I froze to death, unable to find any coins for the meter of my two-bar electric fire.

'That's the story of my life,' he said, with the passion of a man experiencing an epiphany. 'That's what I've been trying to do all my life. Burn with a hard, gem-like flame.'

It was only on the train home later that day that I realised the quote contained two words which exercised an irresistible and lifelong fascination for Roy – 'hard' and 'gem'. How could he not be seduced by that quote?

It was to become one of his favourites, joining '*Non Serviam*' on the wall of his cell. I seemed to be sprinkling intellectual icing on the maggot-ridden cake of his self-justification. This was beginning to make me uncomfortable, making me feel that I was some sort of accomplice.

I asked Roy if he felt any regrets at having committed murder. The 'M' word had come out of the closet at last.

'Regrets?' he said, as if he were surprised at such a question. 'No. Why should I? It was either him or me. He was a blackmailer. If I hadn't taken him out of the equation, he'd probably have killed Lady Hudson. But I did cry. Yes, I have to admit I cried. But not for him. For me. I knew that the Pokeskine Sike burn would soon become a sea of troubles.'

By the waters of the burn, he sat down and wept. He was on the verge of becoming hysterical. 'Why, David? Why did you make me do it?' he repeated to himself, to the body of his dead lover and to the indifferent universe. Wright's eyes were staring at him accusingly. He closed them and dragged the young man's corpse into the undergrowth.

He wearily started to pull out the bloodstained ferns.

'I thought I might burn them, but I decided it was easier to throw them into the burn.'

He started to collect clumps of the bloodiest ferns and throw them into the river, which became his Rubicon, though briefly it was as bloody as the Tiber. *(OK, I know I'm throwing in a lot of Roman references here, but why else study Higher Latin? I knew it would come in handy some day.)*

'Oh David, David my boy, your troubles are over. Mine have just begun,' he said to the bloody corpse as he did his best to conceal it in the undergrowth.

The ground was frozen. It was too cold to dig. He straightened Wright's arms before rigor mortis set in completely.

He was trembling. 'I had only an hour or two until Her Ladyship returned, but every moment was an eternity.'

He had crossed the line between the light and the dark. His sparkling career as a jewel thief had suddenly morphed into the murderer's heart of darkness. The genie of violent death was out of the bottle, and its thirst for blood would prove insatiable.

I made one more attempt at asking him how it had felt to take human life. After a reflective pause, he replied, 'Murder's like sex. You always remember the first time.'

27

Murder Most Foul

If the sun and moon should doubt, they'd
immediately go out.
> William Blake, *Auguries of Innocence*

WHEN IT CAME TO slipping him the money in the cigarette packet, I performed as abjectly and as adroitly as usual. So much for my resolution that this time I'd be brave. On the train home I felt uneasy, as concerns about the morality of the project continued to gnaw away at my conscience. The tapeworm of doubt about the purity of my motives had been lurking from the beginning, but now I could feel it growing and slithering through my intestines. On the face of it, the project was going wonderfully well, better than anyone could have expected, with Roy opening up and revealing his life and his philosophy in a way that I felt was both entertaining and thought-provoking.

Yet I was now asking myself if I was I being corrupted by the very thing I had set out to expose. The questions buzzed around my brain like a swarm of angry bees. Was I being seduced by the glamour of evil? That was the very opposite of my declared intention. I was meant to be exposing evil, not celebrating it.

Was I glorifying a murderer? Was I complicit now, casually breaking the law by smuggling him money? Had his will triumphed over mine? Would I have helped him dispose of a corpse if he'd asked me to, like his other accomplices?

I started to worry that I was glorifying the psychotic murdering bastard. I was increasingly convinced that he was corrupting me. I was putting cash into the cigarette packet like a humble acolyte with no will of his own.

Now that we'd reached the first murder, a dividing line had been crossed and my relationship with Roy underwent a fundamental change. The pretence that we were two colourful vagabonds, bohemian kindred spirits cocking a snook at the staid Establishment, gave way to the sombre reality. He was a cold-blooded killer, and I was treating him like a rock star – which made me his groupie.

I tried to dispel such brooding thoughts on the train by downing a couple of whiskies. When I got back to my flat in Glasgow, I felt drained. I collapsed into bed and fell into a fitful sleep. I woke up in the middle of the night bathed in sweat. I'd been dreaming about a river of blood.

◊

I spent the next few weeks in the newspaper archives researching Roy's murders. Every grisly detail helped to strengthen my resolve: on my next visit I would not put any cash into the cigarette packet.

The day of that visit dawned and as the train raced towards Full Sutton I hoped I would have the guts to stick to my decision. I put the thought of how he might react to the back of my mind. I didn't want to look like a nervous wreck throughout the interview.

When I arrived, he welcomed me with his usual over-the-top bonhomie. We sat down and he told me that since my last visit he'd given 'the Wright business' a great deal of thought. The master of self-justification reiterated that 'Wright was a scheming, blackmailing murderous bastard. He'd have killed the old lady if I hadn't killed him first. They should have thanked me instead of locking me up.' He glossed over the tiny detail that he was actually locked up for killing *several* people.

He concluded that 'Killing was my destiny. It was in my stars. Whatever will be will be,' he stated emphatically, before launching into a very convincing Doris Day impression as he gave an impromptu rendition of 'Que Sera, Sera', which he described as 'one of my favourite songs'.

If he'd put on a blond wig, I would have sworn it was Doris herself.

If this spontaneous performance had taken place on one of my earlier visits, I might have been taken aback, but I thought that nothing Roy could do now was capable of shocking me. In an hour or so, I'd find out just how wrong I was.

'That song was used in a Hitchcock film, wasn't it?' I asked.

'Yes,' he replied. '*The Man Who Knew Too Much*, starring Doris Day and James Stewart. I've often thought that *The Man Who Knew Too Much* would be a great title for my autobiography.'

He winked and added, 'Maybe even better than *Beautiful Lies*. They'll never let me out of here because *I'm* the man who knew too much. Mountbatten, Boothby, the Cabinet papers . . . I know all their dirty little secrets.'

He resumed his narrative where he'd left off — hiding Wright's corpse in the undergrowth beside the burn: 'I realised I had less than an hour till Lady Hudson came home. I raced to my quarters and had a much faster bath than I was used to. It was as if I was in one of those films where they speed up the action. I scrubbed myself so hard I nearly took off the top layer of skin. I was trying to get rid of blood, hair, the smell of gunpowder, everything.'

He scrubbed as vigorously as Lady Macbeth trying to get rid of that damned spot. But it was another female Scottish aristocrat — Lady Hudson — who was dominating his thoughts at the moment.

When she arrived back that night, she immediately noticed the gash on his face and asked how it happened.

'I slipped getting out of the swimming pool, ma'am,' he replied.

She seemed satisfied with this explanation and told him she was having guests round that evening. They'd be drinking champagne. When Roy went to fetch it, he found only empty bottles.

'Fuck it!' he said. 'It was only then I realised Wright had drunk them the night before, when he'd tried to kill me.'

He made a quick dash to the nearest off-licence to buy replacements. They didn't have the same type in stock. Characteristically, he bought a better brand.

At dinner, when Lady Hudson commented that the champagne tasted 'somewhat different', Roy claimed that Wright had finished off several bottles of her usual brand to celebrate the new job in Torquay that he had left to take up.

He impressed her Ladyship and her guests by eloquently expounding on the superior virtues of the champagne they were drinking. One of the guests mentioned that champagne was a gift of the good French earth.

It was the good Scottish earth that was dominating Roy's thinking. He knew that after the dinner party guests had left his real job would begin: that of disposing properly of David Wright's body, which he had left in a location that was all too easy to find.

As one of the guests lit up a cigarette, he realised that to his horror he had left his own lighter at the crime scene. He had a moment of panic as he told himself that he had to find it. But he went on pouring champagne with the nonchalance of a man who didn't have a care in the world.

Later, in the twilight, under an eerie moon, he made his way back to where he had hidden the corpse.

'I've never felt lonelier than I did at that moment,' he said, 'as I knelt beside his corpse, scouring the grass for my lighter.'

He had brought a shovel with him, as well as a small torch that he was trying to use discreetly so as not to advertise his presence. He was taking a big risk. It would be difficult even for his silver tongue to explain what he was up to, roaming the estate at that hour with a torch and a shovel. At last he spotted a reflection from the golden lighter. With a gasp of relief he picked it out of the ferns, cleaned it and put it in his pocket.

He stripped off his own clothes to avoid them coming into contact with the dead man. His next step was to strip the corpse. He would incinerate Wright's clothes later.

Naked flesh to naked flesh, like lovers in the moonlight, the grotesque twosome stumbled towards the edge of the burn in a macabre dance of death.

'I learned a lot about rigor mortis that first time,' Roy said with the seasoned air of a professional.

'The limbs were locked into position. I would never have guessed rigor mortis would make a body so difficult to manoeuvre. It was like moving a mannequin.'

Naked, he waded into the freezing waters of the burn and shoved Wright's face down onto its stony bed. He shivered as he recalled the moment.

'It was so cold! Everything was cold. The whole world seemed to be freezing over.'

Roy's new Ice Age began with him being unable to dig the frozen ground and continued with him digging a trench in the bed of the stream. He thrust Wright's corpse down and stood on it as he covered the body with stones. As he did so, he talked incessantly to himself. At one point he tearfully cried out, 'Why, David? Why did you get so greedy?'

As dawn broke, the exhausted Roy finished his labours and walked up to the top of the riverbank to contemplate his work. He was horrified to see that the mound of stones was clearly visible to the naked eye. He was too tired to do anything about it. It would have to do for the time being. He wearily made his way back to the big house.

Later that day, his domestic chores done, he took Lady Hudson's Labrador Tessa out to the burn to see if she could detect the body. She made straight for the mound of stones and started whining.

'My heart sank. I knew I had to bury him deeper,' he said.

That night, he was back at his grisly task. Again, he stripped off completely 'to make it difficult for the forensic people'. The body that had so recently been warm and responsive against his own was now cold and rigid – a thing rather than a person. As he dug the trench deeper, memories of happy times with Wright came flooding back and Roy's tears flowed copiously. He shouted at the corpse, 'You fool, David! We could have been so happy here. You ruined it for both of us.'

It was the longest night of his life. He was terrified Lady Hudson would wake early and send out a search party. Dawn was breaking once again as he completed his macabre task. He washed himself in the freezing waters of the burn and put his clothes back on. He looked back from the bank and this time there was no mound to be seen.

The warm bath he luxuriated in when he got back to the house was the most welcome of his life. After little more than an hour's sleep, he took Tessa out for her morning stroll. She ran through the burn without stopping and Roy heaved a huge sigh of relief.

He resumed his normal life, buying drinks at the local pub and lighting cigarettes with his gold lighter. Once or twice he looked at it morosely before going back to laughing with the regulars.

A few weeks later, John Wooton came on a visit and spent a pleasant weekend. Roy introduced him to Lady Hudson as his brother, reminding Wooton not to mention his real surname to her Ladyship, as 'Major Wooton' was his referee and she would smell a very large rat. Roy told Wooton he would soon be ready for 'the big clear-out' of her valuables.

But the best-laid plans 'gang aft agley' (that is, often go awry), as Robert Burns, Scotland's greatest poet, wrote in Dumfries, just up the road from Kirtleton House.

Roy's plans went awry on the night he got back from the pub and heard the telephone ring. He picked it up, but Lady Hudson had answered it a split second before on the bedroom extension. He put his hand over the receiver and listened. A voice asked her Ladyship if she was employing a butler called Roy Fontaine. She said she was. The anonymous caller said, 'You are in grave danger. For your own safety you should know that he's a liar, a thief and a con man.'

Taking a huge puff on his Romeo and Juliet cigar, Roy told me, 'I recognised the voice. It was Colin. Hazel's son. The little bastard.'

The caller put the phone down, leaving Lady Hudson in a state of considerable agitation. Roy tried desperately to decide what to do next. He heard Her Ladyship's bedroom door creaking open. He stood at the foot of the stairs as she emerged.

She was gazing down on him, wondering how she could have been so wrong about this man in whom she had placed so much trust.

'May I help you, madam?' Roy enquired, with as much brightness as he could muster in the circumstances.

'No,' she replied brusquely, closing the door and locking it behind her. Roy heard her making another call. He picked up the extension and listened once again. She was calling the local police station, asking that some officers come round immediately.

All he could do now was to wait for them to arrive. He had to put out of his head the thought that a few hundred yards away lay the bloody corpse of his victim. He knew that the police would already have checked out his criminal record. Fortunately it was a record completely devoid of violent crime, so they would not be searching the woods for any bodies – not yet anyway. He worried that they might bring dogs, better trained than Lady Hudson's in the detection of a bloody corpse.

The police arrived quickly. He was soon summoned to a room in which Lady Hudson sat, flanked by two officers. One of the policemen confronted him with his criminal record, accusing him of being a thief and a con man. Roy claimed that he had reformed and moved on, which was in a sense true. He was no longer just a thief and a con man. Now he could add 'murderer' to his resumé.

Lady Hudson confirmed that there had been no thefts – but she didn't want a criminal, reformed or otherwise, on the premises. Roy was told to pack his bags and leave immediately. He demanded, and got, three months' wages in lieu of notice. He had no choice but to accept the offer of overnight accommodation in a police cell.

As the door clanged shut behind him, he silently vowed revenge.

Needing a base, he rented a cottage in Newton Arlosh, Cumbria, just over the border. He posed as Robin Thomson, accountant and nephew of a retired judge. He told the cottage's owner that he was a writer who needed some privacy to write. He told the locals he was recently divorced and nursing a broken heart. He told people whatever they wanted to hear. The one thing he never told them was the truth. He had a genius for making up stories to meet the needs of the moment. If he'd been a stand-up comedian, he would have excelled at improv.

Whilst staying in the cottage, he answered an advertisement in *The Lady* magazine for a butler to Sir Walter Scott-Elliot of Sloane Street, London.

Sir Walter was the 82-year-old former Labour MP for Accrington, Lancashire. He was an old Etonian of Scots descent, and both he and his Anglo-Indian wife Dorothy liked Scots. They had met lots of them in India, and they made damn fine servants. They were mightily impressed by Roy at his interview, and he secured the post. They didn't bother to check his references.

Sir Walter had a colourful background. He had enjoyed a distinguished military career, serving as a Captain in the Coldstream Guards in the First World War before becoming a successful merchant in India, where he met his second wife Dorothy, a pukka memsahib from a very wealthy Indian family. Twenty-two years his junior, she was what was quaintly known in those days as a 'woman of colour'. Certain elements of society disapproved of such unions, but Sir Walter was never one to shy away from controversy.

His first wife had been an even more controversial choice. In 1939, just before the Second World War broke out, he had married the German Baroness Maria Alice von Groeller, who worked at the German Embassy in London. Hitler was not amused, believing she was well placed to pass on Nazi secrets to the British.

The German Ambassador Joachim von Ribbentrop discreetly told her that if she went through with the marriage she'd be murdered – or, more accurately, since the Nazis loved to be thorough, she'd be drugged, smuggled out of the country, tortured and then murdered.

She and Sir Walter courageously told von Ribbentrop where to stick his Nazi threats and the marriage went ahead. He was doing the decent thing in marrying her, enabling her to stay in the United Kingdom, thereby saving her from having to return to the land where she would almost certainly have been killed. Theirs was a true marriage of convenience.

Roy was fascinated by this Nazi connection – which came as no surprise given his admiration for Hitler. He told me that 'occasionally I would try to get the old man to talk about it, but he would clam up whenever the subject of his first wife was mentioned'.

In 1948, when the Nazis had been well and truly vanquished and the Baroness was safe from their murderous embrace, the marriage was annulled and Sir Walter was free to marry the young Indian woman with whom he had fallen head over heels in love. He continued to serve his country with distinction after the war, when he was given a senior post with the Ministry of Labour.

Partly because of their shared passion for all things Scottish, and partly because Roy was always congenial and erudite company, he and Sir Walter got along famously from the start.

Roy would accompany him on shopping expeditions to London's best department stores. They would frequently lunch together at Harrods or Harvey Nichols and have afternoon tea at Fortnum and Mason. People seeing them together assumed from Roy's stylish dress and sophisticated manner that the two men were friends rather than master and servant.

Roy hadn't seen Mary Coggle for years. He was delighted to discover through his underworld contacts that she was now working in the Lancelot pub, just along the road from Harrods. It was there that she was lovingly reunited with Roy, her knight in tarnished armour.

The Scott-Elliots were not a healthy couple. Dorothy had chronic arthritis. Sir Walter had failing eyesight and was gradually drifting into senility. He was dependent on a daily supply of painkilling drugs. Unfortunately for him, the man charged with administering those drugs was his butler.

Roy knew that the wealthy couple had bank accounts all over the world. He planned to bleed them dry financially before absconding to Brazil, like Ronnie Biggs, the Great British Train Robber, who was a hero and role model.

Roy looked forward to all those gorgeous brown bodies on the beach – sweet, caramel-coloured young men and women.

He told me that he kept a postcard of Rio de Janeiro's Copacabana beach on the wall of his cell. The longer he was in prison, the more it seemed to be mocking him. He eventually took it down when he finally had to admit that Brazil would remain a sun-kissed mirage.

While in Sir Walter's service, Roy used his new base at Sloane Street to case the wealthy houses in the vicinity. He concluded that it would be possible for a slim cat burglar to go across the rooftops and through the narrow skylights of adjacent houses. It was the kind of thing he would have loved to have done himself in his prime, before his waistline expanded, but now he needed to form an alliance with a younger, fitter, sleeker cat burglar.

He asked Mary Coggle if she knew anyone fitting the description, and in the bar of the Lancelot she introduced him to Michael Kitto, a small-time crook in his late 30s.

At this point in her life, Mary was turning over stolen credit cards and chequebooks on behalf of her clients, many of whom were King's Cross prostitutes. When really short of cash, she was said to turn tricks herself.

Roy and Kitto hit it off immediately. The younger man was in a relationship with a Soho stripper. In his book, the perfect woman was one who would charge other men for sexual favours but give him sex for free.

Roy suspected that Kitto was actually bisexual like himself. He calculated that if he invited the younger man back to the Scott-Elliots' to continue their conversation, it would only be a matter of time till they ended up in bed together.

Kitto accepted the invitation and was amazed at the opulence that surrounded him in the Scott-Elliots' apartment. As far as the projected burglary was concerned, he decided that Roy was right: entry through the neighbours' skylight was possible. After a couple of drinks, he climbed into Roy's large double bed, where a different kind of entry was successfully negotiated.

The two continued their trysts as they planned the robbery. But life, as John Lennon put it, is what happens while you're busy making other plans.

On a cold night in December, when Lady Scott-Elliot was taken into a clinic for four days to receive treatment for her arthritis, Roy met Kitto for a drink and suggested he stay with him that night. Old Sir Walter would be asleep, so in effect they'd have the house to themselves. They went back to the apartment and continued drinking in Roy's room.

When they ran out of Scotch, he suggested they go downstairs and help themselves to his master's cocktail cabinet. As they passed Lady Scott-Elliot's room, she opened the door! They were astonished to see her standing there. The clinic had let her out a day early – a kind-hearted decision that was to have cruel consequences for everyone.

'What are you doing, Fontaine?' she demanded. "You are intoxicated! Who is your drunken companion? Answer me!'

Had he been sober, Roy might have come up with one of his brilliant impromptu ripostes, but in his drunken state for once words failed him. He panicked and knocked her to the ground. She started screaming. Roy didn't want the old man to waken up. To silence her, he held a pillow over her face. She continued to scream as she struggled to get free.

'Help me!' he shouted to Kitto – a measure of just how drunk he was, since when he was sober he never had to ask anyone for help. Kitto came to his aid, and together they pressed the pillow over her face. They raised it to find her panting for breath.

'She's a tough old bird!' shouted Roy, as if he were carving the Christmas turkey. Her arms and legs struck out as she struggled for dear life. Fontaine pressed the pillow down harder, till she was motionless.

When he finally removed it, blood was streaming from her nose.

'I couldn't feel a heartbeat or a pulse,' he told me.

He and Kitto looked at each other, becoming more sober by the minute. Roy started to weep. Kitto put his arm around him, saying, 'I know, it's a terrible thing to take a human life.' He didn't know, of course, that Roy had already taken a human life.

Drying his tears, Roy looked at him bitterly and said, 'No! It's a terrible thing not to have a copy of her fucking signature!'

Roy told him he had devised grand plans to trick her Ladyship into signing legal documents that would enable him to divert many of her assets into his name using a fake power of attorney. In his drunken and distressed state, he didn't do a great job of explaining the details. He said he'd fill Kitto in properly on the plan later. Meanwhile they had a corpse on their hands.

Roy said that for now they should make it look like her Ladyship was asleep. They picked her up, carried her to the bed and tucked her under her silk bedcover.

Suddenly there was a piercing cry from Sir Walter's bedroom. The men stopped in shock before Roy composed himself and went to see his master. Sir Walter was wide awake and asking, 'What was that noise next door, Fontaine?'

'Lady Dorothy cried out whilst having a nightmare, sir, but she is all right now.'

'Is she sleeping soundly?' asked Sir Walter.

'Very soundly, sir.'

Appeased, his master went back to sleep, saying, 'Good man,

197

Fontaine!'

The two killers sat up whilst Roy devised the master plan. He told Kitto that 'the couple were planning a holiday in Italy. I'll redirect their mail to a hotel there.'

'What about the old man?' asked Kitto.

'We need his signature. We'll keep him alive – for now. We'll drive to Scotland.'

'Why Scotland?' asked Kitto.

'Because it's lovely at this time of year,' replied Roy. 'And in Scotland they have the bastard verdict.'

28

The Bastard Verdict

I am not prepared to say on this record that
President Clinton is not guilty . . . Juries in
criminal cases under the laws of Scotland
have three possible verdicts: guilty, not
guilty, not proven. Given the option in this
trial, I suspect that many Senators would
choose 'not proven' instead of 'not guilty'.
That is my verdict: not proven.

Senator Arlen Specter's closed-door
impeachment statement, February 1999

IT IS A SOURCE of pride to many of us Scots that we were one
of the few peoples whom the Romans couldn't conquer. Indeed,
the Romans had to build Hadrian's Wall at the English border
to prevent us from conquering them. I share that Scottish sense
of pugilistic pride and fierce desire to go our own way, but one
of its unforeseen consequences is that Scotland has created a
unique and occasionally eccentric system of law.

Whilst a large chunk of the world sees the logic in having only
two verdicts – Guilty and Not Guilty – the cantankerous Scots
decided to have three: Guilty, Not Guilty and Not Proven. The last
two acquit the accused.

Not Proven is also known as the 'bastard verdict', though it
should be called the 'lucky bastard verdict', since it really means,
'We're pretty sure you're guilty, but we can't prove it, so you're free
to go, you lucky bastard.'

Cynics claim the verdict is perfect for Scotland, a paralysed little country that can't make up its mind about anything.

The term 'bastard verdict' was coined by Scots author Sir Walter Scott, a distinguished writer, though he cannot be entirely forgiven for inflicting the *Waverley* novels on an unsuspecting humanity. If hell has an antechamber, it will no doubt be lined with the *Waverley* novels to give a foretaste of the eternal torment to come.

Scott knew a thing or two about the law, though. He was Sheriff of Selkirk, the Scottish border town. Perhaps the *Waverley* novels were his revenge for the unrelenting tedium of a Scottish legal career.

The bastard verdict enjoyed a surprising resurgence in a very unlikely context when American Senator Arlen Specter tried to vote Not Proven on an article of impeachment of Bill Clinton in the Monica Lewinsky affair. Had Specter succeeded, Not Proven might have become known as the Clinton Verdict (not to be confused with the Clinton Defence, otherwise known as 'Eatin' ain't cheatin''.)

Because the Not Proven verdict carries with it the implication of guilt but no formal conviction, the defendant is often seen as morally, if not legally, culpable. It is a stain on one's reputation, but of course as far as Roy was concerned his reputation was already as stained as a schoolboy's blotter. One more blot was infinitely preferable to a guilty verdict and the hefty sentence that would accompany it. Hence the proposed trip to Scotland.

They put Roy's plan into action the day after the killing of Lady Scott-Elliot, when they hired a car with Kitto's stolen driving licence.

Sir Walter had been dispatched to the Reform Club and Lady Dorothy was upstairs under silk covers enjoying the Big Sleep when the dealer from the luxury car rental firm arrived at the Chelsea apartment. He immediately became suspicious when Kitto gave his own date of birth instead of the one on the stolen licence.

'Fucking amateur!' spat Roy as he recounted the events. 'He couldn't get anything right!'

Quick-thinking as ever, he intervened to save the situation, gently reassuring the dealer that 'my friend is upset because of the recent demise of his younger sister, whose date of birth he has given by mistake.'

Roy, who was posing as the Scott-Elliots' godson, was so plausible that the dealer offered his condolences to Kitto.

Throughout this discussion, Mary sat on the luxurious chaise longue in the warm, centrally heated apartment wearing Lady Dorothy's mink coat and a wig that was as close as she could get to the old lady's hair colour.

Roy had instructed her to say as little as possible, lest she give the game away. He had told the man from the car-rental firm that she was suffering from laryngitis and had to rest her vocal cords. She sat smiling inanely, caressing her coat.

'I hadn't meant her to keep the fur coat on,' said Roy, shaking his head. 'She was starting to sweat like a pig on a spit. All she needed was an apple in her mouth. But nothing could persuade her to take off that fucking coat!'

The dealer thought they were an odd bunch, but in the palatial surroundings of the sumptuous apartment he didn't question them. He was used to the eccentric ways of the British upper class.

'We must have looked like a strange assortment,' Roy told me, 'but all you need to have people grovel before you are smart clothes, shiny shoes and a little bit of jewellery. People are fooled by the props, by the trappings of wealth. Appearance is everything.'

When the hire had been successfully negotiated, they put certain small valuables into holdalls and started loading up the car. Roy wrapped Lady Dorothy in what he called 'a lovely silk bedcover' and Kitto helped him roll her up in a carpet that they left at the top of the stairs. They took a breather, flexing their muscles before carrying her downstairs. She was a surprisingly heavy load.

At that moment, the doorbell rang. They froze. Roy pulled himself together and put the corpse down again at the top of the stairs. He pulled on his butler's jacket and composed himself as he went downstairs. He turned round and saw Lady Dorothy's feet sticking out, visible to anyone looking up from the bottom of the staircase. He sprinted back upstairs and with Kitto's help dragged her and the carpet out of view.

He opened the door and was shocked to see a couple he recognised as close friends of Sir Walter and his wife. The gentleman told him they had been invited round for drinks by Lady Dorothy.

'It was arranged by telephone some weeks ago,' added his wife, helpfully.

Roy thought on his feet, saying there must be some mistake as Sir Walter and Lady Dorothy had both gone out and he knew for a fact that she was not planning to return soon.

He went over to the Appointments Diary that sat on a table in the hallway and said, 'Ah, yes – there has been some confusion. I have you down for next week.'

They were perplexed but convinced by his authoritative manner. They apologised for their mistake and left.

When the coast was clear, he and Kitto loaded Lady Dorothy's body into the boot of the car.

When Sir Walter returned from the club, Roy plied him with whisky laced with pills to further cloud the old fellow's already addled brain. Roy told him they were going on a little trip to Scotland to visit Sir Walter's relatives and that Lady Dorothy was already waiting in the car – which in a sense she was. From now on, Fontaine would feed the old man increased dosages of drugs to keep him dazed and confused.

He helped Sir Walter out to the back seat of the car. Mary was already sitting there. Roy introduced Kitto as their new chauffeur. Sir Walter couldn't remember hiring one.

'Have you dyed your hair, darling?' the confused soul asked the woman he thought was his wife. 'Yes, darling,' she replied in the best posh accent she could muster.

'Why are we going to Scotland?' he asked.

Mary looked at Roy imploringly.

'To see your cousins,' replied Fontaine. 'They've invited you up for the week.'

'Oh, really?' said Sir Walter. 'I must have forgotten. I forget so many things these days.'

I asked Roy, 'Didn't you feel that you were corrupting people like Mary Coggle and Kitto?'

'Corrupting them?' he replied, as if the question were an affront to his dignity. 'Not at all. I taught them ambition. They were small-time nobodies till they met me.'

This domineering aspect of Fontaine's personality was becoming increasingly apparent, emerging from behind his charming facade. It helped steel my resolve that I would not slip the money into the cigarette packet at the end of the session. I kept pushing that thought to the back of my mind, warning it to behave itself, like an adult scolding a mischievous child.

◊

When the carload of the debauched, the demented and the dead set off for Scotland, Mary insisted on continuing to wear Lady Dorothy's mink coat, even though the heating was on full blast in the vehicle. Sweat soon started lashing off her. When Sir Walter dozed off, Roy took the opportunity to say, 'Mary, you're looking most unladylike.' Receiving no response, he added, 'You're sweating like a pig in heat!'

She pulled the coat closer to her. Roy needed her for the moment, but his rage was simmering.

After a few miles, he woke Sir Walter and got him in his confused state to sign blank cheques for 'travelling expenses'.

'It was like handling a child,' said Roy. 'The old man did what I told him to. Now I was the master and he was my servant.'

Roy's dream of turning the social order on its head – with him on top – was finally realised on that icy road to death, the landscape as frozen and unforgiving as the blood in his veins. This desire for social revenge, which had hitherto lain dormant, was finally erupting, the end product of 50-odd years of smouldering class resentment.

When the cheques were signed, Roy let Sir Walter drift back into sleep. As they went through the border territory of Dumfriesshire, the old man woke, gazed in admiration at the passing landscape and said to the woman he thought was his wife, 'I was so happy growing up here. We must visit it on the way back, my dear.'

'Of course, dearest,' squeaked the be-wigged grotesque beside him, in an accent that was one part Belfast, one part Cockney and one part absurd. Roy could only wince as she spoke. Her performance as Lady Dorothy left a lot to be desired.

'She sounded worse than Dick Van fuckin' Dyke in *Mary Poppins*,' he said, referring to the actor's cod English accent.

When they reached the small Scottish town of Lanark, they

stopped at an ironmonger's, where Roy bought a garden fork and shovel. They then drove north, till the Scottish Lowlands gave way to the Highlands.

Shadows lengthened as they approached the remote and eerie Glen Affric in Perthshire, just past the town of Braco. A mist suddenly descended, reducing visibility considerably.

A wind started to howl like a banshee coming to claim a soul. Roy told Kitto to turn down a slip road by the side of Loch Earn. He did so, and they got out of the car. Sir Walter was asleep. 'If he wakes,' Roy told Mary, 'tell him we've gone for a pee.'

He deemed this much kinder than telling the old man the truth. They dragged Lady Dorothy's corpse down an embankment behind a low wall just off the Conrie Road, and quickly got to work with the newly purchased shovel and pitchfork.

The ground was covered in a thin layer of snow, and digging the frozen earth was backbreaking work. After much toil, they succeeded in carving out a shallow ditch, into which they unceremoniously dumped Lady Dorothy's body. They were too tired to bury her properly and settled for covering the corpse with a layer of leaves and bracken.

They went back to the car. While they'd been digging, Mary had obeyed Roy's command to pop pills into the mouth of poor befuddled Walter to keep him in his confused state.

Kitto's mood was sombre, but Roy seemed strangely buoyant, even jocular. As they drove away from Braco, he chortled and declared, in full hearing of the old man, 'They'll never find her there – we're in the Braco beyond!' His companions couldn't even raise a smile.

They stopped off for some rest and relaxation at the Tilt Hotel in Blair Atholl. For the purposes of checking into hotels, he and Kitto decided to pretend they were the Thomson brothers, Roy and Robin. Batman and Robin might have been more appropriate for the twosome who were fast becoming the Dynamic Duo of Death.

They took Sir Walter to his room, whilst Mary remained downstairs and drank. Her performance as Lady Dorothy, never very convincing to begin with, degenerated to the point of farce as she became increasingly intoxicated. So embarrassed was Roy that he concocted a cover story that Sir Walter had married well below his class and now did not like to be seen with his wife, whose behaviour, he felt, did not befit her new social status.

By the time they put Sir Walter to bed, he had no idea where he was. The other three sat up drinking in the adjacent room, discussing what to do with him. They agreed that he would have to go the way of his wife.

It is a measure of Roy's power over the other two that he met with so little opposition. Until they met him, both Kitto and Coggle were very small-time crooks whose idea of crime was stealing a few pounds, or a credit card, or a driving licence.

Like Charles Manson, Fontaine had a way of transforming casual acquaintances into murderous accomplices, as if by a kind of hypnosis.

They got up early the next morning and drove on through the bleak countryside towards Inverness, Roy telling Sir Walter to sign cheques all the while. 'He was literally paying for our company,' Roy said.

Sir Walter was signing his own death warrant. When the old man said he was tired of signing cheques, Roy ordered Kitto to turn down a small dirt track and stop the car.

Roy turned angrily towards Sir Walter and said, 'I'll sign the bloody cheques myself: I've got enough examples of your signature.'

The old man was lucid enough to respond, 'You can't do that!'

Incandescent with rage, Roy shouted, 'I'll do whatever the hell I want!' and dragged Sir Walter out of the car. Kitto got out too and helped pull the old man towards a hedge beside a field.

Sir Walter was wearing a woollen scarf. He fell, and Roy pulled the scarf tight around his neck. The old man gasped for air and choked. Just as the life seemed to be ebbing out of him, he suddenly grabbed Fontaine's wrists.

'It was as though he was calling on the strength of his ancestors,' Roy told me, in a well-rehearsed line that he used often, knowing it would play well with the media around the world. I was already familiar with it from the press cuttings. For Roy, quotability was everything.

With Kitto holding Sir Walter down, Roy pulled the scarf tighter, till the old man's hands became limp and his grip gave way, the life squeezed out of him. In a furious frenzy, Roy kicked him again and again. Telling Kitto that they should leave him to rot, he turned and walked back to the car. Kitto, as ever, followed him.

Just as his attackers were about to drive off, Sir Walter uttered a long, low groan. Roy was dumbstuck. The old man was still alive! Later Roy would put a gloss on these events by saying, 'He was the hardest of all to kill. I admired that. If he hadn't groaned when he did, he might have lived.'

But in reality, there was no admiration, only rage. Roy was not used to having his will thwarted: the stare master had to re-assert his supremacy. He ran to the boot of the car and grabbed the shovel. Gazing unblinkingly into Kitto's eyes, he commanded him to 'follow me and do as I say'.

He strode over to Sir Walter, who lay groaning, and stood on his neck. He handed the shovel to Kitto and said, 'Do it!'

Kitto slammed the shovel against the old man's head. His skull cracked like an eggshell.

I said to Roy, 'But I thought you liked the old man?'

'Oh, I did,' he replied. 'He was a gentleman to the very end. It was all very unfortunate.'

Somewhere in a galaxy far away a mother was lovingly running her fingers through her young son's hair and calling him *'mon parfait gentilhomme'*.

The image of Roy standing on the neck of his former master shocked me as much as anything in his sordid saga. It seemed an evil reversal of the triumph of good, which is represented in Catholicism by the iconic image of the Virgin Mary crushing underfoot the neck of the Satanic serpent.

I asked him what he was thinking at that moment when he stood on the old man's neck. In a chilling voice packed with the accumulated resentments of a lifetime, he said, 'I wanted to break the neck of obedience.'

Only later did I realise that he was quoting *Roberts' Guide* on the need to be firm with servants, 'lest they break the neck of obedience'.

They left Sir Walter's body behind a stone wall in Glen Affric. They were becoming so blasé about death that they didn't even attempt to conceal his corpse.

Later, when body parts were found, it appeared that a fox had abandoned Sir Walter's skull in favour of the fleshier delights of the former Government Minister's leg. A chewed kneecap was found in the bracken. It was a tawdry and grisly end to Sir Walter's life of dedicated service to his country.

Back in the car, Mary took off her wig off and said, 'Thank God that's over. Now I can go back to London.'

Roy told her that she'd better give him the mink coat to sell. They would split the proceeds. Otherwise the police would be onto them in double-quick time. Mary did not respond: she sat in the back sulkily stroking the luxurious fur.

When they reached Edinburgh, the trio checked into the Mount Royal Hotel.

Even 15 years later, when he'd had ample time to reflect on his evil acts, Roy didn't seem to think his murder spree was anything more than a jolly jape. 'The Mount Royal seemed appropriate,' he said. 'I liked the name. Why shouldn't I? After all, I'd been mounted by a royal.'

His mood darkened when he relived the anger he felt at Mary's behaviour: 'There she was in the Mount Royal, swanning around in Lady Dorothy's mink coat, thinking she was impressing everyone, but no matter what she did she was still a fucking sow's ear. She still looked like a wee tramp selling her arse under the railway bridge at King's Cross. She thought she was fooling everybody into thinking she was a toff.'

She'd been drinking from a flask throughout the journey and was already half cut. Noting her continued reluctance to relinquish the mink coat, Roy told her, 'Of course, Mary, do what you like. But let's go back to the cottage first and have a small celebration.'

He looked from the mink coat to Kitto and back again, saying, 'As far as the coat's concerned, I'm sure we can come to some arrangement.'

He smiled at Kitto, who in a later statement said he looked into Roy's eyes and saw the lust for blood.

29

Bloody Mary

A judicious use of the poker is essential to
the well-being of an anthracite fire.
Roberts' Guide for Butlers and other
Household Staff

R OY SMOKED AND SMILED his way through the story of Mary as
if he were a raconteur at a dinner party entertaining the
guests with an amusing anecdote.

He, Kitto and Mary arrived back at the rented Cumbrian cottage
in the small hours of the morning. They sat up drinking and
enjoying flights of fancy as they discussed how they would spend
the blank cheques. Roy said he thought they should rob the Scott-
Elliots' flat in London, as nothing had been reported so far about
the sudden disappearance of Sir Walter and his wife.

The alcohol finally caught up with Kitto, who yawned and went
to bed. Roy asked Mary if she still intended to head back to London
with the mink coat. She said she did. He told her he thought that
was a bad idea. He said she could take it back to London if she
wished, but they would ultimately have to sell it, along with Lady
Dorothy's jewellery.

'There's no way you can swan around King's Cross in a coat like
that without giving the game away,' he told her once again.

Here he met with some opposition. Mary showed the kind of
spirit she had displayed all those years earlier when she had rescued
a bunch of kids from drowning. She said there was no way she was
going to part with the coat.

Roy shook his head as he remembered their heated discussion.

'She was obsessed with that bloody coat. If she'd agreed to sell it, she'd have had her share and everything would have been OK.' That was Roy: in his own head at least, fair to a fault. He said they would discuss the matter again in the morning.

She was tired and went upstairs to join Kitto in bed. She had been sharing her sexual favours with both of them for some time now.

Roy stayed up drinking malt whisky and thinking dark thoughts.

'Why,' he asked himself, 'am I surrounded by fucking idiots?'

He could hear the bed upstairs creaking as Mary and Kitto engaged in love-making, though 'love' is probably not the most accurate description of their drunken exertions.

Perhaps Kitto failed to satisfy her: in any event, when he fell asleep she came back downstairs. Roy was surprised to see her re-appear at the door of the living room, naked under the mink coat. She had put the wig back on again, believing it increased her sex appeal. She sashayed seductively towards him, asking, 'Roy, have you ever made love on a mink coat in front of an electric fire?'

Not surprisingly, he hadn't.

The cottage actually had a log fire, but since they'd been too busy carrying corpses to carry logs they had found themselves using the two-bar electric fire instead.

At this point Roy interrupted the narrative to comment, 'Her mentioning the electric fire almost made me lose my stiffie. There's nothing less sexy than a two-bar electric fire. Unless it's a one-bar electric fire. But, thanks to the alcohol, I was feeling quite randy. A fuck's a fuck, so in my head I blotted out the electric fire and pretended the log fire was blazing away.'

He told her that she looked great in the coat, but she'd look even better naked. She stripped it off and lay down on it. Roy climbed on top of her and they had vigorous sex. Just after the moment of climax, he asked her once again if she'd take the coat with her to London. She said yes, she wanted to show it off to her friends.

'You little fool!' he screamed. 'How many times do I have to tell you? They'll be onto us in a flash. You look ridiculous in it.'

'But you just told me I looked beautiful in it,' she said, slipping the coat back on.

'Shut up!' he shouted. 'I was just after a fuck! I'll say anything for a fuck!'

She started sobbing, saying, 'It's my coat, and no one will take it from me.'

'I've had enough of your nonsense!' he shouted, grabbing the coat. 'Either we sell this or I'll light the log fire and burn it!'

Mary screamed and pulled the coat tight around her. 'No, no!' she yelled, 'I'm not going to let you burn it.'

That was a big mistake. Roy didn't need anyone's permission to do anything.

'Well, Mary, this looks like goodbye,' he shouted in a rage, as he grabbed the poker from the fireplace and crashed it down on her skull.

It hit the thick wig she was wearing, deflecting the blow onto her shoulder with a loud thump.

Stunned and dazed, but still on her feet, she stared at him in horror.

At that moment, Kitto appeared in the doorway, awakened by the sounds of their squabbling.

Mary was moaning, 'Why, Roy? Why?'

Fontaine's answer was to hit her over the head again with the poker. This time there was the sickening crunch of her skull cracking.

She fell to the floor, still clinging to consciousness and a tiny sliver of hope. She looked up at Kitto. He looked away, unable to meet her gaze.

She stared at Roy, begging for mercy as she said, pitifully, 'I won't give you away, boys. Trust me. I won't give you away.' Those were her last words.

Roy yanked the mink coat from her body, saying, 'That'll teach you to be so fucking shallow.' Then he pulled his trousers back on.

Fontaine – for I cannot at this moment bring myself to call him by the chummy epithet of 'Roy' – then picked her up beneath the armpits and dragged her to the couch. She was still breathing as he bound her hands behind her back with one of his ties. He took a plastic carrier bag, placed it over her head and tied it round her neck.

The bag moved in and out with her breath. She was slowly suffocating.

Kitto looked on in grim fascination. Roy turned to him and said, 'Come on, I need a drink. Want one?' Kitto nodded.

Roy went over to the cocktail cabinet and poured a couple of brandies.

They sat sipping their drinks as they watched the plastic bag cease its in-and-out movement. Mary breathed no more.

Roy dragged her pathetic crumpled little figure into the room next door and shoved her under the bed, saying, 'We'll get rid of it tomorrow.'

He then came back to finish his drink.

I had the temerity to suggest this was all a bit callous.

Roy gave me a stare as if I'd said something deeply insulting, and asked, 'Have you ever killed anyone?'

'No,' I answered apologetically.

'If you ever did, you'd need a drink too. I'm only human, after all.'

I was beginning to doubt it.

After a few more brandies, Roy and Kitto collapsed onto the bed underneath which Mary's corpse was lying.

Roy said to his young accomplice, 'It was either her or us!'

Kitto nodded but said nothing. He endured a sleepless night, staring at the ceiling, wondering how in the space of a few weeks he had left behind his sweet stripper girlfriend and his idyllic world of petty crime to end up sharing his life, his bed and his body with a multiple murderer and their female accomplice who was now just another victim.

As Kitto slept above the corpse of his former friend and lover, he wondered if he'd be next. He later said at his trial that he felt like he was living in Agatha Christie's novel *Ten Little Indians*, where characters are murdered one by one till only the killer is left.

Of the five characters who featured as the curtain rose on this drama, only two remained. The phrase 'And then there were two' kept echoing through his troubled mind as he asked himself if he'd be next. He wondered if he should do a runner in the middle of the night, but decided that for the time being he should continue as

Roy's ever-obedient henchman. He wanted to get his hands on the Scott-Elliots' treasures that still awaited them back in the Sloane Street mansion-block apartment, which he and Roy would loot together. Kitto knew it was too big a job for one man. As long as Roy needed him, he was safe.

◊

Of all the heinous deeds Roy committed, the killing of Mary nauseated me most. Whenever I found myself succumbing to his charm I would remind myself of poor little Mary, mother of nine, begging for mercy, only to have her plea fall on deaf ears. The two men who had enjoyed her company and her sexual favours now treated her like a lump of meat to be disposed of as quickly as possible.

◊

In the morning, they wrapped her body in a blanket and put it in the boot of the car, which was again doing double duty as a hearse. Before that, Roy did something that was bizarre even by his own warped standards. I often remind myself of it whenever I'm in danger of forgetting that he was nuts: he dressed poor Mary's corpse in a blue-and-white-striped short-sleeved man's shirt, women's stockings and men's flared trousers. Then he put one earring on her right earlobe. When the bemused Kitto asked him what he was doing, he replied, 'I'm making her look like a lesbian.'

Kitto acted like that was a satisfactory explanation. I didn't. Accepting for the moment the dubious notion that lesbians ever dressed like that – I don't believe they did, even in 1977 – I still had to ask, 'Why exactly did you want her to look like a lesbian?'

'Because it would confuse the cops,' he said. 'It would take them out of their comfort zone and brighten up their miserable little lives by making them think they were dealing with an exotic case.'

(Well, they were, weren't they? Planet Roy was one of the most exotic places in the cosmos.)

He warmed to his theme: 'See, cops know where they are with

gay men. They hate them. End of story. The cops who are gay themselves, of course, have to *pretend* to hate gays. But with gay women, cops don't know what to think. They believe they should hate lesbians, but part of them is turned on by them. Men like the thought of women kissing and fucking each other with strap-ons, dildos, etcetera. This turns the cops on, but they're supposed to morally disapprove of it, so they're in a permanent state of confusion. And a confused cop is a whole lot less likely to solve a crime. See what I mean?'

I did. Sort of. I asked him to continue with the story.

With Mary's body in the boot, they drove along the A74 towards the scenic border town of Lockerbie, which, a decade later, a terrorist bomb on PanAm flight 103 would make synonymous with sudden violent death.

They turned off at a deserted spot where a little rivulet known as the Back Burn ran under a picturesque bridge. It was close to Lady Hudson's estate. Roy told Kitto they'd be robbing her soon.

From the bank, they heaved Mary's body into the river. The current carried the corpse majestically downstream, the man's shirt billowing in the wind as Mary floated away like a cross-dressing Ophelia.

Her clothes snagged on a metal spike that stuck out from the river bed. As a result, the corpse was completely hidden under the bridge.

Congratulating themselves on their good luck, the partners in crime decided to go for a hearty lunch. En route they somewhat cavalierly hid the poker in a hedge by the side of the road.

Robert Roberts in his *Guide for Butlers and Other Household Staff* devoted some of his most colourful passages to what he called the dexterous use of a poker, listing the various uses to which it could profitably be put. Smashing in your lover's skull with it was certainly not one of them.

In Chapter IV, entitled simply 'Of The Poker', he prophetically proclaims:

'I am almost ready to say that I can form my opinion of a man's intellect from his application of the poker . . . An ignorant, meddlesome or nervous person you will often see thrusting in the poker at all adventures, without rhyme or reason . . . on a cold winter particularly, the poker should always be kept out of their reach. They are unworthy of its honors.'

If only Roy had listened.

◊

I pressed him once again on the question of whether he felt any remorse for his victims. He looked baffled for a second, then described their deaths as 'mercy killings'. 'I was doing them a favour,' he said, in the manner of a compassionate doctor performing euthanasia.

'The Scott-Elliots were old and arthritic,' he added. 'Wright had tried to kill me the night before I took care of him: I was acting in self-defence. As for Mary, I saved her from a miserable life of prostitution, of turning tricks with strangers in seedy side-streets around King's Cross.'

Welcome to Roy's world of compassionate, caring killing. Please give generously.

When he suggested a tea break, I gratefully accepted. Trying to psych myself up into Churchillian mode, I told myself this was it: my own personal D-Day.

Now that I had glimpsed the real Roy in all his savage glory, I no longer felt comfortable smuggling cash to him. It made me feel unclean, an accessory after the fact. I knew I had to tell him this and I knew he wouldn't be happy, but at last my will would assert itself and I would no longer be his bitch.

I came back with the tea as per usual, but this time I had added cold water and lots of milk lest he decide in his anger to throw it in my face. My heart was pounding on that long walk back from the tea bar. This time would be different.

Perhaps he could tell from my expression that something was wrong. He seemed to open the cigarette packet in slow motion. As he saw that there was no banknote, his genial expression morphed into the Stare of Death.

Trying not to show the fury that was already raging in his soul, he stared unblinkingly into my eyes and tried to force his lips into something that the guard would mistake for a smile.

'Where's the fuckin' cash?' he said in a quiet yet menacing voice. His eyes did not blink. Neither, for once, did mine.

'There's no money, Roy. You said this wasn't about the money, didn't you? There will be no more money in fag packets.'

There was an ominous silence.

'Why the fuck not?' he growled through gritted teeth. 'I have expenses. I want to buy a chicken!'

Only later did I discover that 'chicken' is sometimes used as prison slang for 'an attractive young male'. Perhaps Roy meant it literally: maybe he really did want to buy a chicken of the feathered variety. Or perhaps he had a different sort of flesh in mind. In any event, I tried to state my case as succinctly as possible, regardless of whether his expenses would be incurred plucking or fucking.

'I don't feel comfortable giving you money, Roy. I never have. That was never part of the deal. You've always said you're not doing this for the money, that you're doing it for your legacy. You're talking to me because you want your story to be told properly. If it's money you want, there are plenty of ghost writers out there you can come to some arrangement with.'

I was so busy making eye contact, trying not to blink, that I didn't notice that in one swift movement he had grabbed my pencil and had cast a lightning-quick glance to the side, to ensure the guard wasn't looking. In fact, the guard had his back to us, talking to the woman at the tea bar. Suddenly Roy thrust the pencil's sharp tip to within a few inches of my eye.

'This'll kill you outright, you cunt!' he rasped.

I knew he had nothing to lose by killing me there and then. He was never going to get out of prison anyway, so what difference would one more death make? He'd no doubt revel at being back in the headlines. I was staring my own death in the face.

Terror was compounded by a profound sense of injustice and anger. Sure, I was too old to win the Somerset Maugham Literary Award (the upper age limit is 35), but I was too young to die, and there was always the Booker. Time stood still. This moment when I felt I was about to be dispatched into eternity felt like the eternal moment mystics are always going on about.

But still I didn't blink. I had promised myself I wouldn't. My heroes didn't blink. Churchill stared down Hitler. Kennedy stared down Krushchev. But neither of them had a sharp pencil held inches from their eye by a serial killer.

This was my own personal Rubicon, my chance not so much to be a hero as to avoid being a coward. I had vowed to myself that I would make my dad proud of me.

Roy must have been surprised. He stared and stared, but I stared back. I was determined to prove that good guys can be Stare Masters too. Suddenly, he blinked and put the pencil back down on the table.

I had won a major battle.

He took a deep breath and spoke like a man trying to keep his emotions in check. 'You're lucky that I've always liked you, Pender, or you'd be dead by now,' he said in a measured tone. 'But I will not tolerate betrayal. I have many friends on the outside who owe me a favour. You understand my meaning?'

I nodded. I understood his meaning.

'Go away, and when you've seen reason, come back here with two large bills in your fag packet. That'll make up for the instalment you missed today. OK?'

It would have been easy to say yes, but my alpha male buttons had been pushed. I wasn't feeling subservient any more.

I stood up, grabbing my pencil before it got a second chance to become a murder weapon.

'No, Roy, it's not OK. I don't like being threatened. These interviews are terminated!'

He looked up at me in disbelief.

I nodded perfunctorily at him and could not resist one final barb before I left:

'Goodbye, *Archie*!' I said.

I turned and started to walk towards the exit. My knees were feeling weak and my legs were like rubber, but I still managed to make it to the door, listening for Roy's footsteps behind me. I could feel his eyes boring into my back.

I told the guard I had a train to catch, and he unlocked the door.

I was determined not to turn around. I didn't want to gaze into Roy's shark eyes, especially now that I felt like live bait. As I walked through another set of blue metal doors the adrenalin rush passed and my sense of pride in standing up for myself quickly gave way to fear. The reality of my new situation dawned. I had just been threatened by a killer. A man who had nothing to lose. A man who had proven skills in the murder department.

I knew that even though he was no longer free to kill in person, he had plenty of scar-faced friends on the outside for whom taking human life was as routine as having a cup of tea.

As I headed towards the train station, I was hoping I could leave behind the world of Full Sutton and its very peculiar inmate. I was hoping that would be the end of the affair, and I'd be left with the memory of an extraordinary personality whose energy and charisma were best described as demonic.

On the train, I had a couple of Glenfiddichs. I was looking forward to the comforting embrace of Glasgow and the furniture of home.

I would tell Bill Bryden that I was leaving the project and that I intended to close the file on Roy. It had been a magnificent intellectual adventure, but I told myself it was over now. The dramatist in me refused to believe it, though, whispering in my ear that we were just at the end of the second act, and the curtain was about to rise on the third, which threatened to be the bloodiest act of all.

The whisky, intended to dull my fears, instead seemed to heighten them. I tried to sleep, but every time we went through a tunnel I broke into a sweat. I eventually did doze off. I dreamed of a tornado. No matter how fast I ran in the encroaching darkness, I couldn't get away from it.

I awoke just as the train crossed the railway bridge over the River Clyde. I had an excellent view of several bridges spanning the river. One of them had an inscription engraved on its stone pillar. It said: 'Be steadfast in the storm'.

I took it as a sign. I vowed I would repeat that mantra to myself every day until Fontaine's fatwa was abandoned – or fulfilled.

30

Dying for your Art

I'd like to achieve immortality through my
work. But I'd rather achieve it through not
dying.

Woody Allen

MY RELIEF WAS SHORT-LIVED. When I got home, I noticed that
the light on my telephone answering machine was blinking.
I pressed it. A strangely otherworldly voice said, 'Pender, I'll
have your balls for garters.'

My heart was pounding. I listened to the message again and
again, as if mere repetition would make it go away.

I was trying to identify the voice as Roy's, of course. It didn't
sound like him, but I couldn't be entirely sure, given his gift for
mimicry. I could not believe he'd be so foolhardy as to call in a death
threat from prison. Were prison calls taped? Were they traceable? I
didn't know. It was more likely that he had contacted one of his pals
on the outside and instructed him to leave the message.

One thing was for sure: whether Roy had made the call personally
or through one of his surrogates, he hadn't wasted any time. He
was a real man of action. He knew how to keep a promise. If
anyone could convert balls to garters he could.

Somehow he had got hold of my home number. I was imagining
all sorts of devious ways he might have done so. Then I remembered:
I was listed in the telephone directory.

My first impulse was to immediately make myself ex-directory,
but the more I thought about it, the more I reckoned that to do so
might goad him into taking some more drastic course of action.

Perhaps the calls would function as therapy, as a kind of safety valve allowing him to vent his spleen. Besides, I could collect the messages and use them in evidence if necessary. I asked myself if I should call the police – or would that be pulling the tiger's tail and further provoke the psycho?

The scariest thing was that Roy knew where I lived, as evidenced by Wee Toe's visit. Was Toe out there even now, in some dark alley – my back lane, perhaps – sharpening his blade?

I was exhausted and drained. I desperately wanted to go to sleep. I checked all the latches on the windows and double-bolted the doors. Every gust of wind, every tin can blowing in the street, felt like an approaching assassin, a harbinger of death.

I lay in bed looking at the ceiling, having secreted a large serrated bread knife under the pillow beside me, my hand grasping it as if I had rigor mortis – an unwelcome thought that bubbled unbidden to the forefront of my troubled mind.

As a writer, I had signed up for *La Vie Bohème*. I had lived that bohemian life in my London bedsit. But I did not sign up for *La Mort Bohème*. The bohemian death was going a bit too far.

I can endure suffering for my art. Indeed, I remain particularly fond of the joke about the artist who tells his audience, 'I've suffered for my art. Now it's your turn!' But *dying* for your art is a different thing entirely.

After several hours of looking at the ceiling, wondering if my killer could come in through the skylight, I fell into yet another troubled sleep, my second of the day. I woke up a few hours later bathed in perspiration. It was to be the beginning of several months of night sweats and daily washing of the bed linen. I'd have been as well going to sleep in a sauna and saving on the laundry bill.

On that first night, I dreamed I had been killed and that my writing was being discussed posthumously by a panel of critics on *Art Attack*, Scotland's late-night Arts review. Those of you who know the programme will be aware that after a successful pilot episode, viewing figures plummeted as people realised that, despite its title, *Art Attack* was not a medical drama.

In the dream, my murder had been announced, and the answering machine's death threat was replayed to the nation in the hope that someone would recognise the voice. The critics showed little compassion for the dead. Prominent amongst them was Becky Farr, who dissed my entire output as 'sophomoric, sentimental and cloying'. She was much kinder about the taped death threat itself, which she praised as 'commendable in its directness, honesty and economy of expression'.

Even though I was now officially dead, from whatever astral plane I was on I found myself wondering if she'd have been more generous if I'd asked her out on that date.

When I awoke the next morning, I felt strangely elated. I think it was my surprise and delight at being alive. The grim reaper had not come for me in the night. I pulled the sodden bedclothes off, stuffed them into the washing machine and had a long bath as I quickly formulated my survival plan.

I told Bill Bryden that the Roy Fontaine project was no longer viable owing to Roy's emotional instability. I didn't mention the death threat, as I didn't want to escalate my own personal crisis.

Bryden took the news philosophically. He told me he had anticipated problems in dealing with a paranoid schizophrenic. We would just have to chalk it up to experience. He put his arm round me and said, 'I know how disappointing this must be for you, but hold onto the truth of Kipling's great poem, *If*.' He started quoting it:

'If you can meet with triumph and disaster and treat those two . . . dipsticks just the same . . .'

I was grateful I had a boss who was so understanding, despite having invested so much time and emotional energy in the project.

I had to reconcile myself to spending the foreseeable future in a state of high anxiety. Now I knew how Salman Rushdie felt when the fatwa was taken out on him, but at least he had the protection of highly trained bodyguards from the intelligence services. I was on my own.

I decided that reporting the matter to the BBC or to the police would only escalate the tension by angering Roy and raising the stakes, making my job infinitely more difficult and possibly unsustainable.

Fortunately, my brother owned a flat that he rented out in

Glasgow's West End. With his blessing, I moved in without telling anyone I was no longer at my old address. Any scarfaced henchman with murder on his mind who arrived on the doorstep of my home would be disappointed. Only my brother knew the perilous reality of my situation, though even with him I played down the severity of the threat.

For the next three months, I received a threat every couple of weeks, either by telephone – where 'Pender, I'll have your balls for garters' became the mantra of choice – or in the shape of mysterious cards, featuring hearts with needles through them and faces with the eyes gouged out.

They were all postmarked in Glasgow, and there was never any accompanying text save for the words 'You're dead'.

They scared the hell out of me.

To throw any hitman off the scent, I decided to change my appearance.

I started to do things I had never done before, like growing facial hair. Throughout my life I'd worked on the assumption that men with facial hair had something to hide. Now that I had facial hair of my own there was something I couldn't hide: my embarrassment.

I realised why I'd never grown a moustache: a hairy caterpillar now claimed squatter's rights on my upper lip. It drooped down to my chin, where it clung to my face like an unlucky upside-down horseshoe. I began to look like a Mexican bandit. *Viva Zapata!*

Determined to change my wardrobe too, I began dressing like I was about to fly into battle with the Luftwaffe. I started wearing a Royal Air Force greatcoat that my Auntie Lizzie had given me years earlier, when she described it as 'Carnaby Street style' – though 'thrift shop style' might have been more accurate. She palmed it off on me when she couldn't find anyone daft enough to buy it.

Lizzie ran a second-hand clothes shop and 'bric a brac emporium' a few hundred yards from Glasgow's main street market, the Barras (that's the Barrows in English). The shop was in Glasgow's Gallowgate. Yes, the street really did have gallows back in the day, and Glaswegian gallows humour came along with it. I once heard one of Lizzie's customers describe life in the East End of Glasgow as 'a downhill struggle'.

Lizzie had the best of intentions: Douglas Bader, the Second World War flying ace, was a hero of hers. Despite losing his legs in a flying accident, Bader went on to distinguish himself in the Battle of Britain, thereby becoming the subject of a very popular film, *Reach for the Sky*.

Lizzie assured me that all the 'young yins' (trans. 'young ones') were wearing Second World War Royal Air Force greatcoats. She created the impression that the 'young yins' was an exclusive club to which I would only be invited if dressed according to her diktats.

Since her own taste had ossified around the Edwardian era and her definition of contemporary male beauty was Tiny Tim, a large-nosed American singer and one-hit wonder with a penchant for woolly hats (or beanies, as the Americans call them) complete with pom-poms, I should have anticipated trouble. At least I no longer looked like Zapata. Now I looked like Douglas Bader, with legs.

I consoled myself with the belief that if I were attacked by a scarfaced henchman in a dark alley, my greatcoat might soften the blow of the knife.

Just when my attempt to disguise myself seemed to be working, just when I thought I could tough it out, just when I thought my paranoia was on the wane, a sinister character re-entered my life, like an intimation of mortality.

◊

It was a warm afternoon in late summer, and I no doubt cut a curious figure, sweltering in my greatcoat with rebel strands of pasta puttanesca clinging to my moustache. It was nearly two months since I had walked out on Roy. I had just enjoyed a convivial lunch at a bar-restaurant called the Big Blue on the banks of Glasgow's River Kelvin, which shares its name with Lord Kelvin, the scientific genius who defined the concept of temperature. Mine was about to rise dramatically. Terror does that to you.

For the first time in the weeks since I had last seen Roy I was feeling relaxed. So relaxed, in fact, that I didn't spot the figure lurking on the park bench. Many homeless people and alcoholics (or 'jakeys' as they are known in the local parlance) used to sit there.

I often gave them money for 'food', which was of course their code word for drink.

Suddenly a guttural voice slashed the air like an open razor: 'Hey, Pender! Ah've goat sumthin' fir ye!' it shouted.

I turned. The creature jumped up from the bench and propelled itself on its spindly legs towards me, like an evil mutant spider in a low-budget horror film. That's when I recognised it. After Roy, it was the creature in the whole wide world that I least wanted to see. It was Wee Toe.

He was holding a long brown cardboard cylinder. I assumed that it contained the murder weapon he intended to use on me.

Pretending I hadn't seen or heard him, I turned back and walked as fast as I could in the opposite direction. Then I ran for it.

He started to run after me, shouting, 'Stoap! Stoap! Pender, Stoap!' I was already mentally trying to match the voice to the one on my answering machine, but in the circumstances it was difficult to make a definitive judgment.

Despite the greatcoat and the heat I broke into a trot, reckoning I could get to my office and comparative safety within a few minutes. I sprinted along the riverbank, past derelict graffiti'd walls spray-painted with FKB (Fuck King Billy) and FTP (Fuck The Pope), monuments to the great sectarian divide which bedevils our thrawn wee nation and has led to much spilling of blood. In my present plight, the spilling of blood was not a welcome thought.

Wee Toe's pursuing tread was getting louder. He was gaining on me. But then he wasn't wearing a heavy RAF greatcoat. It took him less than two minutes to catch up with me, on a deserted riverside path with not a soul in sight.

'Whit the fuck are ye runnin' fir, ya daft cunt?' he asked, with his customary verbal dexterity.

'Oh, hi Toe,' I said chummily, as if I'd just noticed him, sweat dripping in rivulets onto my moustache. 'I've taken up jogging recently. It's important to keep fit at my age.'

As he raised the brown cardboard tube towards me, I flinched, convinced he was about to pull out whatever weapon it was concealing.

'He wants you to have this!' he said, unscrewing the tube's lid. I braced myself for the fatal blow, thinking I'd rather be shot than stabbed. Put yourself in my position, dear reader. Which would you prefer? I had decided shooting was quicker and less painful, other things being equal.

From the tube he produced neither gun nor knife but some sort of canvas rolled up and held by an elastic band.

I gasped a huge sigh of relief, mingled now with just a little curiosity, as he removed the band and opened out the canvas. It was a painting. A watercolour of a Glasgow street scene, and it was a street I knew well. It was the Gallowgate, just along from Auntie Lizzie's shop.

I was stunned. Had Roy forgiven me? Were we back to flowers and baskets of fruit? Would we get together again after our acrimonious break-up? Would we become an on-again, off-again couple – the Richard Burton and Liz Taylor of true crime?

The painting was signed in a squiggle I couldn't decipher.

I said to Toe, 'Thank Roy very much for going to all that trouble.'

'Roy?' he said aggressively, starting to do his foaming-at-the-mouth trick. 'Whit the fuck has Roy got to do wi' it? This is fae fuckin' Billy!'

'Fuckin' Billy?' I said, baffled.

'Billy Toe Elliot. Big Toe.'

The penny finally dropped. I was looking at a gift from Wee Toe's hero and mentor, Billy 'Toe' Elliot, aka Big Toe.

Big Toe, as you may recall, had allegedly cut off his victim's toe before killing him.

Once again I found myself looking nervously at the cardboard tube. Maybe it was some kind of warning. Maybe along with the painting there were a couple of toes in there too, or perhaps a whole foot. Come to think of it, it was the right size and shape for an ankle. I was beginning to feel like Brad Pitt in the movie *Seven*, being handed Gwyneth Paltrow's head in a box.

'That is fuckin' beautiful,' added Wee Toe, staring at the painting like an enraptured art critic. 'Pure dead brilliant, so it is!'

'Yes, it's . . . very good,' I said, enormously relieved that it didn't depict me in a coffin.

'It's the Gallowgate, isn't it?' I said, trying to keep my scar-faced acquaintance sweet. He nodded.

'But why is he giving it to me, Toe?

He had stopped frothing at the mouth. I took that as a good sign.

'It's a present. Billy's the Best of Gallowgate.'

'You're right,' I said enthusiastically, grateful that I was still alive: I was prepared to praise this painting as if it were the *Mona Lisa*. 'This really does represent the Best of Gallowgate.'

'Naw, no' the Best. The Beast!' said Wee Toe, an alarming fleck of froth re-appearing at the corner of his mouth. 'The Beast of Gallowgate. That's what they call Billy.'

'Really? Sorry, Toe. My mistake.'

'It's a' right,' he said, 'but Ah've goat tae be oan ma way,' he said. 'Ah've goat tae get up the clinic.'

'Of course' I said. 'You wouldn't want to miss the clinic.'

I hoped I'd struck the right note of concern.

'Ah need tae ask the doctor if the powder kills the eggs as well.'

I was prepared to let the remark pass, but he clarified it for me.

'Crabs are a cunt.'

I backed off, in case they could jump.

Wee Toe waved, grunted and walked off.

No sooner had I arrived back at my office than the phone rang. A gravelly working-class voice said, 'Hello, Paul – I'm Billy Elliot. But you can call me Toe. Big Toe. I hear you're working with Roy Fontaine.'

'I was, yes,' I replied cautiously.

'Don't worry,' he continued, 'I'm not asking you to write the story of my life. I've written it masel'. I just want your comments. Ah've wrote it as a stage play called "Glasgow Boy". I'll send it tae ye. I hope ye appreciate it, bein' a Glesga boy yirsel."

'Fuck me,' I thought, 'I should be getting a retainer from HM Prison Service.' What I actually said was, 'Thank you, Toe, I look forward to reading it.'

He said he would call me the following week for my reaction.

As soon as I put the phone down, I called Moira the BBC librarian and asked for his file. Twenty minutes later she delivered it, quipping, 'What is it with you and convicted killers?'

My heart sank as I read that Billy Toe Elliot was said by many to be Scotland's most dangerous killer. 'Even more dangerous than Roy?' I asked myself. Moira was right. How many killers does a script editor need in his life?

Billy had launched the Category A theatre group with fellow Barlinnie Special Unit inmates Jimmy Boyle and Hugh Collins. Boyle and Collins were fast becoming celebrated sculptors, and Billy wanted to be appreciated as a writer.

He was jailed in 1983 for murdering rival heroin dealer Robert Kane after accusing him of cheating on a drugs deal. Scarily, the death took place in the very landscape he had painted for me as a present.

I promised myself not to be too harsh on his script. Fortunately, I did actually think it showed talent. There must have been something in the Special Unit's water.

When he called me a week later, I gave him my comments, which to my relief he accepted gratefully. He subsequently had his plays produced in Scotland and even wrote a screenplay for *Taggart*, the successful TV cop show. I like to think that my Category A Prisoners' Mentorship Scheme paid dividends.

Big Toe said he was looking for a journalist who would campaign for his release on the grounds that he had been rehabilitated in the Special Unit. I recommended Paul Foot, who was also campaigning for Roy.

Later, it occurred to me that if the journalist succeeded, the headline would be: 'Foot Frees Toe'.

◊

This involvement with Big Toe had an unforeseen effect. Two days after talking to him about his script, I left my brother's and went back to my own flat to collect the mail. As I did so, the phone rang. The caller ID said: 'Unknown number'. After some hesitation, I decided to pick it up.

'Is that you, son?' said the warm, avuncular voice, which this time was unmistakably Roy's.

I was tempted to put the receiver down, but decided not to. I was curious about what he would have to say. Besides, even Roy hadn't worked out a way of killing over the phone.

'Have you got time to talk for a minute, son?' he said affectionately. I told him I did.

'Good. Then let me finish telling you my story. Come and see me. Just one more time. I'm spoken to the Governor, and he'll permit an extended session. It'll give me enough time to finish my tale and tell you my secret.'

'Your secret? What secret?'

'Well, if I told you it wouldn't be a secret any more, would it?'

He was up to his old tricks. I thought the alleged secret was probably a bluff, but I couldn't be sure. And scary though it would be to re-enter the lion's den, I desperately wanted an end to hostilities and to hear him complete his saga.

There was a long pause while I thought about it.

'OK, Roy,' I said. 'One more visit. On certain conditions.'

We laid down clear parameters. If there were no more threatening messages or cards, we'd meet in three weeks' time. Roy feigned surprise at the news of the threats but said he'd look into the matter and use his influence to prevent such behaviour recurring.

We also agreed that no money would change hands. And by mutual consent it would be our last meeting.

'Agreed. You won't be sorry, son,' he said, his voice choking with emotion. 'I'll make out the visiting order tomorrow.'

I put down the phone, enormously relieved, even excited. It sounded like he needed closure too. I wanted to hear the end of his story. And if there really was a secret, so much the better.

A few days later, the visiting order arrived at my home address, enclosed in a greetings card bearing the inscription 'Your friend Roy'.

The card showed a man with a smiling face. There was something about that card and that face that struck me as odd.

Then I realised what it was: the eyes hadn't been gouged out.

31

My Brother's Keeper

And the Lord said unto Cain, Where is Abel
thy brother? And he said, I know not: Am I my
brother's keeper?
   And God said, What hast thou done? The
voice of thy brother's blood crieth unto me
from the ground.

Genesis 4: 9-10

FOUR WEEKS LATER I was standing in the visitors' centre, being
hugged warmly by Roy as I tried not to gag on his aftershave.
It was just like old times. The important difference was that we
had the place to ourselves, under the watchful and sympathetic
eye of the guard, who may or may not have been Roy's lover.
'Our Roy' was receiving the special privilege of an extended
session. There had been no more threats by phone or mail since
we'd spoken on the phone.

'Forget about the last visit, son. We both said things in anger.
Let's put all that behind us.' That was the closest he came to an
apology.

'By the way, you were right about the cash,' he whispered. 'I
spoke to a lawyer about it and he said slipping me money could
have got you into serious trouble.'

'I'm glad your lawyer gave you such wise advice,' I said, smiling.

'Oh, he's not my lawyer,' laughed Roy. 'He's a qualified lawyer
all right, but he's in the cell next to me.'

'What's he in for?' I asked, surprised. I assumed it would be some
white-collar crime, like forging a conveyancing certificate.

'Oh, he chucked his wife off the Eiffel Tower,' added Roy with an enigmatic smile. 'See Paris and die,' he added with a chuckle.

I was back on Planet Roy.

We settled down to business. Not wishing to take any unnecessary risks, I took notes with a very small, very blunt bookie's pencil. Since the '2B or not 2B' incident I had taken to gripping my pencil like a drowning man clutching a piece of driftwood.

He lit one of the Romeo and Juliet cigars I'd brought for him and resumed where he left off.

After dumping Mary's body in the burn, he and Kitto drove back to Edinburgh, left the car in a side street and hired a new car using a forged driving licence.

That done, they decided to celebrate Christmas.

While normal law-abiding folk had been celebrating the season of goodwill by wrapping presents, the gruesome twosome had been wrapping corpses. Deciding it was better to receive than to give, they made a quick dash south to loot the Scott-Elliots' apartment.

Once they were satisfied that there was no evidence of police activity, Roy opened the door discreetly with his key.

'I felt like Aladdin re-entering his cave,' he told me, with a nostalgic glint in his eye. I didn't have the heart to remind him that Aladdin didn't kill the cave's inhabitants.

Roy and Kitto started stuffing their loot into large suitcases. If anyone spotted them they could pretend the cases were part of the Scott-Elliots' travel luggage.

Their haul included original paintings, Dresden china, silverware, rare books, valuable coins and priceless Chinese jade ornaments. Roy had a network of fences throughout the country. He would waste no time in disposing of much of this in exchange for large amounts of cash.

In the meantime he got rid of those pesky incriminating clothes in which he and Kitto had committed murder. He burned them in the Scott-Elliots' fire. He kept the mink coat, though, got a decent price for it and breathed a sigh of relief that he'd never have to look at it again.

Concerned relatives of the Scott-Elliots had meanwhile alerted the police, whose car flashed past Roy and Kitto as they drove away from the apartment with their booty. Luck was once again on their side. Roy was entitled to believe he was leading a charmed life.

In celebratory mood, they drove to Staffordshire, to join Roy's sister Violet and her husband for Christmas, buying presents for them en route. Now feeling invulnerable, Roy told Kitto that he was already planning a heist that would give him even greater satisfaction than the one they'd just pulled off at the Scott-Elliots'. He'd liked the Scott-Elliots, after all, whereas he was still furious with his next proposed victim – Lady Hudson.

He told Kitto they would 'clean out the old bag's mansion of all its treasures. Then we can fly to a warm, sunny country, where, unlike this godforsaken dump, it doesn't freeze the balls off a brass monkey for eight months in the year.'

Roy had Brazil in mind. He was creatively visualising himself sharing a sundowner on the beach with his hero, the Great Train Robber Ronnie Biggs. To complete the perfect evening he would then rub Ambre Solaire onto the glistening torso of a beautiful young man.

Kitto enthused about the plan, partly because he realised that as long as Roy needed him for another job, his life was reasonably secure. As soon as he had enough cash he'd split, but of course he was keeping that quiet for the time being.

Now that they had some cash in hand they relaxed and bought themselves new suits. They arrived at Violet's house looking like the two successful antiques dealers they were pretending to be.

Violet had never met Kitto before. She thought that 'Robin', as he was calling himself, was a cut above the kind of lowlife types with whom her brother often associated. Roy told her in the kitchen that his friend had never been in trouble with the law. 'Robin' generously gave her a lovely set of earrings and even bought a present for her husband – a matching set of aftershave and soap.

They were asked to stay for Christmas dinner. All was going festively in the Yuletide spirit of goodwill until Violet revealed that Donald was coming to dinner. Roy's face immediately darkened, but he consoled himself with the thought that another pair of hands could be very useful in robbing Lady Hudson, with the added benefit that 'Donald was dumb enough to be controlled'.

When his brother arrived, having recently been released from prison for again molesting a young woman, Roy hid his distaste and gave another one of his fine bravura acting performances. He exuded bonhomie and even simulated a degree of brotherly love, despite the fact that, as he put it, 'the wee tramp hadn't even washed his hair, which was long, lank and bedraggled, as if he'd chopped off a bunch of rats' tails and glued them on his fucking napper. And he'd obviously been drinking before he arrived. He was bevvied and looked like a jakey! He should have been ashamed of himself! Violet got him to take a shower, by hinting that he might want to freshen up.'

While Donald was showering, Roy had a discreet word with Kitto, who agreed that it would be good to have three pairs of hands to clean out Lady Hudson's mansion.

All was sweetness, light and Christmas joy as they sat down to savour the flesh of the turkey that Violet's husband was carefully carving. As that flesh was being torn asunder, so too was the fabric of the clothes covering Mary's battered and broken flesh. Melting snow had swollen the current in the Back Burn and the metal spike could hold her no longer. Her corpse drifted out from under the bridge into full view, till it wedged between some large boulders.

The tearing of that fabric presaged the tearing asunder of the fabric of Roy's life. His luck was turning. His crimes were being discovered.

The policemen in the car that had passed them near the Scott-Elliots' apartment were greeted by a scene of ransacked devastation. When they burst open the door, they smelled smoke. Embers were still glowing in the fireplace. Their first thought was that someone had tried to set the place alight. They didn't know yet that the flames had destroyed the evidence of murder.

◊

While Roy and Kitto were enjoying their festive feast, a very unseasonal sight spoiled the otherwise picture-postcard perfection upon which young farmworker Duncan Kerr was gazing that Christmas Day as he drove his tractor over the Back Burn bridge:

he saw a bloodied corpse wedged between two large boulders in the burn.

Within an hour, the area was swarming with policemen. Soon grateful Scottish press men, relieved that their slow news day had suddenly gained dizzying momentum, were writing about the mysterious, oddly dressed woman whose battered body had washed up in this idyllic corner of Scotland. She had no identifying marks on her body, and they soon christened her 'Mrs Nobody'.

Less than two weeks later, on 3 January, the still unidentified body of Mrs Nobody would be buried in a sad little ceremony in the village of Annan, Dumfriesshire.

Belfast Mary, mother of nine, had as mourners only the sombrely dressed gentlemen from the Dumfries Co-op Funeral service and a handful of police officers.

Roy never showed any regret about killing her. He claimed he'd elevated Mrs Nobody to a kind of posthumous celebrity status, pointing out that the burn in which they had dumped her body was now known as Bloody Mary's Burn. It didn't seem to cross his mind that she might have preferred to remain alive and anonymous.

A few hundred miles south, the man who always wanted to be Mr Somebody continued to plan his next crime.

After enjoying Christmas dinner, he discreetly invited Donald to join the team. The young man felt that his prayers had been answered. He had always craved the approval of his big brother. At last he was being allowed to participate in one of Roy's great adventures.

When the Christmas party was over, the happy band of Roy, Kitto and Donald took their leave and headed north in the hired car.

They arrived in Carlisle, where they would stay the night. Roy suddenly became fixated by the number plate of their new car, the one they'd hired in Edinburgh. Up till now he'd been too busy to notice it. But as he stood in the falling snow gazing at the Ford Granada's plate – YGE 999R – he turned and said to Kitto, 'That's got to go! It's bad luck.'

When Kitto asked why, since their luck so far had been very good, Roy pointed out that 999 is the number you dial for the police. He'd no doubt have been much happier with 666 – the number of the Beast and a favourite of his hero Aleister Crowley.

'999,' said Roy, 'feels like we're inviting people to call the cops. It has to go!'

With more important things to think about, he delegated the task of acquiring false number plates to Kitto, who claimed to have some expertise in that area from his early days as a car thief. Kitto said he'd sort it out the next morning.

It had been a long drive from Violet's house, and the three hungry criminals decided to have a festive Chinese meal in a local restaurant, at the end of which they each got a fortune cookie. Roy's said: 'You will be well rewarded in your next venture', Kitto's that 'Your plans will bear rich fruit' and Donald's that 'A big surprise awaits you'. Donald was delighted, mistakenly assuming that the surprise would be a pleasant one.

In the morning, Roy went to a joke shop, where he bought three Dracula masks for the Hudson heist – to conceal their identities and to 'frighten the shit out of the old bag'. He had never forgiven her for sacking him. After all, he had never stolen anything from her. Sure, if you wanted to split hairs you could point out that he'd killed a fellow employee and buried the corpse on her estate, but as Roy said, 'She didn't know that when she sacked me, did she, the unreasonable old bitch?'

He got hold of a bottle of chloroform from one of his corrupt doctor associates, 'to keep the old girl quiet if necessary'.

Meantime, 500 miles away, forensic experts were finding bloodstains in Lady Dorothy Scott-Elliot's bedroom. *(A slash cut from the Dracula masks here, please, Herr Director! OK, OK, it was only a suggestion!)*

Scotland Yard was now combing the country for the Scott-Elliots and their servant. Wags in the force were already calling the investigation 'The Strange Case of the Disappearing Butler'.

An alert was immediately put out for the car hired by the Scott-Elliots' 'godson'. It was found in a street in Edinburgh. Unfortunately for the investigation, the vehicle had been returned to the local branch of the car-hire firm and an over-zealous employee had given it a full wash and vacuum, thereby removing any possible forensic evidence.

Blissfully unaware that the net was closing in on them, Roy, Kitto and Donald drove to the cottage in Cumbria. They celebrated the run-in to the New Year with a drink in their local bar, the Joiner's Arms.

After only a few drinks, Donald started shooting his mouth off about how he and his friends were planning something really big. Roy was incensed. He suggested they go back to the cottage and continue drinking there.

They did so, and Roy poured some drinks. They tried on the Dracula masks, and he talked about the plan for robbing Lady Hudson's, saying, 'If she has guests, we'll need to tie them up.'

Eager to impress, Donald told his big brother that in prison he was shown a great way to tie someone up so that they could not escape.

'I can show you how to do it,' he said. 'All I need is six inches of string. Do you have any?'

This was a bit like asking Jack the Ripper if he had any sharp knives.

Kitto said he could use his pyjama cord, which was in the bedroom, and Donald went to fetch it.

Roy sipped his whisky and said, 'Did you hear him in the pub? He can't keep his big mouth shut.'

'He's another Mary!' replied Kitto.

'Exactly,' replied Roy menacingly. Each knew what the other meant.

Donald returned with the pyjama cord and put his hands behind his back, saying, 'Make sure you turn their thumbs outwards. Come on, Roy, tie my thumbs together.' Roy needed no second invitation. He enthusiastically obliged.

Donald then took his shoes off and asked his brother to tie his big toes together. Roy did so.

'There!' said Donald, lying on his front. 'You push them down on their face and loop their feet through the circle made by their hands.' Roy followed his brother's instructions to the letter.

'I can't believe how easy he made it for us,' Roy told me. 'He was an idiot to the very end. This was the dumbest thing he had ever done. Even dumber than stealing the Salvation Army tuba.'

Despite the fact that he was lying like a trussed chicken, Donald was grinning, happy to be of service to his big brother who stood staring down at him contemptuously, years of festering hatred welling up inside.

The young man was trussed in the foetal position. Roy thought there was a certain poetic justice in this, since he had hated his brother since the latter had been in their mother's womb.

'You can untie me now,' said Donald, with just a hint of anxiety. But Roy didn't untie him: instead, he went into the kitchen and came back with a little brown bottle and a cotton-wool pad.

'What's that, Roy?' his brother asked, his voice now trembling with fear.

'You're about to find out, ya pervy wee bastard!' replied Roy, nodding to Kitto, who pressed down on Donald's back. The two killers seemed to know instinctively how to act in synch, like interlocking gears in the machinery of murder.

Fontaine poured some chloroform onto the pad. Then he bent down and put it over his brother's mouth. Donald choked and started struggling so hard that the pyjama cord burst. He managed to turn on his back and grab Kitto, tearing his nails down his face. He wasn't going gently into that good night. Roy poured more chloroform onto the pad and pushed it hard onto his face till the struggling ceased.

Roy liked to boast that it was Britain's first confirmed murder by chloroform – a source of great pride for him, ever conscious of his place in the history books.

He started to strip the lifeless body, showing no hint of emotion, as if he were undressing a mannequin in a shop window. He felt something in Donald's pocket, and took out a photo of their mother. She seemed to be staring at him accusingly. He held his head in his hands and tears rolled down his cheeks. Kitto looked on, amazed at this rare display of emotion.

Roy spoke to the photo: 'Mother – oh mother, forgive me. I didn't want any of this.'

He stared at Donald's corpse for a moment as he drew himself together again. Kitto was about to console him when he reverted to his usual hard and efficient self. He stuffed the photo into his pocket and barked out an order: 'Come on – let's put this thing in the bath!'

'Why?' asked Kitto.

'It delays the onset of rigor mortis,' Roy replied. 'Makes the body easier to handle.' He had never forgotten the lessons he'd learned while disposing of David Wright's corpse. Keep the body supple and easy to manoeuvre at all times.

They carried the corpse to the bath and submerged it in water.

'OK, so he was dead,' Roy told me. 'But at least he was fuckin' clean. Cleaner than he'd ever been in his life.'

I asked him how it felt to kill your own brother. He spat his answer back at me: 'He was *not* my brother! He was my *half*-brother! How many times do I have to tell you? He was a dirty filthy pervert! Low-life scum. How could he be a true brother of mine? The world is better off without him!'

'So you have no regrets at all?' I asked.

He thought for a moment and nodded his head. Maybe there was a conscience in there after all, I told myself.

I was soon disabused of that quaint notion.

'I have to admit I regretted putting his body in the bath. I was worried the death might have been attributed to drowning. That would have denied me my place in the annals of crime.'

He felt absurdly grateful to the pathologist who ruled at the autopsy that the cause of death was chloroform and not drowning, as had been at first suspected. After all, deaths by drowning were ten a penny. It took vision and a touch of class to create a death by chloroform.

The next morning, Kitto could hear Roy singing away merrily in the bathroom.

'You sound happy!' he said, as he approached.

'Yes,' replied Roy chirpily, 'I'm just having a quick bath.'

Kitto looked through the open bathroom door and saw Roy splashing away happily, like a kid with a rubber duck, in the bath that overnight had served as a storage facility for his brother's corpse, which now lay on the bathroom floor, wrapped up in plastic sheeting.

Kitto stared in disbelief. Sometimes Roy was too weird, even for him.

The thought that it might be necessary to do a runner sooner rather than later rose to the surface of his consciousness, like the bubbles in Roy's bizarre bath.

32

The Butler Did It

Alas, poor country! Almost afraid to know
itself.
      It cannot be call'd our mother but our
grave.
                    Shakespeare, *Macbeth*, Act 4, Scene 3

FOR THE TIME BEING, Kitto decided it was in his own best interests
to be as compliant as possible, at least until he got his hands
on some of Lady Hudson's loot. He readily agreed to Roy's plan
to dump Donald's body in Scotland, again with a view to taking
advantage of the Not Proven verdict. Roy helpfully suggested
'somewhere near Dunbar' – a picturesque village in the south-
east of Scotland.

'It's nice up that way. Lovely views of the sea,' said Roy, as if he
were planning a family vacation – which in a sense he was. Just
because one member of the family had rigor mortis and was
wrapped up tight in a plastic sheet was no reason to spoil the holiday
mood. Roy was determined not to let a detail like that mar his
enjoyment.

They drove north with the now traditional body in the boot. A
normal human being might have felt slightly uneasy at having the
trussed-up corpse of a sibling in the car, but Roy was not as other
men, and the word 'normal' was not in his lexicon. He was in a
good mood. On crossing the border he broke into an impromptu
rendition of his old favourite, the patriotic Scottish anthem 'For
These Are My Mountains'.

'I used to love the Alexander Brothers,' he chattily informed the bemused Kitto, who had never heard of them. The singing brothers were famous in the Scottish sense – i.e. unknown throughout the rest of the world.

'I've always liked a man in a kilt,' Roy added.

Kitto was in no mood to discuss the sexual allure of Highland dress. He wanted to dump the body as quickly as possible, but Roy told him that they had learned that disposing of a corpse is heavy work, particularly when it involves digging up frozen earth. He reminded him of how difficult it had been to 'plant the old man'.

'To build up our strength,' said Roy, 'we should have a slap-up meal and a drink. A nice glass of red wine or a good malt will heat us up quite the thing.'

The issue was settled when a flurry of snow started falling.

'If this weather keeps up,' Roy added jauntily, 'we might just have to dump the wee bastard's body in the Firth. Though that's probably too good for him. I'd like to be buried at sea myself, actually. What about you?' he asked his companion matter-of-factly. Kitto didn't really want to think about his own death at this precise moment, but it was an occupational hazard of hanging out with Roy.

'I'm not bothered, Roy,' he answered non-commitally. 'When you're dead, you're dead. What does it matter where you're buried?'

'I'll bear that in mind,' laughed Roy, nudging the younger man in the ribs like it was all a great big joke. Kitto failed to see the funny side.

As the snow continued to fall, they decided to check into the nearest hotel. It was to prove to be yet another apparently small decision with enormous consequences. You could argue that the snow defeated Roy Fontaine, just as it had defeated his heroes Hitler and Napoleon, forcing them to retreat from their advance on Russia. Berwick was a long way from Moscow, but General Winter was to prove victorious here too.

They arrived at the Blenheim House Hotel in North Berwick, a scenic seaside town located on a promontory at the eastern end of the Firth of Forth. Looking out to the islands of the Firth and the majestic Bass Rock, the town enjoys its own micro-climate and has beautiful sandy beaches, a picturesque harbour and a bustling high street. Just the place to relax and unwind before disposing of a corpse.

They checked in as the brothers Roy and Robin Thomson,

though the Brothers Grim might have been more appropriate. They signed the guest book under the watchful eye of the hotel's landlord, Mr Norman Wight, who thought he noticed a momentary hesitation when the younger 'brother' signed.

In years to come, Roy uncharitably insisted on referring to the landlord as 'Basil fuckin' Fawlty', in honour of the cantankerous, bad-tempered, guest-hating hotelier so memorably portrayed by comedian John Cleese in the British sitcom classic *Fawlty Towers*. The ever-vigilant Mr Wight noted that the two were travelling very light, with just a holdall for luggage, despite the fact that they were claiming to be en route to Australia.

Berwick is a border town, and Mr Wight had a border town mentality. He knew the border attracts vagabonds and thieves, so he decided to check them out, starting with their car. Kitto had, as promised, acquired new car number plates, but he had made the crucial mistake of not obtaining a matching tax disc, a fact which 'Basil' noted with great interest. It confirmed his suspicions that they were up to no good. He immediately called the police and was subsequently delighted when his suspicions were confirmed.

When the cops checked out the licence number, they found that it was registered to a Mothercare van in the south of England. Mothercare! The store that supplies all things pertaining to babies and maternal love. The Oedipal killer who had never forgiven his brother for being born, the jealous sibling who had dumped his brother's body in the boot, was finally to be unmasked, courtesy of Mothercare.

Roy's run of good luck had come to an end. His Faustian pact had expired, having gone the way of all such pacts. The Devil was calling in his debts, just as he had done with the other stare masters, Roy's mentors Adolf and Aleister. They had done their deal with the devil too, who had promised them everything from eternal gratification to a Thousand-Year Reich.

Instead, Adolf got a bullet in the brain in a Berlin bunker, whilst Aleister, the self-styled Great Beast, died a beastly death in a decrepit seaside boarding house. That's the problem when you make a pact with the devil: sooner or later Satan always welches on the deal.

But Roy didn't blame the cloven-hoofed one. For him, the villain of the piece was the alert and observant hotelier Mr Wight.

'Basil fuckin' Fawlty was a nosy meddling cunt!' he said through gritted teeth. The intervening years had not lessened his sense of outrage.

'*Now, Roy,*' I thought, '*don't mince your words. Say what you think.*'

He continued: 'There we were, sitting in front of a blazing fire, innocently enjoying our meal and our brandies [presumably he meant as innocently as you can with a corpse in the boot of your car] when these two cops walked in! Basil fuckin' Fawlty had phoned them! He was so uptight I wouldn't be surprised if he was reporting toddlers in his fuckin' breakfast room for nicking straws for their milk! He should have got a life. Instead, as a result of his meddling, *I* got life. There we were, patronising his establishment, spending our money – OK, it was somebody else's money, but so what? It was still money. Meanwhile, what was he doing? Snooping around our car, checking out the task disc, phoning the cops! Paranoid cunt!'

Roy took a breath and re-lit the cigar he'd left in the ashtray.

'He even searched our rooms while we were at the cop shop and found a batch of rare coins I'd hidden in an envelope. I wanted to sue the cunt for invasion of privacy, but I had too much on my plate!'

Roy found this abuse of the hotelier's noble calling disgraceful: if he'd espoused any of the tenets of Christianity, he might even have called it sacrilegious. Throughout his criminal career, Roy had seen hotels in a romantic, almost mystical, light, as places of sanctuary. His attitude was that of a medieval outlaw seeking refuge in a church beyond the reach of secular authority. As he saw it, the hotelier grassing him up to the police was like the Abbot of Locksley turning Robin Hood in to the Sheriff of Nottingham.

When the police asked the two men why their car had false licence plates, Kitto started sweating. Roy maintained his composure.

'I'm sure there is a perfectly innocent explanation, officers,' he said, and asked the policemen if they'd care to join him and his brother in a brandy.

They replied, 'No, thank you, sir, we're on duty,' but they were so impressed by his calm and confident demeanour that they sat down and had soft drinks at an adjacent table while Roy and Kitto finished their meal.

'I have cursed myself time and time again for being over-confident,' Roy said. 'I should've dumped the corpse before dinner.'

Had Robert Roberts been advising his young gentlemen friends on how best to rid themselves of a corpse, he would surely have recommended disposing of it before the appetisers. Roy and Kitto failed to do so, and you might say that they got their just desserts.

When the meal was finished – and Roy suspected that it might be the last decent meal he would have for a long, long time – he asked if he could go and make a quick phone call to the friend who had loaned him the car. He felt sure the entire matter could be cleared up very quickly.

'I was planning to do a runner, of course,' he confided. But the police were insistent that he and Kitto accompany them to the station.

Once there, Roy knew that he was about to be searched. He asked if he could go to the toilet, and was allowed to do so. In his pocket he had a plan of Lady Hudson's estate and a compromising list of names and addresses of where he was going to resell the goods.

He flushed them down the toilet, put down the lid of the seat, stood on it, and reached up to a small window. He managed to squeeze himself through – but not before leaving a pound note 'for the cloakroom attendant'. It was those little touches, after all, that made him who he was.

He rushed down the street and hailed a passing car, using his old trick about having to race to his wife's hospital bedside. The car was not going in the direction of the hospital, but he was dropped off at a taxi rank, where he gave the taxi driver the same story. As the cab sped to Belhaven Hospital in Dunbar, the police found that Roy had escaped and put out an all-points bulletin for every cop in the area to be on the lookout for him.

(Here, Herr Director, we can cut from the speeding taxi to a young police constable opening the boot of Roy's car. We go in close on his horrified face.)

DC Donaldson opened the boot. Inside was an odd bundle of plastic sheeting. He tugged on it. As it unwrapped he found himself staring at a corpse.

It was the corpse of a young man wearing only underpants, a plastic bag tied over his head. The body was trussed like the Christmas turkey the victim had enjoyed with his killer just a few days before. The minor motoring offence was now a major murder investigation.

When Roy's taxi arrived at Belhaven Hospital, he went into the reception area and re-emerged to tell the driver that his wife had been transferred to a hospital in Edinburgh.

As the taxi set off, Kitto was being confronted in the police station with the discovery of the body in the boot of his car. He was told things would go better for him if he were to cooperate.

Kitto said he was relieved that he now had the chance to get everything off his chest. He began telling the whole sorry tale – for which Roy would never forgive him. 'Betrayed again,' he said, shaking his head.

On the outskirts of Edinburgh, Roy's taxi was stopped at a roadblock. Two policemen looked inside at the passenger who was puffing confidently on a cigar. He matched the description of the suspect. The taxi driver said that the poor man was in a terrible hurry to get to his wife in hospital.

The policemen asked Roy his name. 'Mr Thomson,' he replied calmly. They radioed forward to the hospital, only to find that no 'Mrs Thomson' had been admitted. They knew that Roy was their man. They nodded to each other and said, 'Could you step this way, please?' Roy knew it was over, but before the handcuffs were put on his wrists he insisted on paying the taxi driver.

'A lot of fuss over some false number plates,' he said, bluffing to the end.

On the way to the police station, he politely requested that they stop the car. The two policemen thought he needed to relieve himself. Instead, he stood in his handcuffs and gazed in rapt silence at the Firth of Forth. He breathed deeply and smelled the brine. As the cops looked on in bemusement, he started reciting Masefield's

'Sea Fever' out loud, to the lonely sea and the sky.

It would be the last time he ever gazed upon the sea.

Back at the station, Kitto had admitted his role in the murder of Donald and was spilling the beans about how they had disposed of 'another three bodies'.

When Roy was questioned, he initially protested his innocence, but confronted with Kitto's damning evidence about the four murders his natural showmanship got the better of him. 'Four murders?' he said, holding up all the fingers of his left hand. 'Five, actually.' The policemen looked stunned.

'I have to admit some responsibility in contributing towards the death of five people,' he added.

'You sound like a politician,' said Detective Chief Inspector Shearer, the senior investigating officer.

'Oh no,' said Roy. 'I'm far too honest for that.'

Knowing that the game was well and truly up, he decided to cooperate, in the hope that he might get a lighter sentence.

'This is the biggest case you'll ever have to deal with,' he assured the officers, as if they should be honoured to be part of his adventure. The stage was now his.

He asked for a cigar to help his concentration. They fetched him one. He turned up his nose at it and asked if they didn't have anything better. They didn't. He sighed just long enough to convey his superior tastes, lit up and started weaving his tale of murder, madness and mayhem.

'I felt I was in some way brightening up the dull little lives of those police officers,' he told me. 'After all, their daily grind was small-time crime. The kind of thieves they were used to would steal cars and dump them in the burn. What *I* dumped in the burn was a lot more interesting! I started telling them wonderful stories of my adventures. I was Sinbad.'

He offered to help them find the bodies of his victims and perversely claimed that he would enjoy accompanying them on their search. As the officers began their gruesome work, he chatted away merrily to them as if he were on some sort of treasure hunt. Even when he saw the sickening remains of his victims, he showed no signs of remorse. The police were struck by his lack of emotion.

Detective Chief Inspector Shearer described Roy as 'the oddest character I've ever encountered in a lifetime of police work. In remembering where each corpse had been left it was if he was just playing a game of concentration.'

The findings were grisly. Sir Walter's skull was found some distance away from the rest of his body. Wild animals had banqueted on his corpse.

The gnawed remains of his kneecap were discovered in a remote spot even further away from his body. As Roy nonchalantly put it, 'there were bits of the old man everywhere'.

Lady Dorothy's body was more difficult to locate. The police came close to giving up the search. When the corpse was finally found, it was the most badly decomposed of all.

Wright's body was discovered only five miles away from where Mary's corpse had floated into view. His partly decomposed toes could be seen popping out from the bed of the stream on Lady Hudson's estate, having been nibbled by fish and wading animals.

'I'd recycled Wright,' said Roy with utter contempt for his victim, sounding like a politician stressing his green credentials. 'He was food for the fish. That's all he was fit for. He did more good in death than he ever did in life.'

It niggled Roy that of all his victims, only 'that little runt Donald would look good in his coffin'.

When the thrill of finding the corpses wore off, Roy realised that 'I couldn't face the rest of my life in prison.' He meant it.

Whilst awaiting trial, he made a couple of highly controversial attempts at suicide. His methods showed just how much he had learned from the Nazis, whose leaders found ingenious ways of concealing cyanide capsules on their persons, most notably in concealed cavities in their teeth. Thus did Himmler, Goebbels and Goering take their own lives rather than suffer the righteous vengeance of the civilised world.

Not having access to a Nazi dentist, Roy's methods had to be improvised. He managed to conceal a large supply of powerful sleeping pills in his orifice of choice – inevitably, in Roy's case, his anus.

Our delicate bourgeois sensibilities may be shocked by such a revelation. So were the hardened cops of Musselburgh when they found him in his cell close to death. They rushed him to hospital to have his stomach pumped. No one knew how or where he had obtained the pills.

He recovered briefly, before making a second attempt at suicide using yet more pills from the same discreet source. It was only then that a dedicated doctor performed a very thorough probe and the police realised that the patient had, in Roy's own words, 'made an arse of them'.

Sherlock Holmes, I'm sure, would have realised immediately where Roy was hiding the pills. It would have been a case, surely, of 'alimentary, my dear Watson'.

'I always found it useful in situations of danger to have a suicide kit up my arse,' Roy said in a matter-of-fact way, as though we should all have one. 'You've no idea how useful that orifice has been to me over the years, son. I've had everything but the kitchen sink up there! Doesn't give me as much pleasure as it used to, though. These days mostly all I shove up it is my haemorrhoid cream. I tend to stick to oral these days,' he said wistfully, as if he were pleading the Clinton defence.

In an attempt to brighten up his mood, I told him it was highly creative to try to kill yourself by swallowing an overdose of pills hidden up your rectum. Though the thought repelled me, I was trying to give him points for originality.

◊

The newspapers of the day were full of his murders and suicide attempts. 'Suddenly I was famous,' he said, 'but what good was fame to me?'

He did find a use for it, though. He started a rumour that the prison authorities were trying to poison him, because 'I know too much about the Establishment'.

He was referring principally to his affairs with Mountbatten, Vic Oliver, Lord Boothby et al., not to mention the sado-masochistic Lady Aylwen. The press, afraid of the libel laws, made vague references to unnamed 'gay MPs' Roy claimed to have slept with.

Roy told anyone who would listen that he would not be able to survive in prison. Before he went for sentencing, he requested, with characteristic modesty, that his obituary notice be placed in the *Times* of London. The request, like Mary's body in the burn, was spiked.

He received two life sentences at Edinburgh Crown Court for murdering David Wright and Walter Scott-Elliot. He and Kitto were then tried at London's Old Bailey for the murder of Lady Dorothy on the grounds that she, unlike the other two, had been murdered in England.

He was defended by the very able Mr John Matthew, QC, who argued of the murders perpetrated by his hitherto non-violent client that 'this does appear to have been a sudden orgy of extreme and irresponsible behaviour, alien to his previous character'. Since when could Roy resist any kind of orgy?

He was intensely jealous of the fact that Kitto was defended by the celebrity barrister John Mortimer, a man of letters who was fast becoming famous, having recently created Rumpole of the Bailey, his fictional alter ego.

Mortimer sat though the trial with a damaged ankle, having perhaps listened over zealously to his thespian friends advising him to 'break a leg'. Despite his physical discomfort, he performed astutely as ever.

It was a torment to Roy that throughout the trial he was referred to by his real name. Archibald Hall was taking a terrible revenge. Mortimer pointed out that 'when Hall met Kitto, the latter was 39 and a small-time thief. Hall was 53 and had already committed his first murder.'

Mortimer defended Kitto brilliantly, using an ingenious legal argument that became known as the 'passive homosexual' defence. He claimed that Kitto as the passive homosexual in the relationship was entirely dominated by Roy and had no independent will of his own. He was a mere puppet whose strings were pulled by Roy, the active homosexual.

'In all this,' argued Mortimer, 'Kitto was the servitor carrying out the plan of his leader.' In one sense, Roy was flattered by this argument, as it confirmed his faith in his own ability to impose his will on others.

By a curious quirk of fate, sentencing at the Old Bailey took place on Kitto's 40th birthday. Roy made a moving speech, claiming that 'the longer the sentence the less likelihood of any moral salvage. Doing time, you strive to hold onto the best of what you have been, trying not to become brutalised and embittered. It kills something in you.'

This cut no ice with the unsympathetic judge, who sentenced him to life with the recommendation that he never be released.

'Thanks a fucking bundle, you pompous bewigged cunt!' Roy murmured under his breath, as he tried to come to terms with the fact that he would never taste freedom again.

When Kitto got life with a recommendation that he serve at least 15 years, Roy spoke to him for the first time in months.

'Happy Birthday, Kitto,' he said ironically, before adding with a malicious wink: 'You know what they say: life begins at 40.'

33

The Hunger Artist

'Yonder Cassius hath a lean and hungry look.
Give me men about me who are fat.'
Shakespeare, *Julius Caesar*, Act 1, Scene 2

ROY WAS TO SPEND the first few months of his incarceration in London's Wandsworth Prison, which he detested.

'It was the smell,' he said. 'After spending so long on the outside, I was more sensitive to how prisons smell. It's a mixture of boiled cabbage, disinfectant and shite. Those old Victorian prisons smelled like an old hoor dousing her fanny in cheap perfume.'

He said he wanted to be transferred to a Scottish prison, not because they smelled any better but because he wanted to die in Scotland. At first no one took him seriously. The prison authorities thought he was merely up to one of his old tricks to gain publicity, ingeniously playing the patriotic card. They didn't believe him when he said he would starve himself to death if they didn't transfer him.

He did, though, gain some sympathy amongst certain members of the Scottish public. As they saw it, he may have been a serial killer but at least he was a patriotic serial killer. There's a famous Scottish toast, 'Here's tae us. Wha's like us? Damn few and they're a' deid.' Roy would be too, if he kept his promise.

The press loved the controversy. He was still capable of hitting the headlines, even from behind bars. Many people thought it was just publicity-seeking bravado, but what followed proved that his belief in the power of the will was no mere theory.

He cast himself once again in the pose of his Red Clydesider hero John Maclean, whose own hunger strike was aborted with forced feeding. The authorities were no longer legally permitted to force-feed, and Roy saw his opportunity. By starving himself to death, he would secure his place in history. His legacy would be guaranteed.

He planned his hunger strike like a military operation with very clearly defined objectives, yet he made it sound like a joke: 'Son,' he said, 'have you heard the one about the Scotsman, the Irishman and the Jew?'

I said I hadn't.

He told me that the two great starving rivals he had to beat on his anorexic path to glory were Jewish and Irish – namely, Jesus Christ (who fasted for 40 days and nights in the desert) and IRA hunger striker Frank Staggs (60 days in prison).

Roy vowed that he'd beat both of them. He'd relegate them to silver and bronze in the starvation Olympics, Roy's own version of the Hunger Games.

He was particularly keen on taking the title from an Irishman. It was a matter of national pride.

'I set out to prove that anything a Mick can do, a Jock can do better.'

He started refusing all food, restricting himself to a pint of water a day. His weight dropped rapidly, and the prison authorities realised he meant business. They moved him to Wakefield prison, where they had a special hospital unit that could monitor his condition. Over the course of the next few months, his weight dropped from 190 pounds to a skin-and-bone 88 pounds. Respiratory problems ensued. He had to be put on an oxygen machine.

As I write this, I am stuffing myself with assorted pastries. I can hardly countenance the kind of willpower it must have taken to fast as he did.

He signed a form stating that he did not wish to be resuscitated in the event of losing consciousness. His blood count dropped to the lowest ever recorded in a British prison.

Ever-loyal Ruth Holmes re-emerged from the shadows of his past to visit him several times a week, despite the fact he'd made her consent to a divorce years earlier that had broken her heart. His ability to inspire devotion even in people he had treated badly was astonishing.

The Government sent Lord Caithness, a suitably Scottish peer, to try to dissuade him from his course of action. Caithness told Roy he would not be transferred to a Scottish prison because the government 'would not give in to blackmail'. This line of argument failed to persuade him to end his hunger strike.

Roy told me that as he got closer to death he started having hallucinations featuring the people he'd killed. He wasn't so sure they *were* hallucinations. He believed his victims were waiting for him in the Great Beyond, plotting revenge. Worse than that, his mother had started to appear, asking him how he had gone so wrong. How could he have killed her beloved Donald, his own wee brother?

He was slipping towards death. The prison service had made plans for his burial. The emaciated, skeletal Roy, by now looking like a concentration camp corpse, received the Last Rites from the prison pastor on the day everyone believed would be his last. It was Christmas morning.

As he was given the final blessing, his eyes opened, startling everyone.

'Soup,' he said, in a barely audible whisper.

'In the end, it was mother who saved me,' he told me all those years later. 'She said it wasn't time for me to die. She told me I had to survive and try to make amends. I had to seek redemption. That's the word she used. Redemption. As she spoke, I could hear singing in the background – songs of hope, salvation, rebirth. Then she told me to eat some soup.'

Carols and seasonal hymns of glad tidings were being sung in the prison by a visiting choir. It was a year to the day since Mary's body had been found in the burn. Roy always did have an immaculate sense of timing.

The warders, who were planning to bring in a wooden box, brought him a bowl of soup instead. Roy sipped it and smiled. He had gone 84 days without food, setting a new record.

The pastor offered him Communion, but he refused. I asked him why.

'I'm not a hypocrite, son. It wasn't God who saved me; it was my mother. I would find redemption in my own way, by my own rules. It wouldn't be through religion, but through art.'

As if in possession of some superior knowledge, he smiled at me and winked.

◊

When his weight started to return to normal, he was not transferred to Scotland, which the Government felt would have been a sign of weakness on its part, but to Full Sutton, where he settled into life as prisoner E14989, listed as Archibald Thomson Hall, but known to all as Roy the Boy.

He was popular with his fellow cons and his jailers. Worldly-wise, upbeat, always entertaining, never dull – thereby practising Mrs Cheyney's Gospel of Hospitality – he was regarded as a father figure by many of his fellow inmates.

He was put in Wing C, the lifers' wing, with 80 other prisoners including Dennis Nilsen, the dismemberer of bodies whose response to the privations of the bedsit, as we have noted, was even more extreme than my own.

Like Roy, Nilsen was Scottish, as was Ian Brady the child-killing Moors murderer. When I commented on the high incidence of Scots amongst Category A serial killers, Roy smiled, puffed his chest out in mock pride and said, 'Thank fuck we're still good at something!'

He was allowed to keep a pet bird, a cockatoo, which he cheekily called Hooch in honour of the contraband whisky the prisoners manufactured. Hooch, like his master, had had his wings clipped. Man and bird both knew they would die in prison. They sat in the endless gloom of the cell trying to cheer each other up, dreaming of freedom and of flight.

I asked him once again if, during those endless empty nights in a barren cell, he ever regretted the actions that had brought him there.

'Of course,' he replied. 'I could have been a captain of industry. A man of power and influence. I feel remorse for a wasted life.'

'Actually, Roy, I meant remorse for the lives of the people you killed.'

He shrugged as if to say, 'Not that hoary old chestnut again,' and replied, 'Que sera, sera. It was my destiny,' as if that were the last word on the subject.

'But Roy, five people lost their lives at your hands.'

He looked at me for a moment as if I had insulted him, then shrugged.

'Looking back on it,' he said, 'I can see the funny side.'

'Funny? Roy, what was funny about it? There's nothing funny about murder!'

'Are you tellin' me Mary in the wig wisnae funny?' he replied. 'She was funny and pathetic at the same time. Don't mix me up with Nilsen and the rest of those butchers! They're sick. They're psychos! I'm not like them. I'm an artist. All they did was kill people. I did so much more! I will leave a legacy.'

I had to respond.

'A legacy, Roy? Not one you can be proud of, surely?'

'I know what you're saying, son, but I would like to make my mother proud of me, despite everything. She might forgive me for all the bad things I did if I could somehow show people the good things as well.'

He paused for effect.

'I haven't told you the full story of how she talked me out of starving myself to death.'

He stared at me intently, but not in his usual intimidating fashion. This was an inviting, open stare. It was not the Stare of Death.

'I've never told anyone the whole truth,' he added.

'Is this the secret you promised me?' I asked, still suspecting it was a ploy.

He nodded, adding in typically provocative fashion, 'A man without a secret is a man without a soul.'

The fate of his soul seemed to be concerning him greatly.

'If I meet Mother in my next life I want to be able to tell her that at least I tried: I did my best to make amends. To find redemption.'

I wasn't sure where he was planning to run into his mother. I was hoping she wasn't in the place he was going to, unless she was wearing an asbestos suit.

'Do you believe in reincarnation?' he asked me suddenly.

His question reminded me that I was imposing my own belief system on him: he didn't believe in the Heaven and Hell of Christianity. He believed in reincarnation, so he and his mum could presumably run into each other anywhere, hopefully in suitable life forms. It would be a bummer if she came back as the rat-catcher and he as the rat.

'No, Roy,' I replied candidly. 'I don't believe in reincarnation. Though I may have done in a previous life.'

He laughed.

'See? I've missed you, son. You're funny. Funny as fuck! That's why you have to write my story.'

He moved his chair towards me and whispered conspiratorially. I suspected that the secret was about to be revealed.

'On my hunger strike, just as I was about to die, I had an . . . experience. There was a dazzling light. I was in a long corridor. Everything was shimmering, bathing me in beautiful beams of light. Suddenly my mother appeared like a shining angel. She said it was too early for me to pass to the other side, that I had to stay alive and find redemption. She had foreseen my destiny, she said. I would meet a special person. A person who would make me a crown of diamonds.'

He placed an invisible crown on his head.

'For years I wondered what her words meant, but as soon as I met you I knew.

'Destiny had brought us together, just as she said it would. That's why I saw *The Bogie Man*. That's why you met Roy Rogers. That's why you went to Rothesay, like me, and skimmed skiters. It doesn't make sense if you don't write my story. That's why I got so upset when you left. It was as if you were calling my mother a liar. You're the one she foretold. You're the chosen one: the one who'll make me a crown of diamonds.'

'What's a crown of diamonds got to do with me, Roy? I'm not a jeweller.'

'Don't be so fucking literal, son! You're a writer! Use your imagination! She was speaking poetically. It was a near-death experience, not a fuckin' public service announcement! Don't you get it? She meant you would redeem me by writing about me!'

'But, Roy, the BBC has abandoned the project!'

'So what? The crown of diamonds isn't a TV show! It's the book you're going to write about me!'

'The book?' I said, surprised. Up till now we'd always talked about a film or a TV serial. We'd never mentioned my writing a book.

'Yes,' he said excitedly, warming to his theme. 'Every chapter should be a jewel in the crown! Fuck the crown of thorns. Fuck that joyless Christian obsession with martyrdom, suffering, death and blood. They can have their crown of sorrow. Make mine a crown of joy!'

I was pretending I wasn't impressed by his eloquence, but this was a helluva pitch, and so far I was buying it. His would be a hedonist's crown – a symbol not of self-denial and sacrifice but of self-indulgence and gratification.

I wanted to make sure I wasn't walking into his silver-tongued trap.

'Are you sure you're not making all this up, Roy? All this redemption stuff from your mother?'

'Of course not. Redemption was my mother's word. It's not a word I ever used myself. Except in the old days, of course, when I was redeeming cigarette coupons for gifts.'

I tried to test him. 'If what you're telling me is true, why didn't the near-death experience turn you on to religion, as it does with so many other people? A long corridor of dazzling light . . . it was obviously a vision of heaven.'

'Oh, it was heaven all right, son,' he said, laughing. 'I recognised it immediately. It was the Argyle Arcade!'

As he sat chortling away, I realised that he had found my Achilles heel. I had always wanted to write books, of course, and he knew that, but I had never thought of writing a book about a serial killer. Although perhaps, on reflection, I had. Hitler was the biggest serial killer of all.

Roy saw that he was getting to me.

'See, son, I made people feel more alive.'

'You mean – when you weren't killing them?'

'I wish you'd stop bringing that up!'

'I have to, Roy. I'm a stickler for detail.'

'OK, son, have it your way. When I wasn't killing people, I made them feel more alive. They had boring lives till I came along. I was the jewel in the crown. They bathed in my radiance.'

The man's narcissism knew no bounds, but it was, in its strange way, refreshing. It reminded me of how much I had missed our conversations. What did I expect from a serial killer? Modesty?

Deciding to indulge his Messianic fantasies, I quoted Jesus Christ: 'I am come that ye shall have life and have it more abundantly. As somebody once remarked.'

There was a pause before he replied, 'I remember my father reading that to me. If only the Church had practised what Christ preached, I would have signed up in a heartbeat. But I don't have to believe in Christ to be a Christ-like figure, do I?'

(Wow, Roy! Just when I'd almost forgotten how nuts you are.)

'That's right, Roy. You don't.' I knew he would go on denying the existence of God, except possibly when applied to himself.

He started to get maudlin. 'I'd like to be remembered for the joy I brought to people.'

'The joy?' I said, failing to disguise my disbelief.

'Yes,' he said defiantly. 'The fun, the vitality.'

Obviously I didn't look convinced.

'You're thinking I brought people death, aren't you?'

'Something like that, yes.'

'But I want to be remembered as a life-enhancing figure, not a bringer of death. Even though, of course,' he added quickly, 'I did bring death. Does that make any sense?'

I thought for a second.

'Yes, Roy, strangely enough, it does.'

'Promise that you'll write something that will show the funny side of me as well as the . . . other side. Tell me you'll show the light as well as the dark, the life as well as the death, the joy as well as the sorrow. Please tell me you'll do it!'

Once more, I tried not to be swayed by his eloquence. I knew how he used his honeyed words to seduce and manipulate.

'I'm sorry, Roy, but I've moved on to other things. Somebody else can write your story. There are plenty of ghost writers out there.'

A ghost writer seemed ideally suited to the subject matter. After all, Roy had turned five sentient human beings into ghosts. I had spent the last few months trying to avoid being added to their number.

'A ghost writer could never capture my voice the way you can,' he said. 'It's the difference between love and sex.'

I must have looked at him with a degree of disdain. The image of love and/or sex with Roy wasn't doing a lot for me.

Seeing this, he quickly added, 'I need a real writer. I need you! It *has* to be you!'

He was trying to flatter me, of course, appealing to the writer's ever-fragile ego.

I decided to drop my bombshell. I hadn't really planned on telling him, but now seemed like the moment.

'Roy, I'm flattered, but I don't have time. I've written a script, and I'm going to America to try to sell it.'

'Is the script about me?' he asked.

'No, Roy, it's not.'

He seemed disappointed.

I explained to him that during the period of our estrangement, I had gone to Edinburgh, representing the BBC at a media conference. In the bar of the hotel that was hosting the event I met an Irish woman named Evelyn who told me her father had done a remarkable thing when she was a little girl: he had fought church and state to get her out of an orphanage where she had been unfairly incarcerated.

In a frenzied ten-day period of intense creativity, to take my mind off the Roy situation, I hid out in the Glasgow University Men's Union library and wrote a screenplay about those events, on the grounds that an uplifting story about a father's love would be less likely to result in my balls being converted into garters than a story about a psychopathic serial killer. A nice Irish convent girl was less likely than Roy to employ a scarfaced minion to nail my head to the floor.

I had swithered about letting Roy know about my trip to America, in case the golden streets of California were paved with friends of his who had graduated from Barlinnie to Alcatraz. Now that I had told him, there was a pause. He sounded sad.

'America, eh, son? Well done. I never made it, but that's the way it goes. Send me a postcard. Say hello to Barbra Streisand for me, eh? She's my favourite singer.'

'I will, if I get the chance.'

He sighed. 'I know you're a busy man. You can write the book when the time is right. Promise me you'll do that.'

I paused. The prospect did, I have to admit, intrigue me.

'Roy, if I ever do write a book about you it won't be the typical true crime book. It will be my book, not yours.'

'I know that, son. That's fine. It's your book, but it's my crown. Deal?'

'I'll need to think about it, Roy.'

He launched into a monologue designed, no doubt, to soften me up. I let him ramble on to get it out of his system, keeping my thoughts to myself.

'If I'd a son, I'd like him to be like you.'

(If I'd a father, on balance I'd prefer if he weren't a serial killer.)

'What did I do to lose your friendship?'

(You threatened to kill me, Roy. That'll work every time.)

'You're funny, son! You read the same stuff I do! You get me like nobody else could. You're the only friend I've got!'

He was becoming maudlin.

'Will you promise me that you'll at least think about writing my story? Even after I'm . . . gone? I don't want to spend my 80th birthday in prison. I'll make sure I die before that happens. I'll rot towards the millennium.'

He was making me feel melancholy.

'Don't talk like that, Roy!'

'What have I got to live for? Talking to you was my last great adventure. Now there are no adventures left.'

He sank back in his chair. His shoulders sagged. He seemed to age visibly in front of me.

'I'm Scheherazade!' he said, with profound sadness.

'The Arabian Princess who told stories to stay alive?'

'Aye, for fuck sake, son, I don't know any other Scheherazade, do you?'

I remembered in a vague way the story of the vengeful king who slept with a different virgin every night before executing her the next morning, and of how Scheherazade saved her life by spinning him wondrous tales of adventure, which became *The Arabian Nights*.

'She created Sinbad,' he said. 'And Ali Baba, and all the others. Just like I created all my characters.'

'*Including Roy,*' I thought, but I didn't voice the thought, not wanting to risk reminding him he was Archie.

'My life was a great adventure, but if you don't write my story it has meant nothing. People will think I'm just another killer.'

There was a cough from the other side of the room.

'Time's up, gentlemen,' said the guard. The words suddenly had an ominous finality.

Roy looked at me pleadingly.

'Please, son, make me something that will sparkle after I've gone into the darkness. Something that would make my mother proud. Something she could call a work of art. So that she wouldn't think having me was a complete waste of time.'

Despite myself and my awareness of his ability to fake emotion, I was touched. 'All right, Roy, I promise. When the time is right.'

He stepped forward, shook my hand and gave me a bear hug. I almost gagged on his aftershave.

'Thanks, son. Now I can die with some hope.'

The guard coughed again and rattled his keys.

'I suppose this is goodbye, then?' he said.

'Yes, Roy, I suppose it is.'

'Say hello to the ocean for me, son. Neptune never took me across it, the unreliable wee bastard.'

'I will, Roy. I will. Goodbye!'

'Goodbye, son!' He was choking up with emotion.

We hugged again as the guard came over to lead me out.

'Bye, Roy!'

'Goodbye, son. It's been a great adventure.'

'It has, Roy. For me too.'

I walked to the door and turned. He smiled, placed an invisible crown on his head, and waved his last goodbye.

On the train home, sipping a Glenfiddich, I wondered why I hadn't realised it sooner. Perhaps because I was fixated on him as Sinbad I'd missed the bigger truth, the most important truth of all. Roy was Scheherazade. All this time he'd been telling me stories to stay alive.

34

Paradise Cove

This day thou shalt be with me in Paradise.
Jesus to the dying thief, Luke 24:43

AFTER THE TRAUMA OF those months, I wanted a change. I wanted to get far away from the world of Scottish serial killers and from the low, brooding Scottish sky. I pined for golden sands. Happy circumstance pointed me towards California: when Bill Bryden left the BBC to concentrate on theatre, I decided it was time for me to go too. One of my last acts was to produce on behalf of the BBC a short film that was written and directed by the Scottish actor Peter Capaldi. Entitled *Franz Kafka's It's a Wonderful Life*, it went on to win an Oscar for Best Live Action Short.

This was Scotland's first Oscar for 45 years, the previous one having been for a documentary about shipbuilding called *Seaward the Great Ships*. Roy claimed that he and his mother were present at the filming of that epic, and that they could be seen in the background cheering a successful launch. In any event, after that triumph the Scottish film industry sank without trace.

I ended up on the night of the Oscars talking to Madonna at the winners' post-Oscars party at Chasen's, the legendary Hollywood restaurant. I'd like to think this was the result of my natural sex appeal and charisma, but it may just have had something to do with the fact that at the time I was holding an Oscar, the world's most exclusive form of penile extension.

You'll no doubt be disappointed to find out that Madonna soon switched her attention to someone else, but the win did have the enormous benefit of enabling me to spend several months in sunny California, on a cultural exchange programme.

One of the last things I did before I left Scotland was to mail a cassette of Barbra Streisand's Greatest Hits to Roy as a farewell present.

I was based at the MGM studio in Santa Monica, where I could study truth, justice and the American way of making films. Every day was as juicy and succulent as a great big fat Californian orange.

There were teething problems. At first, no one could understand my Scottish accent, so I decided to speak more slowly.

'Hell-o, my name is Pa-ul,' I would say with excruciatingly elongated vowels. Suddenly everyone became a whole lot nicer to me. I later realised that they thought I was a recovering stroke victim.

I kept on my flat in Glasgow, of course, and could access my phone messages from across the Pond.

One night I was startled to hear the familiar voice of Roy, sounding maudlin.

'I hope it's all going well for you over there, son. Thanks for the Streisand tape, by the way. I listen to it every night.'

At this point he sang a snippet: '*On a clear day you can see forever.* Not quite as good a voice as her, but not bad, eh, son? Anyway, check out *Hansard.* I'm being abused by the vermin in ermine. It should be a wee reminder to you not to forget my crown of diamonds. Bye, son.'

He put down the phone, and there was a long howling sound. It was probably just the Transatlantic connection, but it sounded like the cry of an animal in pain.

I went online and found what he was referring to in *Hansard*, the record of proceedings in Parliament. The debate concerned the whole-life tariff system and centred on the morality of imprisonment for life with no prospect of release. As the oldest such prisoner in the whole of the UK prison system, Roy was at the very heart of the debate.

He had been moved from Full Sutton to HM Prison Kingston, which was nearer the sea, but his regular appeals for compassionate release were always turned down.

This is an edited transcript of what was said by the 'vermin in ermine' aka the 'noble Lords' in the upper tier of the UK Parliament:

> Baroness Blatch: The noble Lord referred to Roy Hall, or Roy Fontaine, as he is often called. Lord Longford said that it was obscene that a man or a woman should never come out of prison. What is obscene is the way in which so many lives were brought to a cruel end by those very people.
>
> Lord Hylton: My Lords, before the noble Baroness sits down, I urge her to ask her colleagues to reflect on the kind of despair which is likely to be induced in people when they are told that they will never be released from prison and how that despair is likely to be even greater when they appeal and are unsuccessful.
>
> Baroness Blatch: My Lords, I acknowledge readily that there must be a feeling of despair. But I invite the noble Lord to consider along with me the despair of the husbands, wives, mothers, fathers, sisters and brothers of the people whose lives have been snuffed out by those people.

The debate revisited many of the issues that I had wrestled with in my encounters with Roy, torn as I was between compassion for him and revulsion at his deeds.

◊

I had originally intended to stay in California for a few months, but when Pierce Brosnan agreed to star in *Evelyn*, my stay was extended indefinitely. Pierce played an Irish painter and decorator fighting to get his daughter out of an orphanage. There is a scene in the film where his lawyer tells him to wear well-polished shoes in court. That scene was inspired by the tip that the Polish pilot, in his highly polished boots, gave to Roy: 'People always judge you by your shoes.'

In the years it took for all the pieces of *Evelyn* to fall into place, I got work polishing scripts, and I learned how to sell film projects by pitching ideas to studio executives. I even attended a class entitled 'How to Warm Cold Pitches'. Before I went to Hollywood I believed the phrase 'warm cold pitches' referred to Scottish football's winter experiments with undersoil heating.

For the first few years, Roy would send a Christmas card to my Glasgow address and I would send one to him from California. His cards to me usually featured a crown, whilst mine often showed athletic bodies on Muscle Beach. As he 'rotted towards the millennium', as he put it, and my screenwriting career gained momentum, the cards eventually dried up.

I intended sending him a card in late 2002 to celebrate the Christmas release of *Evelyn*, but one morning in September of that year I booted up my computer and was linked automatically to my BBC homepage, only to see Roy's face staring out at me accusingly. The headline read 'Mad Butler Dies In Prison'.

I took a sharp breath as I read:

> A former butler who was at the centre of a notorious killing spree has died in prison. Archibald Hall, who was jailed in the 1970s for life for the murder of five people, died at Kingston Prison, Portsmouth, on 16 September. A spokesman for the coroner's office said that Hall, dubbed The Mad Butler by the press, died of natural causes aged 78.

There followed a brief account of the life I knew so well: an account that certainly did not contain the light, only the dark. To my surprise I felt sad, as if I'd just lost an old friend.

That's when I walked to the beach and threw that large flat stone, a 'skiter', in his honour. As the sun seared my flesh, I found myself remembering one of Auntie Lizzie's favourite sayings: 'You don't miss the water till the well runs dry.'

I felt guilty that I had not thought about him recently, far less written his story. I went home, sharpened my pencil, and wrote down a few disconnected thoughts. I smiled as I remembered his shameless request to have his ashes scattered on Lady Hudson's estate.

He did not wish to be buried in a Christian cemetery. He told me once that George Bernard Shaw would never allow himself to be buried in a Christian churchyard, as the religion's central symbol is the cross, an instrument of torture.

That reminded me of Roy's intense dislike of the Christian crown of thorns, and I once again thought of my unfulfilled promise to make him a crown of diamonds. I'd had no time for that. Life had intervened. I had married and now had a lovely wife and a beautiful little daughter.

Evelyn went on to win a couple of awards, and as a result I received a call from a Hollywood producer who said, 'Gee, kid, I loved your Irish orphanage in *Evelyn*. Can you write me a Mexican one? You give great orphanage.'

It had never occurred to me that the idea was franchiseable. I could be Hollywood's go-to orphanage guy. I should think about where to go after Mexico. Romania, perhaps?

I started work on the Mexican movie. It began with the noblest of intentions – based on the remarkable true story of a wrestling Mexican priest, the project had the commitment of an A-list Hispanic actor, and my script began with a Biblical quote: 'We wrestle not against flesh and blood, but against the rulers of the darkness of this world.'

It ended up, several years and four writers later, reeking of adolescent toilet humour and starring an overweight white comedian in spandex playing Hispanic for laughs. I took my name off it, and it went on to make a ton of money. I could now officially class myself as an abused Hollywood hack, authentically inauthentic.

While all this was going on, Roy Fontaine existed for me primarily as a heap of yellowing papers in a cardboard box in the cupboard. Whenever I saw that box I felt a twinge of guilt at the memory of a promise unfulfilled.

That's how matters remained until in 2007 a talented young film director asked me to play a priest in a promotional trail for a movie he was planning to make. I was helping him with the project and, though I am not an actor, I did it as a favour. It was a Cain and Abel tale where a brother seeks forgiveness for the murder of his sibling. It had an obvious thematic resonance with Roy's story.

I was to scatter the dead brother's ashes into the ocean, whilst intoning, 'Remember, man, that thou art dust and unto dust thou shalt return. We commend his soul to you, O Lord. May he rest in peace. Amen.'

The film's theme of fratricide brought back vivid memories of Roy killing Donald. When the director told me that we'd be filming on the Malibu cliffs near Barbra Streisand's home I found myself thinking once again of Roy.

When I finished rehearsing my lines the night before filming, I poured myself a Glenfiddich, just as I used to do all those years earlier as I read over my interview notes on the train home from Full Sutton. In a perverse act of patriotism I now found myself sitting up late at night with a bottle of malt, toasting the man who had been denied his request to die in a Scottish prison.

I asked myself how many nights Roy had spent in his little cell. I did the maths. It was more than ten thousand and one nights. Scheherazade didn't even come close.

I took out my laptop and did a little googling. I discovered that one month after Roy died, the European Court of Human Rights debated whether whole-life tariff incarceration was inhumane. They decided it wasn't. Even if Roy had lived into his 90s, he'd have remained behind bars.

My online search yielded more revelations. Roy's ghost was said to haunt the ruined manor at Glen Affric, where he'd killed poor old Scott-Elliot. Someone had posted a spooky photo of what purported to be Roy in the manor grounds, his face made up of wisps of smoke.

This was particularly disturbing, as it reminded me of the smoke he'd blown in my direction throughout the interviews as he puffed on his Romeo and Juliets. What could be more apt than Roy coming back as wisps of cigar smoke?

I found these tales of his ghostly presence disturbing, evidence that he had not found peace. Could his restless spirit ever find peace? Did he even deserve to?

I kept thinking of the promise I'd made to him ten years earlier, when I'd said goodbye to him as I walked out of Full Sutton's blue gates into the wide blue yonder of a freedom he would never know again. He wasn't just haunting Glen Affric. He was haunting me.

I went into the cupboard and took out my old interview notebooks. On every second page I had printed the letters 'BDI', which stood for 'Butler Did It'.

Suddenly BDI meant 'beady eye'. I now felt that his beady eye was gazing upon me, following me everywhere, accusingly, asking why I hadn't written that book yet.

That was when my Big Idea came to me, in the pulse of an artery, albeit an artery through which good Scotch whisky was flowing. I had kept all my notes and draft outlines. I fished them out of my highly sophisticated filing system, otherwise known as that big cardboard box in the cupboard.

On those pages I had outlined Roy's entire life and a significant slice of mine. I started reading. It all came flooding back to me. I remembered something he said to Kitto, and I knew what I had to do. Roy's hard, gem-like flame had been extinguished, but it could be rekindled, after a fashion.

I made two copies of everything. I would keep one copy and use it as the basis for the book you are now reading. The other I would take to the beach the next morning. But first I needed a tartan shortbread tin.

The next morning found me bright-eyed and bushy-tailed and heading for the Tudor House on 2nd Street and Santa Monica Boulevard, a shopping mecca for expats. This is where you can get the Cadbury's Flake or the HP sauce that reminds you of dear Old Blighty. For Scots, it's haggis, Loch Fyne kippers or Irn Bru, Scotland's version of an energy drink. I had already purchased a few miniatures of Glenfiddich at the nearby liquor store.

The Tudor House provided me with a tartan tin of Walker's shortbread, complete with views of Edinburgh Castle and a portrait of our national poet Robert Burns, which would please Roy, who liked to travel in the company of great fellow artists.

I was now equipped with the same shortbread and whisky that he had given to his prison chums after his father's funeral.

With my tin, my whisky and my notes on the life of Roy in my briefcase, I headed for Muscle Beach, a brisk ten-minute walk away.

Finding a quiet section of beach near Santa Monica pier, I stood on the spot where Salvador Dali first fell in lust with his Christ of St John of the Cross flexing his soon-to-be-famous biceps on the parallel bars. Verily, I say unto you, this day you will be with me in Paradise.

It was time. I transferred the pages into the shortbread tin and sprinkled the whisky over them, like a priest anointing a corpse. I supplied the requisite gem-like flame from my Zippo lighter, wondering as I did so who had ended up with Roy's famous lighter, the gift from Churchill's son-in-law. With a sudden whoosh, Roy's life went up in flames. 'Ashes to ashes,' I intoned, kneeling by the edge of the ocean he had dreamed of crossing.

It was against the law to light a fire on the beach, but I started one anyway. In death, as in life, Roy was pushing me past the boundaries of the acceptable, towards the dangerous edge of things.

It was as if he were sitting beside me, whispering in my ear, 'Do what thou wilt shall be the whole of the Law.'

The outline of Roy's life, intertwined with mine, went up in smoke. With a breathtaking burst of lilac flame, he was ashes. Soaked in his favourite whisky, he blazed beautifully. In his tartan shortbread urn he was the tin man once again.

Now I had to get to Malibu. Filming started in a couple of hours.

Richard, a local cab driver I'd known for years, ran me to the location with my strange cargo. I asked him to go on a little further, and within a few minutes we were outside the imposing gates of Barbra Streisand's mansion. He pulled down a side road and I got out. Richard didn't ask any questions about my odd behaviour. I was hoping he'd assume I was getting into character for my role, as a good method actor should.

Maybe I was still feeling the effects of the whisky I'd consumed the night before, but I now found myself pointing at a celebrity's clifftop retreat whilst talking to a bunch of ashes in a shortbread tin.

'See, Roy, there's Streisand's house,' I whispered as I lifted the lid off the tin carefully. 'You finally made it to America!'

I tilted the tin at a slight angle, to give him a better view. It was a clear day, and you could see forever.

I turned back and got into the taxi to the location, a few miles down the road, where the props man gave me the urn. I carefully poured the ashes from the tin into the urn and mixed them with prop ashes, which were already inside. I was hoping Roy was enjoying this. He always said that life was a performance. Why shouldn't death be too?

Ten minutes later I stood on a windy bluff from which I could still see Barbra's cliffside home in the distance. The cameras rolled. I intoned, 'Remember, man, that thou art dust and unto dust thou shalt return,' as I poured the ashes out of the urn. They floated gently and gracefully down into the ocean below, like a baby rocking to sleep.

His ashes dissolved into the ocean. In the Pacific sunset he and the flame became one. His hopes and dreams, his triumphs and disasters, his hilarious stings and his gruesome murders all melted away into the fiery water. Sinbad had returned to the sea he loved.

I felt a surge of emotion as I watched those ashes melt into the shimmering haze. My eyes misted over. I was mourning the passing of an old friend, and an old self. At long last, after so many shipwrecks, I hoped Roy would find peace.

On the cliffs of Malibu, no less than on the hill at Calvary, two vagabond souls sought redemption. I wondered if Roy's mother had foreseen that I would need redemption as much as her son. If I could write that book and make that crown, it would be no selfless, altruistic act. Yes, it was intended to give him some sort of redemption, but I needed redeeming too.

Experience had taught me that screenwriting is writing in the sand with the tide coming in. If I could write the book I had promised him, it would mark my return to writing something that might endure longer than a bag of popcorn.

I left the Malibu cliffs that day vowing I would write a luminous life of Roy Fontaine. It would be my bridge to freedom, to a new beginning, to the writing life I had always wanted. If I could succeed in writing that book, I would rescue Roy from the fate of being remembered only as a killer and he would rescue me from being remembered only as a hack. I would save his legacy and he would save my soul.

I had scattered his ashes, but they were my ashes too. The ashes of my old life turning tricks in Hollywood and the beginning of my new life as a writer of books, starting with the one you have in your hands.

Roy, old friend, I have now written the story of your life, and I have tried to make it, as you requested, 'funny as fuck'. I have spent many hours polishing your crown of diamonds.

Let this book be your monument. May it burn with the flame of those jewels which you loved so much. May this book and your life sparkle into eternity.

For art is long, life is short, but diamonds are forever.

Finally, Roy, I hesitate to talk about your end for obvious reasons – you who described yourself as 'the man who put the butt in buttling'. I really would like to keep your posterior out of this, but there is no other way to put it:

Thank you, Roy. In your end is my beginning.

◊ ◊ ◊ ◊